"I've had a front-row seat to Batterson's long vision for the church he leads and the city he loves. This book will inspire you to dream bigger, think longer, and dare to be different."

—BOB GOFF, *New York Times* bestselling author, coach, and chaser of whimsy

"In a world chasing shortcuts and instant success, *Gradually Then Suddenly* invites us into the slow, sacred work of building a Christ-filled life that lasts. With honesty, depth, and visionary insight, Batterson unpacks what it means to live with long vision, faithful obedience, and generational impact. Each chapter challenges the reader to trust God's timing and embrace the unseen, often unnoticed, work of transformation. This is a deeply encouraging guide for Christians committed to legacy over urgency."

—CRAIG GROESCHEL, senior pastor of Life.Church and author of *The Benefit of Doubt*

"Inspiring and encouraging, yet grounding and tangible, *Gradually Then Suddenly* is a guidebook to making the daily choices that lead to the creation of the fulfilling life with God we all deeply desire."

—Annie F. Downs, bestselling author of *That Sounds Fun*

"I learn *so* much whenever I read one of Mark Batterson's books. They are fun and enlightening, and I get ideas, wisdom, and inspiration from them. The stories range from the intensely personal to the historical, all pointing to self-evident Godly truths that hit home and apply to my life, occupation, and relationships. *Gradually Then Suddenly* will inspire you to grow. What a great message!"

—John Harbaugh, longtime NFL head coach of the Baltimore Ravens

"Leadership is all about playing the long game, which Batterson models in his life and writing. I was impacted by the prequel to this book, *Win the Day*. And this sequel, *Gradually Then Suddenly*, will challenge you to dream bigger, pray harder, and think longer."

—John C. Maxwell, *New York Times* bestselling author, speaker, and coach

"I've been challenged and encouraged by Batterson's books, including this one. *Gradually Then Suddenly* speaks to my reality as an Olympic athlete. Hurdlers and sprinters spend many years training for races that last mere seconds, but a gold medal is worth the blood, sweat, and tears. This book will inspire you to go after your God-sized dreams!"

—GRANT HOLLOWAY, Olympic track and field gold medalist, three-time world champion, and world record holder

"Batterson's writing has the rare ability to make you believe big and start small—and this book will push you to do both. I love the metaphor of 'gradually then suddenly.' It captures the key to the best (and worst) patterns in our lives and reminds us to keep moving in the right direction. Packed with fascinating stories, Biblical truth, and Batterson's trademark awe and wonder, *Gradually Then Suddenly* is a book you'll be glad you read—and one you'll want to share with others."

—CAREY NIEUWHOF, author, speaker, and podcaster

"*Gradually Then Suddenly* is an inspiring, motivating, and hope-filled road map for translating vision into reality. There are no empty platitudes here but rather a plan to cast a vision for your life that aligns with God's plans and purposes. God's vision doesn't have a short shelf life—it is international and intergenerational. Thank you, Mark Batterson, for pointing us to disciplined perseverance as we pursue the fulfillment of our vision and dreams and for the sobering reminder that quitting isn't about present-tense circumstances as much as it is about future-tense possibilities."

—DR. CRAWFORD W. LORITTS, JR., author, speaker, and founder and president of Beyond Our Generation

"Mark Batterson has blessed us with powerful lessons from the Lord in *Gradually Then Suddenly*. This book will set your soul and heart on fire to seek and obey the voice of the Lord."

—KEVIN WARREN, president and CEO of the Chicago Bears

"The winding road to a God-sized vision is not for the faint of heart. Mark Batterson's *Gradually Then Suddenly* will inspire you to sustain the gradual pursuit of your dream through parallels from historic moments, the wonders of science, and riveting and diverse testimonies. From well-known giants of the faith to those who are charting a new life from behind bars, *Gradually Then Suddenly* reminds all of us that it's never too late to live a life worth telling stories about!"

—HEATHER RICE-MINUS, president and CEO of Prison Fellowship

GRADUALLY
THEN
SUDDENLY

Mark Batterson

GRADUALLY
THEN
SUDDENLY

How to Dream Bigger, Decide Better,
and Leave a Lasting Legacy

MULTNOMAH

Multnomah
An imprint of the Penguin Random House Christian Publishing Group,
a division of Penguin Random House LLC
1745 Broadway, New York, NY 10019
waterbrookmultnomah.com
penguinrandomhouse.com

Hardcover ISBN 979-8-217-15207-0
Ebook ISBN 979-8-217-15209-4

The Cataloging-in-Publication Data is on file with the Library of Congress.

Printed in the United States of America on acid-free paper

1st Printing

FIRST EDITION

The authorized representative in the EU for product safety and compliance is Penguin Random
House Ireland, Morrison Chambers, 32 Nassau Street, Dublin D02 YH68, Ireland.
https://eu-contact.penguin.ie

Book design by Simon M. Sullivan

For details on special quantity discounts for bulk purchases,
contact specialmarketscms@penguinrandomhouse.com.

Dedicated to National Community Church.

When we began this journey,

I asked God for the privilege of pastoring one church for life.

You are the answer to that prayer.

Praise God for every single person who has found faith with their fingerprint on it.

Thanks to every single person who has invested their time, talent, and treasure.

The best is yet to come!

CONTENTS

PART 3

LONG LEGACY

GRADUALLY
THEN
SUDDENLY

PLAYING THE LONG GAME

"How did you go bankrupt?"

That's the question posed by Ernest Hemingway in his 1926 novel *The Sun Also Rises*. The rather infamous reply? Two ways. Gradually then suddenly.[1]

That's how you go bankrupt, but that's also how you get out of debt. That's how you start a business, write a book, or run a marathon—and a thousand other things. That's how entrepreneurs innovate, athletes win championships, and investors make bank. That's how songwriters, filmmakers, and podcasters produce content. Regardless of craft or career, dreams don't become reality overnight. Reverse engineer any success story, and I daresay it happened two ways—gradually then suddenly.

We love suddenly! Gradually? Not so much. But that's about to change. You aren't just beginning a new book; you're beginning a new chapter of your life. I have no idea what dream you've set your sights on, but this is the day when decades happen.

"When you are born, you look like your parents," said Dr. Crawford Loritts. "When you die, you look like your decisions."[2] Destiny is not a mystery. Destiny is a series of decisions—big decisions and little decisions, predecisions and daily decisions. And every decision has a domino effect. For better or for worse, we look more and more like our decisions every day. The good news? You are one decision away from a totally different life. My prayer is that God would give you the clarity, the conviction, and the courage you need to make that decision.

Your life is perfectly designed for the results you're getting. If you don't like who you are or where you are, don't play the victim. Play the long game! If you do the right things day in and day out, God will show up and show off. The pages that follow prove it. I hope the stories and studies that I share will inspire long vision, long obedience, and long legacy.

Is there a defining decision you need to make?

Is there a God-sized dream you need to go after?

What are you waiting for?

It's time to get started on gradually!

AROUND THE WORLD

At the 1984 Olympic Games in Los Angeles, American swimmer Rowdy Gaines won a gold medal in the one-hundred-meter freestyle, setting an Olympic record of 49.8 seconds. How did he do it? Two ways—gradually then suddenly.

America boycotted the 1980 Olympic Games in Moscow, which means Rowdy Gaines trained for eight years—eight *long* years— for a race that would last less than one minute! Add up all the laps, and Rowdy Gaines swam a total of twenty thousand miles in fifty-meter increments. "I swam around the world," he said, "for a race that lasted forty-nine seconds."[3]

Most of us would love an Olympic gold medal, but very few of us are willing to put on a Speedo and dive into a freezing-cold pool at the crack of dawn every day for eight years. We want success without sacrifice, but there are no shortcuts. The phrase *overnight success* is an oxymoron. Success without sacrifice is short-lived.

Don't settle for fifteen minutes of fame. The name of the game is long obedience in the same direction. That's how you leave a legacy that will outlive you.

> The essential thing "in heaven and in earth" is . . . that there should be long *obedience* in the same direction; there thereby results, and has always resulted in the long run, something which has made life worth living.[4]

Friedrich Nietzsche applied this idea to art, music, and dance. If someone makes something look easy, I guarantee it isn't. Effortlessness is evidence of extra effort. The principle of long obedience holds true for absolutely everything. Success is showing up when others give up. It's no quit. It's consecrating yourself to a cause or a craft or a calling—"No reserves. No retreats. No regrets."[5]

In the pages that follow, I want to help you go after God-sized dreams. By definition, God-sized dreams are beyond your education, beyond your ability, beyond your resources. You can't do it, but God can. Show me the size of your dream and I'll show you the size of your God. God makes big people by giving them big dreams. But the goal isn't accomplishing the goal—it's who you become in the process. Life is a journey, not a destination.[6] My advice? Enjoy the journey—every age, every page, every stage!

Take a learning posture toward everyone and everything.

Cultivate a growth mindset during difficult seasons.

Adopt a GTS attitude—gradually then suddenly.

If your dream doesn't scare you, it's too small. Quit living as if the purpose of life is to arrive safely at death. Go after a dream that is destined to fail without divine intervention. Live your life in a way that is worth telling stories about.

Mike Miller was staring forty in the face when he picked up a copy of my first book *In a Pit with a Lion on a Snowy Day.* "I felt something awaken deep in my spirit," Mike said. "I can only explain it as a dying and a birthing at the same time." Mike didn't even know he had fallen asleep, but the Holy Spirit woke him up with that still small voice: "Do you want to spend your forties telling stories from your thirties? Or do you want more stories?"[7]

Are you making a living or are you making a life?

Is your ladder leaning against the right wall?

Are you living your life in a way that is worth telling stories about?

This is your wake-up call.

IT'S ONLY IMPOSSIBLE UNTIL IT ISN'T

Almost everything is impossible, until it isn't.

When I started training for my first marathon, it felt impossible. I could barely run three miles, and I'm using the word *run* loosely! My pace was slightly faster than a sloth. But the impossible became possible. How? Gradually then suddenly! I did seventy-two training runs over six months totaling 475 miles. Then, and only then, was I able to run a 26.2-mile marathon.

In the Lewis Carroll classic *Through the Looking-Glass,* Alice says, "One *can't* believe impossible things." But the White Queen pushes back, "I daresay you haven't had much practice.... When I was your age, I always did it for half-an-hour a day. Why, sometimes I've believed as many as six impossible things before breakfast."[8]

Is there something impossible you're believing for? You can't pull it off before breakfast, that's for sure! But if you practice half an hour a day, the impossible will become possible—gradually then suddenly. "There are three stages to every great work of God," said Hudson Taylor. "First, it is impossible, then it is difficult, then it is done."[9]

A few years ago, I wrote a book titled *Win the Day*. If yesterday is history and tomorrow is mystery, all you can do is win today. That book was built around a simple premise: *Almost anyone can accomplish almost anything if they work at it long enough, hard enough, and smart enough.*

If you're 5′3″ and you want to play in the NBA, the odds are against you. But don't tell me it can't be done, because Muggsy Bogues played fourteen seasons. He had to train harder because he was smaller than his taller competitors, but that work ethic proved to be the secret to his success. Muggsy recorded 146 double-doubles during his NBA career. And even at 5′3″, he blocked thirty-nine shots![10]

There is an old axiom in martial arts: *A black belt is a white belt that never quit.* It's true of everything, isn't it? The way you accomplish anything is one day at a time, but here's the catch—you have to do it for *years* on end. That's what makes *Gradually Then Suddenly* a sequel of sorts. The rest of this book will solve for a simple yet exponential equation:

LONG VISION × LONG OBEDIENCE = LONG LEGACY

In the opening section, we'll reimagine long vision. In the age of immediacy, long vision is a lost art. We want success to happen at the speed of light, but success happens at the speed of a seed. Long vision is daring to dream beyond the dash on your tombstone. It takes time and eternity into consideration. It's doing what you do with the third and fourth generation in mind. Show me your vision and I'll show you your future!

In the second section, we'll reverse engineer long obedience. We want to do amazing things for God, but that's not our job. God is the one who does amazing things for us! Our job? Old-fashioned obedience. It's living for the applause of nail-scarred hands. Long obedience is the key that unlocks our potential and God's promises. It's the key to miracles, the key to breakthroughs, the key to success.

In the final section, we'll explore long legacy. Legacy is not what you accomplish. Legacy is what others accomplish because of you. Simply put, success is succession. It's growing fruit in someone else's garden. Just as we drink from wells we did not dig, we dig wells for the third and fourth generation.

THE BRACHISTOCHRONE CURVE

In 1696, a Swiss mathematician named Johann Bernoulli posed this question: Given two points A and B on a plane, what is the shape of the curve between the points that results in the shortest travel time for a frictionless ball acted on only by gravity?[11]

The answer is obvious, isn't it? The shortest distance between two points is a straight line! Not so fast. The *shortest distance* doesn't equate to the *fastest time*! Those are two very different things. The shortest distance may be a straight line, but the fastest time is called the brachistochrone curve. Roller coasters and skate parks use the brachistochrone equation to maximize momentum. How? They design a dip that leverages potential energy called gravity.

If you ride the roller coaster called life long enough, there will be ups and downs that tie your stomach in knots! We get discouraged by the downturns, but those dips are often blessings in disguise. They are when and where and how we learn valuable lessons. They also produce grit, which is a synonym for gradually then suddenly! The fastest path to your goals is *not* a straight line—it's a brachistochrone curve.

When I was fourteen years old, the primary objective of my life was dunking a basketball. I wore elevator shoes to build my calf muscles and did box jumps for plyometric training. Trust me, I have the scars on my shins to prove it. I tried everything, but the breakthrough didn't happen until I broke my right ankle. Wait, what? Our high school had three floors and eight periods, which meant I was hopping up and down the stairs on my left leg—all day, every day—for six weeks! When I broke my ankle, I thought my season was shot. The reality? That broken ankle proved to be a brachistochrone curve! How so? My left leg got twice as strong bearing all of my body weight. The first time I dunked a basketball, it was with a cast on my right ankle.

"The Dip is the secret to your success," said Seth Godin. Those dips come in lots of shapes and sizes—a difficult divorce, a dark night of the soul, or even a broken ankle. "The people who invest the time and the energy and the effort to power through the Dip—those are the ones who become the best in the world."[12]

DREAM DEFERRED

I felt called to write when I was twenty-two, but I didn't write my first book until I was thirty-five. Those thirteen years felt like forever! In my early thirties, I despised my birthday because it felt like an annual reminder of a dream deferred.

Ever felt that way?

Like your dream is getting further and further away?

Like you're falling further and further behind?

It felt like I was falling behind the bell curve, but it was a brachistochrone curve! During that thirteen-year dip, I read three thousand books. That's how I learned to write—by reverse engineering those books. I wrote hundreds of message manuscripts, I posted thousands of blogs, and I gained lots of life experience—

good, bad, and ugly. I didn't know it at the time, but I was gaining potential energy with every book, every sermon, every experience.

In retrospect, I'm glad I didn't write a book at twenty-two because I would have had to write a book at twenty-three to retract what I said at twenty-two. Truth be told, my writing would have lacked gravity. Or maybe I should say, gravitas.

I've written twenty-five books in the last twenty years, which sounds fast and furious. More than ten million copies have been translated into dozens of languages, but it happened gradually then suddenly. There is no way I could have kept that pace without the brachistochrone curve—*slower* proved to be *faster*!

Technically speaking, *Gradually Then Suddenly* took four months to write. That's the amount of time I allot to every writing season. But packed into these pages are thirty years of blood, sweat, and tears. I didn't know it at the time, but I started writing this book when I was twenty-two. And that's true of whatever dream God has put in your heart.

KINGFISHER

Many years ago, I was part of a gathering at Glen Eyrie Castle in Colorado Springs honoring the life and legacy of author and pastor Eugene Peterson. Eugene pastored in Bel Air, Maryland, for nearly three decades. He also authored more than thirty books. I had the honor of endorsing his final book, *As Kingfishers Catch Fire*.

Eugene's happy place was a cabin in Montana that his father built in 1947. He accumulated a lifetime of memories in that place, but that's also where his imagination ran wild. That lake house is where Eugene would rest and recover from the wear and tear of leadership.

At the Glen Eyrie Castle gathering, Eugene told a story I will long remember. He was sitting on his dock one day, watching a kingfisher do what it does. As the name suggests, few birds are better at catching fish. Eugene actually counted the number of attempts it took. "It took thirty-seven tries to catch a fish," said Eugene. "And he's the kingfisher!" Eugene paused, then asked a pointed question: "How many times have you tried?"[13]

Is there a dream you've given up on?

Is there a breakthrough you've stopped believing for?

Is there is a miracle you've stopped praying for?

Most of us fail for lack of trying—we give up on gradually. When was the last time you tried something thirty-seven times? For the record, Eugene Peterson's first book, *A Long Obedience in the Same Direction,* lived up to its title. "Seventeen publishers rejected it," wrote Eugene. Even worse? "I was advised that it was irrelevant to the concerns of contemporary North Americans."[14]

Fast-forward a few decades and Eugene's paraphrase of Scripture, *The Message,* has sold twenty million copies and counting. That is rare air in the publishing world, but let me ask the obvious question: What if Eugene had given up after the tenth or twelfth or seventeenth rejection letter? He would have gone to the grave with his music still inside him. Or maybe I should say, thirty books still inside him.

When you experience seventeen rejections, how do you react? Do you second-guess yourself? Or do you try, try again? When you fail thirty-six times, do you give up? Or do you double down? Only you can answer those questions!

What if the Israelites had quit circling Jericho on day six? What if Naaman had dipped in the Jordan River only six times? What if the disciples had stopped climbing the stairs to the upper room on day nine? The short answer is *nothing.* They would have left those miracles on the table. Those miracles are very different, but they happened the same way. They happened two ways—gradually then suddenly.

Pablo Picasso was born in Málaga, Spain, on October 25, 1881. He showed a proclivity for painting at an early age. According to his mother, his first word was "piz, piz"—a shortened version of *lápiz,* the Spanish word for "pencil."[15] His formal education in art began at age seven, and Picasso didn't put down his pencil until his death at the age of ninety-one.

More than four decades into his career—already a world-renowned artist—Pablo Picasso was dining at a restaurant in Paris when a patron recognized him. That woman asked him if he would sketch something on a napkin for her, and Picasso obliged. Then he said, "That will be $10,000." A little surprised, the woman said, "But you drew that in thirty seconds." To which Picasso replied, "No, it has taken me forty years to do that."[16]

Whether Picasso was joking about the asking price, I do not know. But every piece of Cubist art that Pablo Picasso ever produced was a benchmark in his body of work. Each piece was an evolution of creative expression.

Picasso's magnum opus, *Guernica*, measures 11.5 feet tall and 25.5 feet long. That monumental painting only took him thirty-five days to produce—May 1 to June 4, 1937.[17] But the imagery and allegory depicted in that painting took a lifetime to imagine. That painting would not have been the same if Picasso had attempted it in his twenties or thirties or forties. And the same could be said for whatever it is you do.

If you find yourself in a midlife crisis, can I alleviate some pressure? The Swiss psychiatrist Carl Jung believed that life *begins* at forty! "Up until then," said Jung, "you're just doing research."[18] Of course you're also earning compound interest along the way!

"Compound interest is the eighth wonder of the world," Albert Einstein is attributed with saying. "He who understands it, earns it. He who doesn't, pays it." Are you earning it, or are you paying it? And I'm not just talking about money! Compound interest applies to everything, including art. How do you earn compound interest? Two ways—gradually then suddenly!

It's true of surgeons who perform the same operation hundreds of times. It's true of lawyers who try similar cases in court. It's true of baristas who pull shots, producers who mix and master music, sprinters who hurdle, and professors who lecture. It's true of you and whatever it is you do.

There are no cheat codes spiritually, relationally, or profession-ally. No one gets a 20 percent discount on the ten-thousand-hour rule. Regardless of what you do, it's probably going to take seven-teen rejections and thirty-seven attempts! It'll take patience and time—but if you fall in love with gradually, time flies!

Ready or not, here we go.

PART 1

LONG

VISION

n 1791, President George Washington commissioned a French architect named Pierre Charles L'Enfant to draft a plan for the capital city. That original map—the L'Enfant Plan—is now enshrined in a Plexiglas case breathing argon gas at the Library of Congress.[1] That plan was the genesis of Washington, DC. More than two centuries later, I live in the revelation of that plan.

When I run the National Mall or walk our dog around the Capitol or navigate Dupont Circle, I'm keenly aware that my reality—the streets I drive on and the parks I play in—first existed in the imagination of Pierre Charles L'Enfant. And that's true of absolutely everything. Don't miss this: *Everything is created twice!* The first creation always happens in the imagination, which is an expression of the image of God. The second creation involves blood, sweat, and years.

When it comes to the city where I live, the first creation was putting pen to paper and creating the L'Enfant Plan. The second creation has taken two centuries of manual labor, physical material, and billions of dollars. The nation's capital was built gradually then suddenly, but it started with long vision.

When L'Enfant presented his plan to George Washington, the sixty-eight square miles that comprise the capital city consisted of swampland and farmland. Few people saw much potential, but L'Enfant saw "a pedestal waiting for a monument."[2] L'Enfant had long vision, but he wasn't the first.

On June 5, 1663, a farmer named Francis Pope acquired four hundred acres of land that included Jenkins Hill. More than a century later, Jenkins Hill would be renamed Capitol Hill. Francis Pope named his property Rome, which many people thought was a playful pun on his last name. But Francis Pope was a prophet in plain clothes.

> It is told of this dreamer, that he predicted a greater capital than Rome would occupy that hill and that later generations would command a great and flourishing country in the new world. He related that he had a dream or vision, in which he had seen a splendid parliament house on the hill, now known to us as Capitol Hill, which he purchased and called Rome, in prophetic honor of the great city to be.[3]

That vision—the Pope Prophecy—predates the Declaration of Independence by 143 years! How did Pope see the far-distant future? The short answer is long vision.

Not long ago, I had the privilege of touring the Capitol Dome. We climbed 343 steps to the top of the rotunda where we got a close-up view of *The Apotheosis of Washington*—the 4,664-square-foot fresco painted by Constantino Brumidi in 1865. Then we ducked through a door to the outdoor observatory where we were treated to a panoramic view of the city.

As I looked out over the city, I thought about the opening sentence from the book where I discovered the Pope Prophecy— *Standard History of the City of Washington from a Study of the*

Original Sources. It's a pedestrian title, but the opening sentence packs a punch.

> As the beholder looks upon the Capital of the Nation today, with its wide, shaded streets, magnificent buildings, restful parks, costly monuments, and thousands of trees, it requires a vigorous play of the imagination to picture the swamps and forests which they have replaced and to realize that where is now the teeming population of a metropolitan city were once the teepees and campfires of the primitive Indian inhabitants.[4]

As I stood on that observation deck and prayed over our city, I couldn't help but think of Francis Pope and Pierre Charles L'Enfant. If only they could see the city now! Then it dawned on me—they saw the city before the rest of us! How? With long vision!

TO THE THIRD AND FOURTH GENERATION

On the Swedish island of Visingsö, there is a forest with "immensely tall and unusually straight oak trees."[5] Three hundred thousand trees occupy nearly nine hundred acres, but the origin of that forest was shrouded in mystery because oak trees are not indigenous to that island. A hundred and fifty years after those acorns turned into oaks, the origin story was unearthed in a rather unusual way.

In 1980, the Swedish Navy received a letter from the Forestry Department notifying them that the ship lumber they had requested was ready. The Swedish Navy had no earthly idea what the Forestry Department was talking about. But after a little digging, it was discovered that in 1829, the Swedish parliament made an unusual request. Anticipating a shortage in lumber—and recognizing that oaks require 150 years to mature—the Swedish parliament had the foresight to order that 300,000 trees be planted on the island of Visingsö and protected for the Swedish Navy.[6]

That's long vision—vision beyond your resources, beyond your ability, beyond your death date. We have a hard time believing God for cities, but God says, "Ask me, and I will make the nations your inheritance."[7] God's vision is always bigger and better than ours! It's international and intergenerational. What God does for us is never just *for us*; it's also for the third and fourth generation.

Does your vision revolve around you? If it does, it'll be short-lived. Why? Because selfishness eventually short-circuits. A God-given vision always revolves around others. Long vision is digging wells and planting gardens for the next generation.

What wells do you need to dig?

What trees do you need to plant?

According to rabbinic tradition, after God told Noah to build an ark, the first thing Noah did was plant trees. Why? Given the size of the ark, it would take a boatload of planks to build it. Noah planted trees that took forty years to mature. Then and only then was he ready to build the ark. If you're going to dream big, you have to think long. You have to stretch your faith past the parameters of your lifespan.

SUPER GENERATION

The monarch butterfly is the only species of butterfly that migrate like birds. They spend their summers in the northern United States and their winters in Mexico, but it takes four generations of monarch butterflies to make this annual migration. It takes three generations to make the three-thousand-mile journey north. Stop and think about that—three generations of butterflies never reach their destination! All they do is help the next generation of butterflies get a little closer to the goal. That's how they fulfill their destiny.

The average lifespan of a monarch butterfly is six weeks, with one curious exception. The fourth generation can live up to eight months. That generation—called a super generation or Methuselah generation—manages to make the migration all the way south, back to the place where their great-great-grandparents were hatched.

That four-generation life cycle raises so many questions. Why do monarchs migrate north in the first place? How do they know where to go? And how does the fourth generation find their way home? Those questions pique my curiosity, which I explored in my last book—*A Million Little Miracles*. For the purposes of this book, that migration paints a picture of long vision. Each generation is tasked with getting the next generation a little closer to the goal.

"I know the plans I have for you," declares the LORD, "plans to prosper you and not to harm you, plans to give you hope and a future."[8]

We love that promise, but it's easy to overlook the context. The Israelites were prisoners of war in Babylon. A false prophet named Hananiah told them they would be there for only two years. The problem with that false narrative was this: If you have a two-year mindset, you don't even unpack your suitcase. You rent the city. Jeremiah relays a very different strategy: "Seek the peace and prosperity of the city to which I have carried you into exile. Pray to the LORD for it, because if it prospers, you too will prosper."[9] How did they do this? By planting gardens and building houses. Why? Because God wanted them to play the long game!

It's estimated that the average lifespan in the sixth century BC was thirty-five.[10] So a seventy-year vision represented two generations. God was telling these exiles to do what they did with the

third generation in mind. Why? Because that's what super generations do.[11] Long vision is doing things that will make a difference
seventy years from now!

In 2014, National Community Church purchased a $29.3 million
city block on Capitol Hill that we branded the Capital Turnaround.
It sits on the southeast corner of a 4.7-mile prayer circle I prayed in
1996. The fact that we purchased it eighteen years to the day, from
the day, of that prayer walk is no coincidence. When we started
redeveloping and repurposing that 100,000-square-foot building,
we dug 109 micropiles forty-feet deep to reinforce the 1891 columns.
Why? So we could build on top of the roof deck. If that acre-and-
a-half roof deck were land, the asking price would be somewhere
north of $25 million. There is very little land left on Capitol Hill, and
they aren't making more of it. A $1 million investment to leverage a
$25 million roof deck makes perfect sense, but here's the catch: We
have no plans to build on top of the building. Then why did we do
it? Because the next generation might want to!

WHAKAPAPA

There is a concept in Māori culture called *whakapapa*.[12] You are one
link in the long chain that is human history. You represent a moment in time situated between two eternities—the eternal past and
the eternal future. It's an exhortation to be a good ancestor.

Whakapapa is represented by the rope of life. It's an actual rope
with three interwoven strands—black, silver, and red. It's a con-
tinuous spiral that is two-directional. "At the same time as the spiral is going forward," says an old Māori proverb, "it is returning."[13]

All of us have two biological parents—a mom and a dad. We
have four grandparents and eight great-grandparents, but that's
where most of us stop the thought experiment. Go back ten generations, and we descend from 1,024 ancestors. Go back twenty

generations, and we have 1,048,576 ancestors. That's why, according to geneticists, all of us are at least fiftieth cousins. What's up, cuz!

In 1999, adidas ran an advertisement celebrating *whakapapa*. It began with the oldest living member of the All Blacks—the famous rugby team that represents New Zealand. The former All Blacks captain, Charlie Saxton, was eighty-six at the time. He put on his old jersey, but in the ad, he's reincarnated as Fred Allen, a captain and coach that followed him. In chronological order, with successive jerseys, the ad celebrates the lineage of leadership.

"You don't own the jersey," said one All Black. "You're just the body in the jersey at the time." The punch line at the end of the ad packs a punch: "The legacy is more intimidating than the opposition."[14]

Next time you feel intimidated by the opposition, remember the cloud of witnesses who have gone before you. They hold one end of the rope, and Jesus holds the other.

God's got this.

God's got you.

If adidas ran that ad for the kingdom of God, I imagine Elijah taking off his jersey and giving it to Elisha. For the record, Elisha performed twice as many miracles as Elijah. If success is succession, then Elisha's miracles are Elijah's legacy.

"What you leave behind is not what is engraved in stone monuments," said another All Black, "but what is woven into the lives of others."[15] Long vision is not just brick and mortar; it's flesh and blood. It's seeing God-given potential in other people. It's kneeling down so the next generation can stand on your shoulders.

OVERSTORY

In the world of ecology, the tallest trees in a forest form a canopy that is called the overstory. It provides shade for the understory—

all the vegetation that grows beneath the uppermost layer of foliage. If you walk through the woods, it's the understory that you interact with. But make no mistake, it's the overstory that determines the destiny of every living thing beneath its umbrella of branches. The overstory is always writing the understory! And what's true in the world of ecology is true of our lives.

We get our narratives from our families of origin, and that includes false narratives. Those origin stories set the tone, set the table, set the trajectory of our lives. If you don't like your understory, maybe it's time to tap into the overstory! When you are adopted into the family of God, you get grafted into the story of God. Scripture is our script cure. That overstory starts rewriting false narratives and overwriting negative narratives. It reveals your true identity and destiny. If you give God full editorial control, the Author and Perfecter of faith will start writing His story in and through your life.

When I get discouraged, it's usually because I'm too focused on the understory. I fixate on the dramas and melodramas of my life. That's when I need to fix my eyes on Jesus. Even more than a vision *from God,* I need a vision *of God.*

Long vision starts with remembering the future. That may sound like a contradiction in terms. How can you remember the future if it hasn't happened yet? We've got a cheat sheet called the book of Revelation. If you're discouraged, make a beeline to the back of the book. Don't lose faith in the end of the story—the overstory!

I know politics are incredibly polarized right now, but the kingdoms of this world are becoming the kingdom of our Lord and of His Christ.[16] Administrations come and go, but the kingdom of God is forever. The day is coming when every nation, tribe, people, and language will worship around God's throne. Long vision begins with the end in mind and works backward. We believe for the redemption of all things—heaven invading earth.

Read the Bible cover to cover and there is one inevitable, undeniable, incontrovertible overstory: *God is God, and I'm not.* Someday I'll stand before the judgment seat of God, and you won't be on it. And neither will I. My advice? Quit playing God. And while you're at it, quit playing the victim. Start playing the long game, and it starts with long vision.

CHAPTER 1

SIXTEEN MILES UPSTREAM

n December 1970, an American agronomist named Norman Borlaug was awarded the Nobel Peace Prize for his contribution to the world food supply. If you've never heard of him, you aren't alone. Most agronomists fly under the radar, but Borlaug is credited with saving more than one-eighth of our planet's population! In addition to the aforementioned Nobel Peace Prize, Dr. Borlaug was awarded the Presidential Medal of Freedom and the Congressional Gold Medal. He is one of only seven people to have received all three awards.[1]

In 1933, Adolf Hitler became chancellor of Germany while Franklin Delano Roosevelt was elected president of the United States. During the Second World War, Roosevelt and Hitler loomed large on the world stage. Very few people, for better or for worse, have had more impact on more people than Roosevelt and Hitler, but Norman Borlaug is one of them.

That same year, 1933, a nineteen-year-old Norman applied to the University of Minnesota but failed his initial entrance exam. Despite that inauspicious start to his academic career, he wasn't given to giving up. "Borlaug had a penchant for hastily deciding on some goal, heedless of its plausibility," said one biographer, "then working relentlessly to achieve it."[2] Borlaug was cut from the cloth called gradually then suddenly.

Norman Borlaug overcame that failed entrance exam and earned his bachelor of science in forestry while wrestling his way into the National Wrestling Hall of Fame. He went on to earn his PhD in plant pathology at the University of Minnesota in 1942.

While millions of men his age were shipped off to the Eastern Front to fight against the Third Reich, Borlaug felt called to fight a very different battle—world hunger. Dr. Borlaug took a research post at the International Maize and Wheat Improvement Center in Mexico where he cultivated a high-yield, disease-resistant variety of wheat.

In December 2006, both houses of Congress passed the Congressional Tribute to Dr. Norman E. Borlaug Act. According to said act, "the number of lives Dr. Borlaug has saved [is] more than a billion people."[3] Let that sink in for a second. A billion people! Very few have saved more lives than Norman Borlaug, and most people have never even heard of him. That includes the people whose lives he saved.

Norman Borlaug's compound impact on the twentieth century is tough to tabulate. He certainly deserves the awards and accolades he received, but legacy involves multivariable calculus. Borlaug is credited with saving a billion lives, but credit is complicated because it never belongs to one person.

"Is *all* that we see or seem," wrote Edgar Allan Poe, "but a dream within a dream?"[4] It's a rhetorical question, but the implied answer is *yes*! Every dream has a genealogy—it's a dream within a dream. So let me play a little game called connect the dots.

MENTORING CHAIN

In 1943, the vice president of the United States, Henry Wallace, grew concerned about an impending worldwide food shortage. Wallace, who had also served as secretary of agriculture, helped establish a research station in Mexico whose sole purpose was addressing food insecurity by creating hybridized wheat for arid climates. It was Wallace who appointed Borlaug to run that research center.[5] So Henry Wallace deserves partial credit for Borlaug's success, does he not? He's the one who saw potential in Borlaug. He's the one who opened the door of opportunity. But if Henry Wallace gets partial credit for that Nobel Prize, you have to trace the food chain.

In 1891, George Washington Carver became the first Black student admitted to Iowa State University.[6] After completing his master's degree, he became their first Black faculty member. During his undergrad years, Carver had a professor of dairy sciences who invited him over to his house on weekends. That professor, Henry C. Wallace, had a son named Henry A. Wallace. George Washington Carver used to take young Henry on "botanical expeditions" that instilled in him a curiosity for creation, a love for plants, and a vision for humanity.[7]

If Henry Wallace gets partial credit for influencing a future Nobel Prize winner named Norman Borlaug, then George Washington Carver gets partial credit for influencing a future vice president named Henry Wallace. But wait, there's more.

When George Washington Carver enrolled at Iowa State University, Joseph Budd served as head of the horticulture department. Budd had a daughter, Etta May, who taught art. She didn't just have an eye for art; she had an eye for talent. She said of Carver, "Painting was in him." Under her tutelage, Carver painted *Yucca and Cactus*, which won honorable mention at the 1893 Chicago World's Fair.[8] "I am greatly indebted [to her]," said Carver, "for whatever measure of success has come to me."[9]

George Washington Carver may not have saved a billion people like Norman Borlaug, but he did save the agricultural economy of the South by introducing crop rotation. Why did he pursue agronomy rather than art? "Miss Budd advised me to take up agriculture in order to render a greater service to my people."[10]

If George Washington Carver gets partial credit for influencing Vice President Henry Wallace—who influenced a Nobel Prize winner named Norman Borlaug—then Etta May Budd gets partial credit for influencing Carver.

We could play this game all day! What game? The long game. I love stories, but I love backstories even more because they reveal the overstories. Every dream has a genesis story, as does every dreamer. All of us were influenced by someone who was influenced by someone who was influenced by someone else.

Long vision is a long throw lens—it always aims at the third and fourth generation. But long vision also looks at life through a wide-angle lens. It always thinks ecosystem. It not only considers the consequences; it recognizes that there will always be unintended consequences.

SECONDHAND INFLUENCE

In 2014, the city of New York used a computer program called ClaimStat to map and index roughly thirty thousand annual insurance claims. The city had paid out $20 million in settlements for playground injuries, so investigators decided to examine what was happening upstream. They discovered that one swing was responsible for five broken legs because it was hung too low! "All someone needed to do was go out and raise the swing six inches, and the big problem would have been eliminated."[11] Note to self: Some really big problems have six-inch solutions!

Most of us tend to focus on downstream symptoms rather than upstream causes. That's true of medicine and marriages and mental health. Instead of solving for symptoms, long vision looks for long-term solutions. The irony? The solution is often as simple as raising a swing six inches!

Our actions and reactions have second, third, and fourth generation impact. Of course, the same is true of inactions. Like secondhand smoke, secondhand influence has real-world implications. For better or worse, we are more influenced by more people than we think. And whether we know it or not, people are watching us. That includes the little people who live in our homes called children.

One of the most mortifying moments for parents is when your kids say something inappropriate and they're quoting you! Kids are parrots. That said, nothing is more gratifying than your kids giving expression to the values you modeled for them. Either way, the apple doesn't fall far from the tree!

All of us have been negatively impacted by poor choices made centuries ago. We are also the beneficiaries of blessings we did nothing to deserve. We hint at these secondhand blessings when we celebrate Memorial Day or Independence Day. Freedom is not free. It was secured by soldiers whose names we'll never know.

Remember the Golden Rule? "Do to others what you would have them do to you."[12] When you bless someone, it doesn't just bless the person you're blessing. That's a shortsighted take on the Golden Rule. Why? It always has a domino effect. When I do marriage counseling, I hope it has a positive influence on husband and wife. But I'm also cognizant that it will impact their kids in tangible and intangible ways.

A few years ago, I started a coaching cohort with pastors. Why? Because pastors need pastors! If I mentor twelve pastors, I'm not just influencing twelve people. I'm indirectly influencing the thousands of people they lead. Influence is exponential.

Can I bring that idea down to earth?

MAKE SOMEONE'S DAY

Art Buchwald was a Pulitzer Prize–winning columnist for more than half a century. In one of his columns, he told a very pedestrian story about riding in an NYC taxi with a friend. When they got out, his friend said to the driver, "You did a superb job of driving." The cabbie was skeptical at first. "Are you a wise guy or something?" To which his friend said, "No . . . I admire the way you keep cool in traffic."

When the cabbie drove off, Art asked his friend, "What was that all about?" His friend said, "I am trying to bring love back to New York." Art said, "How can one man save New York?" Art's friend explained the method to his madness:

> I believe I have made that taxi driver's day. Suppose he has 20 fares. He's going to be nice to those 20 fares because someone was nice to him. Those fares in turn will be kinder to their employees or shopkeepers or waiters or even their own families. Eventually the goodwill could spread to at least 1,000 people. Now that isn't bad, is it?[13]

"But you're depending on that taxi driver to pass your goodwill to others," Art objected.

"The system isn't foolproof," his friend admitted. "I might deal with ten different people today. If out of ten I can make three happy, then eventually I can indirectly influence the attitudes of 3,000 more."[14]

Long vision is perceiving God-given potential in others. It's Etta May Budd seeing potential in a young student named George Washington Carver. It's George Washington Carver taking a young Henry Wallace on walks through the woods. It's Henry Wallace appointing Norman Borlaug to his research post in Mexico. They didn't know it, but by influencing one person, they were saving a billion lives!

Long vision sees the image of God in others. It's treating them as the apple of God's eye. It's making people feel seen, heard, and loved. It's always looking for opportunities to make someone's day. And sometimes it's as simple as a smile or a kind word.

REMOTE FUTURITY

There is a hundred-year-old photograph that hangs in our offices at National Community Church. Four men in top hats are standing on a dirt road surrounded by farmland. That dirt road is now Pennsylvania Avenue. In that picture is a fire station—Engine Company 19—that was built in 1910. Right behind it is a white house on a hill, the first residence built east of the Anacostia River. The four men in top hats would have had no idea what that house would become, but it was their vision that made our vision possible.

In 1996, a Black police officer named Sammie Morrison and a white pastor named Scott Dimock turned that home into the Southeast White House—a house of reconciliation for all people. We inherited that house many years ago, and we're doing our level best to stand on Sammie's and Scott's shoulders. That includes weekly reconciliation lunches, mentoring programs, and community gatherings.

The Southeast White House is in Ward 7, an underserved part of our city where many of the statistics we want to change come from. How do you change statistics? You don't just treat the symptoms. You go upstream. You disciple the next generation by giving them a dream. Or in this case, a Dream Center.

For many decades, there was an abandoned apartment building that sat vacant right behind the Southeast White House. But God gave us a vision—a long vision. "You will be called Repairer of

Broken Walls," said the prophet Isaiah, "Restorer of Streets with Dwellings."[15] That prophecy is our testimony. We purchased that dilapidated apartment building for the back taxes and invested $5.5 million turning it into the DC Dream Center.

The mayor of DC cut the ribbon on August 23, 2017, and we've been serving that part of our city ever since. The DC Dream Center operates sixty-four programs that impact thousands of kids. It's a place where generational curses are broken. It's a place where hope becomes habit. It's a place where God is birthing dreams in the next generation. Like every other dream we've ever had, the DC Dream Center has a genealogy. It was originally inspired by Tommy Barnett, Matthew Barnett, and the LA Dream Center.

There is a word—*futurity*—whose etymology traces back to the third act of Othello.[16] The Scottish writer Sir Walter Scott took that word and coined a phrase—"womb of futurity."[17] It's a metaphor for infinite potential. It's a place of endless possibilities. That's what the Dream Center is. That's what the Dream Center does.

We're not just trying to build a church. We're dreaming bigger and thinking longer—we're trying to bless a city to the third and fourth generation. If you want to change statistics, you have to change tactics. If you want to bless a city, you have to go sixteen years upstream.

We're bold enough to believe for Zechariah 8:5: "The city streets will be filled with boys and girls playing there." The best way to break generational curses is to bequeath generational blessings—one child at a time.

Miracles always start sixteen miles upstream!

A GREAT DISTANCE AWAY

One of the most momentous days in the history of Israel was the miraculous parting of the Jordan River. After wandering in the wilderness for forty years, the people finally set foot in the Promised Land. They crossed the Jordan opposite Jericho, but that isn't where the miracle happened.

> Now the Jordan is at flood stage all during harvest. Yet as soon as the priests who carried the ark reached the Jordan and their feet touched the water's edge, the water from upstream stopped flowing. It piled up in a heap a great distance away, at a town called Adam.[18]

If you look at a map of ancient Israel, Adam was about sixteen miles upstream from Jericho. That is where the miracle happened. That is where the breakthrough began. Such is life! Miracles often seem magical, but most miracles happen gradually then suddenly. Reverse engineer them, and they almost always start sixteen miles upstream. Or maybe I should say, sixteen years.

My first book, *In a Pit with a Lion on a Snowy Day,* was published in 2006. But that book was first conceived in my spirit sixteen years prior to publishing it. When I was nineteen, I heard Sam Farina preach a message about a guy named Benaiah who chased a lion into a pit on a snowy day and killed it. When I heard that message, a thought fired across my synapses: *If I ever write a book, I'd love to write a book about that story.* That was the genesis of my first book and its sequel, *Chase the Lion.* Those books took only about four months to write, but they were sixteen years in the making.

For better or for worse, what's happening downstream is always the byproduct of what happened upstream. And that's true in big and small ways. Some people hesitate offering their opinion in the executive boardroom because of what happened in a fourth-grade classroom. They raised their hand, gave the wrong answer, and their classmates laughed out loud. The laughter died down, but it never really died. The feeling of embarrassment keeps them from taking risks three decades later.

Most of us are Pavlovian prisoners to painful moments in our past. If you let your conditioned reflexes dictate your decisions, they sabotage success. Judas didn't betray Jesus after the Last Supper. The genesis of his betrayal happened when he was a little boy. "In the ancient shadows and twilights where childhood had strayed," said the poet George Russell, "the world's great sorrows were born and its heroes were made. In the lost boyhood of Judas, Christ was betrayed."[19]

Long vision isn't just the foresight to see far into the future. It's hindsight that finds perspective in the distant past. It understands that history shapes destiny. It recognizes that testimony is prophecy. The purpose of this book is to help you tap your future-tense potential, but you have to reconcile past-tense pain to do so.

The lost boyhood of Judas doesn't excuse his betrayal, but it does put it into perspective. We don't make decisions based on present-tense pros and cons. Our decisions are subconsciously framed by past-tense experiences. We don't react to current circumstances. We react to our entire lives! If you leave past-tense pain unresolved, it'll bite you in the back. Usually at the most inopportune times!

THE TRAJECTORY OF GRIEF

On June 30, 1860, then–bishop of Oxford, Samuel Wilberforce, attended the thirtieth annual meeting of the British Association for the Advancement of Science. Seven months prior to that gathering, Charles Darwin had published *On the Origin of Species*. That book took the world by storm and divided the scientific community into two camps: evolution vs. creation. That's a false dichotomy, by the way. Our capacity to evolve—spiritually, emotionally, relationally, intellectually, and genetically—is evidence of intelligent design.

It was at that science association gathering that Samuel Wilberforce became famous for one little quip. He asked his intellectual adversary, Thomas Huxley, if it was "through his grandfather or his grandmother that he claimed his descent from a monkey."[20]

Samuel Wilberforce and Charles Darwin were diametrically opposed in their cosmology, but they shared one thing in common. Both of them endured the heartbreaking loss of loved ones. Darwin lost two daughters and a ten year-old son to disease. Wilberforce lost an infant and an adult son, and his wife died while giving birth to their sixth child. What does that have to do with their beliefs? More than you think. It was grief that "pushed them in opposite directions."[21]

Before setting sail on the HMS *Beagle* to the Galápagos Islands, Charles Darwin studied theology at Christ's College with the intent of becoming a clergyman. Why Darwin lost his faith is not certain, but the loss of loved ones played a role. "Darwin was unable to reconcile the fact of his daughter's painful death with the idea of a just cosmos ruled by a benevolent deity," said one biographer. "Even before her death he had been moving away from the faith of his youth; it was gone forever by the day of the funeral."[22]

When I meet someone for the first time, I picture them as a thousand-piece jigsaw puzzle. The first time we meet, I'm seeing a snapshot. It's easy to judge the book by the cover, but that fails to take into account the pain of their past. Again, a painful past doesn't justify bad beliefs or bad behavior. But it does help put it into perspective. Just as dreams have a genealogy, so do nightmares. At the end of the day, grief pushes us in one of two directions—toward God or away from Him.

Which direction are you moving and why? How have past-tense experiences shaped your present-tense feelings and future-tense dreams? May God give you the self-awareness—prophetic insight and prophetic hindsight—to connect those dots. That self-awareness will help you discern your adaptive strategies and defense mechanisms. It might even help you know what it's like to be on the other side of you!

AUDIT YOUR ANCESTRY

Along with his quick wit, Samuel Wilberforce was known for his sanctified stubborn streak. He was unwilling to compromise his convictions, even if they contradicted popular opinion. Where did that conviction come from? It was more caught than taught.

If the name Samuel Wilberforce sounds familiar, it's probably because of his famous father—William Wilberforce. It was William Wilberforce who was instrumental in taking down the slave trade in Great Britain. "God Almighty has set before me two great objects," he said, "the suppression of the slave trade and the reformation of manners."[23]

The apple didn't fall far from the tree!

Everybody is born into somebody else's story. That's true of Charles Darwin and Samuel Wilberforce, and it's true of you. We stand on the shoulders of the previous generation, and it's our responsibility to give the next generation a leg up. If you compromise your convictions, you're also compromising the next generation.

Have you ever audited your ancestry? I'm not talking about your family tree, per se. I'm talking about the overstory you were grafted into. For some, it's a generational curse you need to break. For others, it's a generational blessing you did nothing to deserve.

One of my earliest memories is hearing my grandfather Elmer

Johnson pray for me. He had a habit of kneeling next to his bed at night, taking off his hearing aid, and praying for his children and grandchildren. He couldn't hear himself, but everybody else in the house could. My grandfather died when I was six, but his prayers did not. There is no expiration date on prayer! There have been moments in my life—decades after his death—when I've been the beneficiary of blessings I did nothing to deserve and the Holy Spirit has whispered these words: "Mark, the prayers of your grandfather are being answered in your life right now!"

I can't tell my story without telling that story. In a sense, his legacy is my destiny. I wouldn't be who I am—genetically or spiritually—without Grandpa Johnson. The same is true of Samuel Wilberforce and William Wilberforce. The same is true of Norman Bourlag, Henry Wallace, George Washington Carver, and Etta May Budd. The same is true of you.

THE REST OF THE STORY

The apostle Paul ends his epistle to the Romans by naming names— no less than twenty-eight of them. Each person profiled influenced Paul's life in some form or fashion. Paul is giving credit where credit is due. Phoebe was the gospel patron who helped fund his missionary journeys. Priscilla and Aquila risked their lives for him. And then there's someone named Rufus.

Greet Rufus, whom the Lord picked out to be his very own; and also his dear mother, who has been a mother to me.[24]

Does the name Rufus ring a bell? Most scholars believe that the Rufus in Romans is the same Rufus mentioned in Mark's gospel. It was his father, Simon of Cyrene, who carried the cross of Christ.

A certain man from Cyrene, Simon, the father of Alexander and Rufus, was passing by on his way in from the country, and they forced him to carry the cross.[25]

We have no idea how old Alexander and Rufus were, but there is no way they forgot this moment on the Via Dolorosa. This was the day when decades happened. If Judas betrayed Jesus because of his lost childhood, this is the opposite of that. There was something about watching their father carry the cross, then seeing Jesus hang on it, that left a permanent imprint on their souls.

For many decades, Paul Harvey hosted a radio segment called *The Rest of the Story*. In his inimitable voice, Paul Harvey would share little-known facts about well-known people. Then he would connect the dots between the backstory and the overstory. The story of Rufus would have made for an epic episode. He makes a cameo appearance in the gospel story, entering and exiting the stage in one verse. But Rufus is the rare extra who gets a curtain call. Paul is writing to the Romans many decades later, which means that little boy is now a grown man. According to Eastern Orthodox tradition, Rufus went on to become the bishop of Thebes.[26]

All of us could name names, like Paul did. And I would challenge you to do just that. When was the last time you thanked the people who have impacted your life? I recently tried to track down the surgeon at MedStar Washington Hospital Center who saved my life on July 23, 2000. His name? Jesus! I'm not even kidding. The *J* was pronounced like an *H*, but it felt like a God wink. After two days on a respirator because of ruptured intestines, God gave me a new lease on life. More than a quarter-century later, I think that surgeon deserves a thank-you!

Who do you need to thank?

Whose dream was the catalyst that conceived your dream?
Is there someone who made a sacrifice that changed your life?

BEGIN WITH THE END IN MIND

In 1996, we launched National Community Church with a core group of nineteen people. We've had the joy of serving tens of thousands of people over the last three decades, but I'm especially grateful, eternally grateful, for the original core group—Jay and Cari, Joe and Esterlin, Dick and Ruth, John and Janet, David and Paula, Bill and Sandra and Jeremy. They helped get National Community Church off the ground. And as we often say at NCC—once a shareholder, always a shareholder!

Our very first Easter, only forty-three people showed up. But I was over the moon because we had never had more than thirty, let alone forty! Almost three decades later, we have the privilege of hosting the Easter Sunrise at the Lincoln Memorial where thousands gather on those historic steps as the sun rises over our nation's capital. It has become a Washington tradition unlike any other, but let me give credit where credit is due. The Easter Sunrise is *whakapapa*—it's a sacred trust we inherited from pastor Amos and Sue Dodge.

In 1979, Amos was praying on the National Mall when he had a thought that he thought was a thought: *What if we hosted an Easter sunrise service at the Lincoln Memorial?*[27] Only 127 showed up that first Easter, but that's when and where the miracle began. When they handed the baton to us, we inherited forty years of faithfulness! And someday, we'll hand that sacred trust to someone else! Such is the kingdom of God—each of us is one link in the chain of church history.

It's not about us.

It's about the name above all names!

At that name, every knee will bow and every tongue will confess.

Long vision begins with the end in mind. The day is coming when every nation, tribe, people, and language will worship around the throne of God. The day is coming when we'll cast our crowns before that throne. Long vision is living this day—and every day—in light of that day. The end goal? The endgame? To hear the heavenly Father say, "Well done, good and faithful servant."[28]

CHAPTER 2

THE LOST WEEKEND

O n September 26, 1953, an artist named Herb Ryman was painting at his home in Hollywood when he received a phone call
from an old friend, Walt Disney. In a rather urgent voice, Walt
asked Herb to swing by his studio immediately. Herb wasn't sure
what the rush was all about, especially on a Saturday. But Walt
Disney had an idea, and he knew that some ideas have a short shelf
life. If you don't capture them quickly, they evaporate forever.

Fifteen minutes later, Walt met Herb at the studio gate. He
wasted no time casting vision for an amusement park—an amusement park unlike anything the world had ever seen. When Herb
asked to see a drawing of the park, Walt Disney said, "*You're* going
to do it."[1]

Roy Disney was scheduled to pitch the amusement park to potential investors the following Monday. He had crunched the
numbers, but Roy also knew that a picture was worth a thousand
words. And in this instance, millions of dollars. When Walt told
Herb they had two days to produce a prototype, he resisted the
idea. "It'll embarrass both you and me," said Herb. "I'm not going
to make a fool of either one of us."[2]

With tears in his eyes, Walt Disney said, "Herbie, this is my
dream."[3]

Over the next forty-two hours, Walt Disney painted word pictures and Herb Ryman did his best to draw them. The net result was an aerial view of Disneyland that looks remarkably close to the real thing. That weekend—known as the Lost Weekend—was the genesis of Disneyland.

Long vision becomes reality gradually then suddenly, but it often begins the way Disneyland did. There is a moment of conception when a single-cell dream is conceived, but you have to act on the idea in a hurry. You have to steward ideas the way you do dollars and cents!

Take captive every thought to make it obedient to Christ.[4]

I'd rather have one God idea than a thousand good ideas. Good ideas are good, but God ideas change the course of history. The challenge? Ideas are escape artists. If you don't capture them, it's as if they never existed. That's why I consider journaling a spiritual discipline.

When I write a book, I don't merely type on my keyboard. I worship God with the twenty-six letters of the English alphabet. It's all about taking thoughts captive. How? By putting them into words, sentences, paragraphs, and chapters.

If you're a musician, you take thoughts captive by combining lyrics and melodies. If you're an artist, you put brush to canvas. If you're a lawyer, you write the brief. If you're an entrepreneur, you pitch the business plan. If you're a CPA, you file the tax return.

EVERYTHING IS CREATED TWICE

Since its opening on July 17, 1955, Disneyland has welcomed more than 800 million guests. It's impossible to calculate the memories that park has made possible or the imaginations it has inspired. But like everything else, Disneyland was created twice.

When Walt Disney's daughters were very young, he took them to Griffith Park in Los Angeles. While watching them ride the merry-go-round, Disney first conceived of an amusement park where parents and children could make memories.[5] That dream lay dormant for many years, but that was a day when decades happened.

I can't overstate the importance of this principle already introduced: *Everything is created twice.* The first creation is spiritual while the second creation is physical. The first creation is internal while the second creation is external. The first creation happens in the imagination, while the second creation involves time, talent, and treasure.

Some of us are better at creativity—the first creation. Others are better at tenacity—the second creation. Either way, the key to the first creation is praying like it depends on God. Prayer is how we get God ideas. Prayer is how we write history before it happens. Praying is a form of dreaming, and dreaming is a form of praying. It's a virtuous cycle—the more you pray, the bigger you dream. And the bigger you dream, the more you have to pray! Of course, you can't just pray like it depends on God. You have to work like it depends on you—that's the second creation.

The metacognitive capacity to imagine the future is part of the *imago Dei.* Imagination is the birthright given to us by the One whose image we bear. That is what enables us to architect cities, engineer moon shots, and code software. When we give expression to our creativity, we are mirroring what the Creator did day one, day two, day three, day four, day five, and day six. Of course, Walt Disney did this better than most.

If you've ever visited a Disney amusement park, you're walking around inside Walt Disney's imagination. That's where Tomorrowland was first conceived. And even if you don't consider yourself a creative, it's still true of you and me. Imagination is the incubator where ideas come from, and ideas can come from anywhere if you're looking for them.

THE MOST METICULOUS PLACE ON EARTH

Long vision is telescopic, but it's also microscopic. It never loses sight of the big picture, but no detail is too small. Disney may be known as the most magical place on earth, but it's also the most meticulous place on earth. And in my book, meticulous begets miraculous.

Do you know why the water is dyed green on the Jungle Cruise? To hide the tracks beneath the water.[6] Does that kind of detail really matter? It did to Walt Disney! That's why the park pumps different aromas called Smellitzers into different parts of the park.[7] Main Street smells like cookies while the Pirates of the Caribbean ride smells like fresh sea air.

Disneyland has more than 130 dining options that serve thousands of pounds of turkey legs, corn dogs, and the iconic Dole Whip every single day. If you've ever worked in the food industry, you're wondering how the park isn't overrun with rodents. The answer is two hundred feral cats who are given free rein to prowl the park by night.

A few years ago, I got sucked into one of those social media rabbit holes that turn into a time warp. The post posed a question: *Why aren't there mosquitoes at Disney World?* No mosquitoes? That was news to me, but come to think of it, I couldn't recall a single mosquito bite while waiting in line for Space Mountain.

What makes that feat so amazing is that Disney World was built on a swamp! That didn't discourage Walt Disney; it actually animated him. "It's kind of fun," said Walt, "to do the impossible."[8] So how did they do it? They hired General William "Joe" Potter to oversee their Mosquito Surveillance Program.[9] A graduate of

MIT, General Potter had served as governor of the Panama Canal Zone. He employed lessons learned from his time wearing a panama hat.

One, there is no standing water in Disney's parks. Everything is designed so that water cannot pool, and there is a vast drainage system beneath the park. Where there is water, you'll always find a fountain to keep the water moving. Two, they use a garlic spray throughout the park. It's subtle enough that humans don't detect it, but mosquitoes are repelled by it.[10] And three, they keep chicken coops all around the resort. Those chickens get blood tests to see if they've been exposed to any mosquito-transmitted pathogens. That tips the staff off to any part of the parks that need a little extra attention.[11]

THE LAW OF REQUISITE VARIETY

Disney's attention to detail is legendary, but they may have been leapfrogged by their subsidiary—Pixar. Before filming *Ratatouille*, animators flew to France where they spent six days dining in Michelin-starred restaurants, touring kitchens, and interviewing chefs. Sign me up! Of course, they also ventured into the sewer system to study Parisian rats.

Before animating *Up*, they took a field trip to Venezuela because they wanted to see Tepui—the tabletop mountain that Paradise Falls is modeled after—up close and personal. They also brought an ostrich into Pixar's headquarters to help animators model the movements of Kevin, the giant tropical bird.[12]

Have you ever seen a Michelin-rated French kitchen? Me neither! Are Parisian rats any different from any other rats? I'm not sure I even want to know. And I wouldn't know Tepui from *Kung Phooey*. Most of us wouldn't know the difference if Pixar had cut creative corners, but their animators would.

"Does this kind of microdetail matter?" asks Ed Catmull, co-founder of Pixar. "I believe it does. There's something about knowing your subject and your setting inside and out—a confidence—that seeps into every frame of your film."[13]

Can I share a pet peeve? Unevenly folded bulletins! Why does it drive me crazy? Because I used to print them and fold them on Saturday nights, so I know it's possible! Can I get one more pet peeve off my chest? Misspelled words on worship chorus slides, especially Jesus! You don't have to be obsessive-compulsive about details, but I do believe excellence honors God. "No crooked table legs or ill-fitted drawers," said Dorothy Sayers, "came out of the carpenter's shop in Nazareth."[14]

When the Pixar team goes on those fact-finding trips, they aren't even sure what they're looking for. And that's precisely the point. "You'll never stumble upon the unexpected," says Catmull, "if you stick only to the familiar."[15]

One key to long vision is getting out of your normal routine. Once the routine becomes routine, you have to change the routine. It's called the law of requisite variety. There is a formula I've employed for many decades now: change of pace + change of place = change of perspective. What you see is determined by where you stand.

When I travel, I do so with great intentionality. And I always come home with fresh eyes. But that doesn't mean you have to travel halfway around the world. Sometimes it's as simple as a prayer walk or short run. Or as my friend Bob Goff likes to say, "Turn your head slightly to the left." You do you, but you have to find ways to reset your mindset.

DOLPHINS IN THE DESERT

If you don't think details are important, I would remind you that twelve chapters in the book of Exodus are devoted to interior design—right down to the color of the curtains, the feng shui of the furniture, and the ingredients in the incense. If those details matter to God, maybe they should matter to us! There is an obscure verse of Scripture that illustrates the importance of aesthetics. When the Israelites were building the tabernacle, one of the punch-list items is rather curious:

> You are to make a cover for the tent of ram skins dyed red and a covering of dolphin skins above that.[16]

Wait, what? Where in the world would the Israelites find dolphin skins in the desert? The answer is the Red Sea. Did you know that marine biologists have identified at least eight species of dolphin whose habitat is the Red Sea?[17]

The Hebrew word translated "dolphin" is somewhat mysterious. Some translations say porpoise or seal or sea cow. But according to rabbinic tradition, the dolphins jumped for joy when God made a sidewalk through the sea. They were cheering on the people of Israel by chirping, but some of those dolphins died during the crossing. God told Moses to keep those dolphin skins as a reminder of that miracle, then they were sewn together as a covering for the tabernacle.[18]

The specificity and intentionality are unmistakable, are they not? But why would God command them to make the covering of the tabernacle out of dolphin skins? Because those dolphin skins doubled as the ceiling of their Sistine Chapel. When the Israelites lost vision, they served as a visual reminder of their wonder-working God. Every time they looked up in worship, their faith was renewed.

What does that have to do with long vision? You can't spell *faithfulness* without the first five letters—our faith is a function of God's faithfulness. If you forget the past, you don't just lose memory. You lose imagination. Testimony is prophecy! If God did it before, He can do it again. "When you see this tent of dolphin skins," said Moses, "remember that we did not . . . become a free people without a lot of help."[19] Long vision is a function of long memory.

GO, SET, READY

In March 1873, *The Atlantic Monthly* published a narrative by Henry James titled "The Madonna of the Future." James told the story of a would-be artist named Theobald. He was well educated and highly trained, but the fear of imperfection paralyzed him.[20]

Any other perfectionists out there? I'm a recovering perfectionist, but one of the things that helped me over the hump is the 80 percent rule. The original inspiration was something Andy Stanley said: "You are probably never going to be more than about 80 percent certain."[21] When it comes to marriage, I might aim a little higher than 80 percent. That said, uncertainty is always part of the risk-reward ratio. Faith doesn't come with a money-back guarantee.

When I feel like someone can do something 80 percent as good as I can, it's time to delegate. When a service is at 80 percent capacity, it's time to launch another one. When I feel like a book is 80 percent of the way there, it's time to hit save and send it to my editor.

Theobald told everybody about his grand ideas, but that's all they ever were. After many years of telling others about what he was going to do, he died a sudden death. That's when it was discovered that his canvas was blank. Theobald never finished because he never started.

Is there something you need to start? The first step is always the hardest, but that's how the journey of a thousand miles begins. Maybe it's time to give yourself a self-imposed deadline. That's what I did with my thirty-fifth birthday—I turned it into a book deadline.

There is an old adage: *Ready, set, go.* I certainly believe in due diligence, but many years ago we inverted the order and turned it into a core value: *Go, set, ready.* I'm certainly not suggesting that you don't count the cost—please do. Failing to plan is planning to fail, and it's a sin of presumption. But there is also a sin of procrastination. When everything is said and done, God is not going to say, "Well *said,* good and faithful servant." He won't say, "Well *thought,*" or "Well *planned,*" either! There is only one commendation: "Well *done!*"

Those who can, *do.* Those who can't, *criticize!* Criticize by creating! Anything less is virtue signaling. It's a form of self-righteousness that is anything but. The opposite of holy is holier-than-thou.

Most of us are educated way beyond the level of our obedience. We don't need to know more; we need to do more with what we know. And we need to do it now! If you wait until you're ready, you'll be waiting the rest of your life.

Lora and I weren't ready to get married—I was twenty-two and she was twenty! A few years later, we weren't ready to have kids. Who is? I wasn't ready to plant and pastor a church in my mid-twenties. We weren't ready to launch any of our eight campuses. We weren't ready to go on mission trips or give to missions. And we certainly couldn't afford to purchase a city block on Capitol Hill worth $29.3 million.

The first creation always happens in the imagination, but the second creation requires risk. Long vision involves as much perspiration as it does inspiration. It takes blood, sweat, and tears. And I might add, years!

GRAND GESTURE

In the 1980s, Jim Carrey was a starving actor trying to land a role. Almost every night, for four years, he would drive to the top of

Mulholland Drive overlooking Hollywood. That was his dreaming place. That's where he verbalized and visualized his future.[22]

In the fall of 1985, Jim Carrey wrote a $10 million check to himself. He postdated it ten years—Thanksgiving 1995. He wrote, "For acting services rendered" in the memo line. Then he kept that check in his wallet for a decade![23]

"Until it's on paper," said Sir John Hargrave, "it's vapor."[24]

That's why I've kept a journal for more than thirty years. It's my dreamcatcher. That's where I pen prayers, ink God ideas, and count my blessings by keeping track of gratitudes.

Write down the vision
And inscribe it clearly on tablets.[25]

The best way to personalize, internalize, and materialize goals is to put them on paper. And while it's unorthodox, writing a check to yourself counts. According to former professor of psychology Dr. Gail Matthews, writing down your goals increases the likelihood of accomplishing them by 42 percent.[26] Written goals hold us accountable. And if you want to up the ante, give those goals a deadline like Jim Carrey did.

In early 1994—less than ten years after writing that check—Jim Carrey was cast as Lloyd Christmas in *Dumb and Dumber*. "So you're saying there's a chance?" Yes, I am. Jim Carrey was paid $7 million for his role in that movie. The next year, he became the first comedic actor to ink a $20 million deal for his role in *The Cable Guy*.[27]

The $10 million check that Jim Carrey wrote to himself in 1985 was more than a wish or a whim—it was a grand gesture. It's a defining decision or dramatic action. Remember the invisible voice in *Field of Dreams* that whispered, "If you build it, he will come"?[28]

The grand gesture was a farmer named Ray Kinsella building a baseball diamond in a cornfield.

It can be a romantic gesture, like getting down on one knee and popping the question. It can be a physical gesture, like taking a "before" picture when starting a new diet or exercise routine. It can be a spiritual gesture, like the one-way missionaries who packed their belongings into coffins instead of suitcases because they knew they would never return.

In October 1989, I walked into the admissions office at the University of Chicago and informed a very surprised admissions officer that they could have their full-ride scholarship back because I was transferring to Central Bible College. Some friends and family second-guessed that grand gesture, but I knew that delayed obedience is disobedience. I knew I was burning a bridge, but that's what made it a grand gesture.

The Bible is full of grand gestures. Noah didn't just build a rowboat—he built an ark that wasn't surpassed in size by another ship until the RMS *Titanic* made its maiden voyage in 1912. When Israel's army retreated from the Philistines during one of their epic battles, a mighty man named Shammah took his stand in a field of lentils.[29] Remember when Peter got out of the boat in the middle of the Sea of Galilee in the middle of the night? And then there were the Ephesians who didn't sell their sorcery scrolls to the local pawnshop; they threw them into a bonfire! What makes that a grand gesture? Those scrolls were worth 50,000 drachmas, which equates to 12.6 million in today's dollars![30]

I have no idea what God-sized goals you're going after, but it often takes a grand gesture to get there. Grand gestures are small steps that turn into giant leaps. Grand gestures end old chapters and begin new ones. Grand gestures are the days when decades happen.

When we planted National Community Church in 1996, our monthly income as a church was $2,000 and it cost $1,600 to rent the DC public school where we met. That left $400 for my salary and all other expenses. We were living offering to offering, and we wouldn't be self-supporting as a church until year three.

Eight months into our plant, I felt like the Lord said, "It's time to start giving to missions." My initial reaction? It's time for people to start giving to us! Have you ever gotten into an argument with God? I certainly did that day, but here's what I've learned about getting into an argument with God: If you win the argument, you lose. If you lose the argument, you win.

I still remember writing our first $50 check to missions because it felt like a *Field of Dreams* moment. That doesn't sound like much money, but it proved to be a tipping point. The month after giving that gift, our income tripled. Coincidence? I think not. I think it was God delivering on His promise—"Give and it will be given to you. A good measure, pressed down, shaken together and running over, will be poured into your lap. For with the measure you use, it will be measured to you."[31] Over the last thirty years, National Community Church has given more than $30 million to kingdom causes that don't have our name on it, but it started with a grand gesture.

A grand gesture turns over the hourglass, but it takes time for dreams to materialize. How much time? That's impossible to answer, but it'll probably take a lot longer than you like. It might seem like Jim Carrey was an overnight success, but if my math is correct, he drove to the top of Mulholland Drive at least a thousand times!

I have no idea what God has called you to do, but faith is taking the first step before God reveals the second. What step of faith do you need to take? What grand gesture do you need to make? The first step might be as simple as writing it down!

A rather infamous Harvard Business School study illustrates the power of written goals. The 3 percent of MBA graduates who had written goals were earning ten times more than the 97 percent who didn't ten years later.[32] That study is infamous because it was fictious, but that doesn't make it untrue! Putting pen to paper isn't an abracadabra, but Southwest Airlines, Shark Week, and Oprah's media empire each started on the back of a napkin![33]

BINDING AND LOOSING

In 1997, National Community Church had moved from a DC public school to the movie theaters at Union Station. One day I was walking home, and as I approached the intersection at 2nd and F streets, I spotted a dilapidated piece of property. That's when and where the still small voice of the Spirit whispered these words: "Mark, that crackhouse would make a great coffeehouse." God idea or crazy idea? It's not always easy discerning the difference, is it? But the million-dollar price tag piqued my curiosity—it was just crazy enough to make me wonder if God was in it.

I started circling that crackhouse like it was Jericho. Five years later—and after about five thousand prayer circles—we purchased that crackhouse for $300,000. The more we prayed, the more the price went down! Even more amazing? After purchasing it, we discovered that four people had offered more money. And two of them were real estate developers. So how did we get it? The short answer is found in Matthew 18:18:

> Whatever you bind on earth will be bound in heaven, and whatever you loose on earth will be loosed in heaven.

Every prayer has to meet a twofold litmus test—it has to be *in the will of God* and *for the glory of God.* If it's not, it's a nonstarter. Prayer is not outlining your agenda to God. Prayer is letting God outline His agenda to you. If you get that backward, you end up with an inverted relationship with God.

The word *bind* is a legal term. Prayer is how we put contracts on things—that's the first creation. Prayer is how we notarize the promises of God. Prayer is how we write history before it happens.

Is there something you need to bind?

Something you need to loose?

Truth be told, we had no business going into the coffee business. And I think that's why Ebenezers has inspired so many entrepreneurs to go after their dreams. This is a little embarrassing, but our business plan was sending one of our employees to work at Starbucks for six months. Somehow, someway, Ebenezers has been voted the No. 1 coffee shop in DC multiple times. We recently started our own roastery, and we're the exclusive provider of coffee beans to our friends and neighbors at Museum of the Bible.

It felt like forever turning that crackhouse into a coffeehouse. Opening our second shop at the Capital Turnaround hasn't been any easier, but binding and loosing happen gradually then suddenly. I don't believe in name it and claim it, but we aren't doing anyone any favors if we don't exercise our spiritual authority. Of course, spiritual authority is always exercised with humility. That combination can move mountains, including Space Mountain.

SEVEN CIRCLES

Less than a decade after opening Disneyland, Walt Disney set his sights on opening a second amusement park in Florida. He secretly started purchasing land in 1964. The next year, he announced plans to build EPCOT—the Experimental Prototype Community of Tomorrow. Disney World opened its doors on October 1, 1971, but Walt Disney died five years before that—December 15, 1966. In other words, Walt never got to see his dream. Or did he?

On opening day, a reporter is purported to have said to Walt's brother Roy, "This must be a bittersweet day for you. It's really sad that Walt never got to see Disney World." Roy's comeback is an all-timer: "If Walt didn't see it, we wouldn't be standing in it."

We're right back where we started—everything is created twice! "Imagination is everything," Albert Einstein is quoted as saying. "It is the preview to life's coming attractions."[34] The second creation takes time, talent, and treasure. And more often than not, a grand gesture of some sort.

Right before releasing my sixth book, *The Circle Maker*, I had a hunch that God was going to bless that book. By faith, we created a foundation called Seven Circles and decided to split royalties fifty-fifty. That book has sold millions of copies, and we've had the joy of giving more than we imagined to causes we care about.

Why has God blessed that book beyond what I would have or could have asked or imagined? The grand gesture of setting up a foundation is one piece of the puzzle. It was a *Field of Dreams* decision—if you establish it, God will bless it. I think the same is true of Ebenezers. God has blessed our coffeehouse because every penny of profit goes to kingdom causes.

Is there a check you need to write?

A foundation you need to establish?

A design you need to draw?

Grab a napkin and get started.

CHAPTER 3

OPPORTUNITY COST

I n the fall of 2008, America was in the throes of the Great Recession. But economic downturns and market collapses don't keep dreamers from dreaming. Four MBA students at the Wharton School decided to disrupt the eyewear industry by offering fashionable styles at affordable costs *online*. That makes perfect sense looking back, but it made no sense to professor Adam Grant. One of those MBA students gave Grant an opportunity to invest in Warby Parker, but he took a hard pass. "If it were a good idea," famous last words, "someone would have done it already."[1]

The founders of Warby Parker trusted their instincts—and they must have hit a nerve in the market—because they had 20,000 orders on their waiting list within the first month of operation. Last time I checked, Warby Parker had a market cap valuation of $2.66 billion.

Looking back on his decision to *not* invest in that IPO, Adam Grant said, "It was the worst financial decision I've ever made."[2] How could it be his worst financial decision when he didn't lose anything? It didn't cost Grant one red cent in *actual cost*. No harm, no foul, right? Not exactly. That's only true if you consider the cost side of the ledger. Adam Grant forfeited millions of dollars in *opportunity cost*.

In the world of finance, an *actual cost* is an expenditure. It shows up on the balance sheet as a liability, and it's relatively easy to account for. *Opportunity cost,* on the other hand, is a hidden cost. It's the loss of potential gain because of indecision or inaction.

"Don't begin," Jesus said, "until you count the cost."[3] Sounds simple enough, but it's not as simple as addition or subtraction! Counting the cost is multivariable calculus—you have to weigh actual costs and opportunity costs. Actual costs are easier to count, so we tend to give them more weight. But it's opportunity costs that offer the greatest risk-reward. Like time, talent, and treasure—opportunity is a stewardship issue.

Make the most of every opportunity.[4]

That exhortation is all-inclusive, including Warby Parker. Long vision is seeing and seizing God-ordained opportunities. Of course, many of those opportunities come disguised as problems. In my experience, divine appointments are not the kind of appointments you schedule. They often happen at the most inconvenient times. Remember the good Samaritan? He saw opportunity where others saw inopportunity. May God give us peripheral vision to see what's really happening around us and the courage to inconvenience ourselves for His glory and the good of our neighbors.

NOTHING VENTURED, NOTHING GAINED

Do you remember what you were doing on May 15, 1997? Why would you, unless that date marks a major life event? It was an ordinary Thursday, but I remember that day because of what I didn't do.

I was contemplating investing in an online bookstore with a strange name—Amazon. At the time, I was reading more than two hundred books a year. Needless to say, Amazon was a booklover's dream! I bought so many books that they sent me a gift. It was a mug that said, "Live as if you were to die tomorrow. Learn as if you were to live forever."

On the day Amazon made its initial public offering—May 15, 1997—I almost invested in the IPO. But instead of investing in Amazon, I decided to invest in a Canadian mining company. Why? I had it on good authority that they were about to strike gold. Yeah, right! If I had been around during the gold rush of 1849, I probably would have been on the first stagecoach to California! That mining company declared bankruptcy not long after, and our entire investment was lost. Meanwhile, Amazon would become the world's largest online retailer.

Not investing in Amazon cost us *nothing*, but nothing doesn't cost nothing. Everything in life is a trade-off. Saying *yes* to one thing is saying *no* to something else.[5] I recently did the math: If we had invested in Amazon at the opening price, a $5,000 investment would be worth $11.4 million today! That's a painful exercise, but it's a healthy reminder. At the end of the day, opportunity costs weigh more than actual costs.

Most of us are pretty good at calculating actual costs. All it takes is addition and subtraction. Calculating opportunity costs is much more complicated because it involves compound interest. That's where long vision enters the equation. It's recognizing that every decision we make, every action we take, is subject to inflation and deflation. Good decisions appreciate while bad decisions depreciate. How? Gradually then suddenly!

Long vision is an eye for opportunity. And despite what the old aphorism says, opportunity does *not* knock. You have to knock on it. And you usually have to knock, knock. Remember Eugene Peterson? He knocked seventeen times before getting a book deal. And that's precisely what Jesus advocated: "Knock and the door will be opened."[6] It's a present imperative verb, which means you have to keep on knocking.

INACTION REGRETS

Psychologists make a distinction between two kinds of regret—action regrets and inaction regrets. An action regret is saying something you wish you hadn't said or doing something you wish you hadn't done. Action regrets can be quite painful, but inaction regrets ache the soul. It's the opportunities we left on the table and left us wondering—*what if?*

According to sociologists Thomas Gilovich and Victoria Medvec, time plays a key factor when it comes to regret. In the short term, we regret actions more than inactions. But it's a coin flip—53 percent to 47 percent. Over the long term, however, we regret inactions more than actions. And it's not even close—84 percent to 16 percent.[7]

When everything is said and done, we may regret sins of omission more than sins of commission. It's the talent we buried in the ground like the servant who played it safe. It's the opportunities we left untapped because we settled for the status quo. It's the sacrifices we failed to make, the risks we refused to take.

The etymology of the word *decide* is the Latin *decidere*—"to cut off."[8] Decisions are difficult to make because you cut off options. But decisions cut two ways. There is an actual cost and an opportunity cost. The actual cost may result in an action regret, but the opportunity cost will result in an inaction regret. The choice is yours, but choose wisely!

If you had one shot, one opportunity, to seize everything you ever wanted, would you capture it? Or let it slip? I know, palms are sweaty, knees are weak, arms are heavy! My advice? "Lose yourself in the music, the moment."[9]

Is there a risk you need to take?

What's holding you back?

I'd rather fail at the right thing than succeed at the wrong thing!

ALL OVER AGAIN

I preached my first sermon at National Community Church on January 14, 1996. The only thing I remember about that message is my opening illustration. I can't remember the original source, but I think I stumbled across it in a *Reader's Digest*. It was a survey of fifty people who were over the age of ninety-five. Add it up and that's about five thousand years of combined life experiences. They were all asked the same question:

IF YOU COULD LIVE YOUR LIFE ALL OVER AGAIN,

WHAT WOULD YOU DO DIFFERENTLY?

Three answers emerged as a consensus. One, they would *reflect more*—stop and smell the roses. Two, they would *risk more*—the greatest risk is taking no risks. And three, they would *do more things that live on after they died.*[10]

Are you living for time or eternity?

Are you living for the applause of people or applause of nail-scarred hands?

Are you building altars to God or monuments to self?

Some people are so busy climbing the ladder of success that they fail to realize it's leaning against the wrong wall. Maybe it's time to reevaluate the risk-reward ratio in your life. How? Audit your regrets.

Auditing your regrets can be a painful exercise, but the only way to leverage regret is to learn from it. And if you don't learn from your regrets, you make the same mistakes all over again. You trade your birthright for a bowl of stew.

"By making us feel worse today," said Daniel Pink, "regret helps us do better tomorrow."[11] In his book *The Power of Regret*, Pink cites some poignant examples:

I regret pawning my flute for thirty bucks.

I regret picking up my first pack of Camel cigarettes in 1999.

I regret bullying kids growing up.

I regret being unfaithful to my wife.

I regret not finding a good therapist ten years ago.

I regret working eighteen-hour days, six days a week.

I regret having an abortion.

I regret that I didn't cuddle more with my kids.

I regret oversharing on social media.

I regret that I let a college counselor convince me I didn't have what it takes to be a doctor.[12]

Some of those are regrets of commission—things that were said or done. Some of them are regrets of omission—things that went unsaid or undone. Either way, you have to learn from those regrets.

What are your greatest regrets—action and inaction?

What have you learned from them?

And what are you going to do about them?

I have my fair share of regrets. This would be a very long book if I shared all of them! But if you redeem your regrets the right way, they can change the trajectory of your life in a positive way.

ESTABLISH BOUNDARIES

When I wrote my first book, *In a Pit With a Lion on a Snowy Day*, I started getting invitations to speak here, there, and everywhere. I was genuinely honored by those invitations, and maybe that's why I said *yes* to way too many of them. I got stretched so thin I felt like Stretch Armstrong.

Leading a growing church is a full-time calling. So is writing a book a year. Throw in speaking engagements all over tarnation and it wasn't sustainable. I was essentially holding down three jobs simultaneously. Plus, we had three young children at the time.

I'm a type 3, "the achiever," on the Enneagram—pedal to the metal. Translation? Every opportunity is an *amazing* opportunity! I tend to overcommit, which leads to overpromising and underdelivering. If you try to be all things to all people, you end up being nobody to no one! Saying *yes* to those invitations was saying *no* to my family.

At one point—a low point—Lora said, "This isn't what I signed up for." She said it graciously, but she also said it in no uncertain terms. At that moment, I knew I had some hard choices to make. I had to reestablish my priorities—family first—by reestablishing some boundaries in my life.

That's when I decided to limit my travel to twelve overnight speaking trips a year, and I've since dialed it back to seven. At the end of the day, I want to be famous in my home. And it's hard to be famous in your home if you're never home! That predecision saved me from myself.

I also asked our stewardship team to limit me to serving on three boards concurrently. Why? It's easier letting someone else say my *no* for me. Plus, I scaled back my preaching to twenty-six weekends a year. Not only does that give me margin to write a book a year, but it has also given room for other communicators in our ecosystem to exercise their gifts.

What regrets do you need to leverage?

What boundaries do you need to establish?

Your health and wealth are largely determined by predecisions— the decisions you make before you have to make a decision. A financial predecision is called a budget. A food predecision is called a diet. If you don't establish healthy and holy boundaries, you'll end up majoring in minors and minoring in majors. The net result is inaction regrets!

Establishing boundaries is hard to do, but it will save you from a ton of regret. It helps us keep the main thing the main thing. At the end of the day, success is not how many people I pastor, how many books I sell, or how many conferences I speak at. Success is when those who know me best respect me most. That's my wife and my kids, full stop.

SO FAR SO GOD

When we were trying to turn a crackhouse into Ebenezers Coffeehouse many years ago, I was garnering support at a community meeting on Capitol Hill. As someone who has lived on the hill for thirty years, I can attest to the fact that local politics are as contentious as national politics.

When I cast the vision for the coffeehouse, I naïvely thought that everyone would rise up and call us blessed. I have since learned that some people love the status quo so much they'd rather have a crackhouse than a coffeehouse for their neighbor.

A few weeks before this particular community meeting, we hosted an Easter egg hunt for kids on Capitol Hill. One of our neighbors complained that we were talking about Jesus too much at the outreach. Really? First of all, we're a church. Second, it's Easter. And third, we underwrote the entire outreach on our own dime.

When I walked into this community meeting, I realized that the woman who registered that complaint was present and accounted for. This is not an excuse, but it put me in a defensive posture. I felt like I was walking on Easter eggshells. Without community support, turning that crackhouse into a coffeehouse would be impossible, so I backpedaled.

After I updated the community leaders on our vision for the coffeehouse, someone in the audience asked the meaning of the name—Ebenezers. No, it has nothing to do with Scrooge! We had chosen that name as a way of honoring God. That's what Samuel called the altar he built at Mizpah. Ebenezer means "hitherto the Lord has helped us." Or as we paraphrase it on our coffee sleeves— *so far so God.*

When the question was asked, I chickened out. I said that it meant "so far so good." But that answer took God out of the equation. Instead of offending this woman, I offended the Holy Spirit. The second I said it, I felt the conviction of the Spirit. I missed an opportunity to honor God by doing the exact opposite.

If you're afraid of offending people, you will ultimately offend God.

If you're afraid of offending God, you will inevitably offend people.

Who are you going to offend? That's one of the most important predecisions you'll ever make! I still regret that cop-out, but I've learned from it. Never again! I'm not going to pull punches when it comes to proclaiming the truth, the whole truth, and nothing but the truth! I won't apologize for who I am or what I believe. Regardless of who's in the room, I'm going to testify to the goodness of God. In a winsome way, of course.

Reliving regret is painful, but not as painful as unprocessed mistakes. Is there a regret you need to AAR—after action review? You can't change your regrets—what's done is done. But you can learn from and leverage them. You can become the opposite of the mistake you made!

THE ETYMOLOGY OF OPPORTUNITY

On August 15, 1987, Howard Schultz purchased a small chain of coffeehouses with a strange name—Starbucks. He almost passed up the opportunity because it felt like a "salmon swallowing the whale."

Have you ever felt that way? An opportunity presents itself, but you shrink from it instead of seizing it? Schultz describes that defining moment this way:

> *This is my moment,* I thought. *If I don't seize the opportunity, if I don't step out of my comfort zone and risk it all, if I let too much time tick on, my moment will pass.* I knew that if I didn't take advantage of this opportunity, I would replay it in my mind for my whole life, wondering: *What if?*[13]

The $4 million price tag was awfully intimidating, but when Starbucks stock went public five years later—June 26, 1992—its market capitalization was $273 million by the closing bell. Not a bad ROI—return on investment. Fast-forward a few decades and there are more than forty thousand stores in eighty-eight countries with an annual revenue exceeding $36 billion.

How did Starbucks end up on every other street corner? Two ways—gradually then suddenly! But it started with a quantum risk. Such is life and leadership. The greatest risk is taking no risks. The challenge? Our aversion to loss is twice as great as our attraction to gain.[14] That cognitive bias, called loss aversion, is a function of our negativity bias.

Are you playing to win?

Or are you playing not to lose?

In the parable of the talents, breaking even is breaking bad. Faithfulness is not holding the fort. Faithfulness is giving God a thirtyfold, sixtyfold, hundredfold return on investment. "We are not of those who shrink back," said the writer of Hebrews.[15] In other words, grow a backbone!

We fixate on sins of commission—don't do this, don't do that, and you're okay. The problem with that is this: Goodness is not the absence of badness. You can do nothing wrong and still do nothing right. It's the sins of omission—failing to tap our full potential—that grieve the heart of God. Why? Because He's the God who gave that potential to us!

GO BIG OR GO HOME

In 2014, a unique opportunity popped up on our real estate radar. A few years earlier, we had purchased an $8 million piece of property with a block of frontage on the 695 expressway that runs through DC. We planned on building a campus there, but we were in a five-year holding pattern because CSX decided to build a double-decker train tunnel under our front yard.

Was I frustrated by the five-year delay? Beyond frustrated, but it was during that God-ordained delay that we discovered that the 1891 Navy Yard Car Barn—right across the street from the property we already owned—was going to list for sale. There was one minor problem: The asking price was $29.3 million.

We didn't have a category for that price tag, but God has blessings in categories we can't conceive of. Our first instinct was to count the actual cost. We could have walked away, and we would have saved $29.3 million. But the opportunity cost would have been far greater! That property felt like a "salmon swallowing the whale," but that's where long vision enters the equation. Long vision counts the opportunity cost—to the third and fourth generation.

An investment firm offered cash for that city block, but we landed the contract. We've spent $25 million renovating and repurposing it as the Capital Turnaround, which is the cost of ministry in an urban context. That's where we gather to worship on the weekends. That's where House of Prayer happens on Thursday nights. That's where we host groups like Celebrate Recovery and Alpha. It's become a church home to thousands of people, but there's an added bonus. Along with all the ministries that operate out of the Capital Turnaround, we host hundreds of rental events every year. If it's a like-hearted partner like International Justice Mission or Prison Fellowship or World Vision, we roll out the red carpet at cost. If it's a concert or a conference, a for-profit organization or a government group, we have rental fees like any other event venue.

Last year, the Capital Turnaround revenue streamed nearly $2 million. At that rate, the rental revenue will earn back our original investment in fifteen years. Of course, the bottom line isn't dollars and cents. We get to show radical hospitality to the tens of thousands of people who circulate through our space for non-church events. When we renovate the east side of the building and open a mixed-use marketplace, the number of people who circulate will multiply thirtyfold, sixtyfold, and a hundredfold.

Why would a church open a mixed-use marketplace? For the same reason we turned a crackhouse into Ebenezers Coffeehouse. The church belongs in the middle of the marketplace! We want to create third places, sacred spaces, where church and community can cross paths. The vision for the Capital Turnaround is to be a place where people can work, eat, play, and pray—and invite their friends to do the same.

When Paul was in Athens, he didn't boycott the Areopagus. He walked into the marketplace of ideas, went toe to toe with some of the greatest minds in ancient Greece, and competed for the truth. How do we do that? We criticize by creating! We write better books, produce better films, draft better legislation, start better businesses, make better music, and create better art—with the help of the Holy Spirit. Faith on Sundays is a thin slice of what it means to follow Jesus. If your faith doesn't work Monday to Friday, it's smoke and mirrors.

REPAIRER OF BROKEN WALLS

Part of our identity, our destiny, as a church is to be a repairer of broken walls. "Your people will rebuild the ancient ruins," said the prophet Isaiah, "and will raise up the age-old foundations; you will be called Repairer of Broken Walls."[16] Our first foray into redevelopment was the crackhouse that we turned into Ebenezers Coffeehouse. That project won a Vision Award from the Committee of 100 on the Federal City:

> For its demonstration of the potential for imagination and creative energy to give new life and purpose to a forlorn building by envisioning a community benefit where others saw blight. The revitalization of 201 F Street, NE, the long neglected, vacant building into the heart of a new vibrant coffeehouse and community center for National Community Church stands as a symbol of the value of adaptive reuse.

If you're going to become a Repairer of Broken Walls, you can't focus on *what is*. You have to see *what can be*. That's one expression of long vision—seeing coffeehouses where others see crackhouses. A decade later, we turned an abandoned apartment building into the DC Dream Center. And a few years after that, we purchased the city block that is now the Capital Turnaround.

In 1891, the Navy Yard Car Barn was the last stop on the red line. That's where streetcars were repaired and rerouted and turned around—thus the name. When we purchased it, the building was carved up into a labyrinth of narrow hallways and small classrooms. We deconstructed all the way down to the original columns; then we reconstructed our vision in phases.

Our auditorium, which seats a thousand people, was a loading dock for deliveries when we bought it. A hundred years before that, it was the garage where mechanics fixed streetcars. But we didn't see what it was. We saw what it could be.

Long vision is seeing through drywall that isn't load bearing. Long vision is seeing through drop ceilings. When we popped the ceiling tiles, we discovered twenty-foot-tall ceilings with enough headroom to add square footage by building mezzanine space.

Long vision is seeing sanctuaries in loading docks. Even more important, it's seeing potential in people and possibilities in problems. Long vision sees opportunity where others see adversity.

LATER IS TOO LATE

When Walt Disney was looking for property to build his first amusement park, several options fell through because word got out about what Walt was up to. He eventually found a 160-acre grove of orange trees that he purchased for $879,000.

Before going public with the location of Disneyland, Walt invited his friend Art Linkletter to go for a drive with him. Art had no idea what Walt was up to, but Walt presented an opportunity during that twenty-five-mile drive to a "sparsely populated part of Orange County." They turned off the main road and "came to a large expanse of land, uninhabited except for a few grazing horses."[17] It looked like land to Art Linkletter, but Walt Disney began to cast vision for what it would become.

Walt began vividly describing Disneyland: the acres of colorful buildings in places called Tomorrowland, Jungleland, and

Fantasyland, the thousands of people parked in huge parking lots.

Walt was getting "more enthusiastic by the minute," but Art couldn't see it. "Who in the world, I mused, is going to drive twenty-five miles to ride a roller coaster?"[18] The answer is 800 million people and counting!

Walt Disney had spent all his cash on acquiring the 160-acre site for the amusement park, but he gave Art Linkletter the first right of refusal on adjoining properties. "I can handle only Disneyland itself," said Walt. "But the land bordering it, where we're standing now, will in just a couple of years be jammed with hotels and motels and restaurants and convention halls to accommodate the people who will come to spend their entire vacations here at my park."[19]

Art Linkletter didn't have a stomach for that kind of risk. Walt Disney warned his friend: "Later will be too late." But Art gave him a hard pass on the opportunity of a lifetime. "I well remember the short walk along the dry, sandy road," said Art many years later, "because that little stroll probably cost me about a million dollars a foot."[20]

God is the God of second chances—it's never too late to be who you might have been. And God can resurrect opportunity like He can everything else. But every opportunity has a shelf life— some shorter than others. Is there a whale you need to swallow? Either you swallow it or it swallows you, like Jonah. In my experience, a dream deferred will eat you alive.

I'm not suggesting that long vision—the road less traveled—is a cakewalk. It's more like *The Pilgrim's Progress*. You still have to pass through the Valley of Humiliation and Doubting Castle, not to mention detours and delays. But the path of least resistance has potholes too, and it dead-ends into the cul-de-sac called regret.

The road less traveled or the path of least resistance? The choice is yours! You can choose present-tense pain called delayed gratification, or you can choose future-tense pain called regret.

Action regrets or inaction regrets?

Actual cost or opportunity cost?

Choose wisely!

CHAPTER 4

CATHEDRAL THINKING

O n August 15, 1248, the cornerstone was laid and construction began on the Cologne Cathedral. Its twin towers stand 515 feet tall—the tallest structure in the world when it was completed. It was surpassed, in case you care, by the 555-foot Washington Monument in 1884. From start to finish, the Cologne Cathedral took 632 years to build.[1]

We refer to the Early Middle Ages as the Dark Ages, but that era was more inspired than we give it credit for. The average lifespan was much shorter—less than half of what it is today—but vision was longer. It's called cathedral thinking, and the best example might be the Cologne Cathedral.

"People in old times had convictions," said the German poet Heinrich Heine, "we moderns only have opinions. And it takes more than a mere opinion to erect a Gothic cathedral."

Everyone has an opinion about everything these days, including things they know nothing about. There is a word for that, by the way. It's among the longest words in the dictionary—*ultracrepidarianism*. It's expressing opinions outside the scope of one's knowledge.[2]

Can I ask a few questions? There are no easy answers to these questions, but I hope they prompt honest evaluation. What percentage of your attitudes and opinions are a regurgitation of social media and news media? And what percentage is a revelation you're getting from God's Word? Are you being conformed to the world around you? Or are you being transformed by the Spirit of God within you? Are you giving in to popular opinion, peer pressure, and political correctness? Or does Scripture get the first and last word?

Opinions are a dime a dozen, but opinions don't change people's minds or lives. A person convinced against their will is of the same opinion still, but let me flip that script. One person with uncompromising conviction has the potential to change the course of history. Historymakers aren't swayed by groupthink. Their conscience is their compass. They don't take their cues from trending hashtags. They're motivated by convictions that defy circumstance and happenstance. Long vision is a function of conviction, and the deeper the conviction, the longer the vision.

The goal of the gospel is not simply going to heaven—it's an open heaven. It's heaven invading earth. The Lord's Prayer is our MO: "Your kingdom come, your will be done, on earth as it is in heaven."[3] Our mission is to mirror what's happening in heaven.

Do we need a vision *from God*? No doubt. Without a vision the people perish.[4] But even more than a vision *from God*, we need a vision *of God*—a vision of God high and exalted. A low view of God is the cause of a hundred lesser evils. A high view of God is the solution to ten thousand temporal problems.[5] We are called to be supernatural solutionaries, but it starts by getting in sync with God's Word and God's Spirit.

LEGION

In Mark's gospel, Jesus encounters a man who was oppressed and possessed by demons. He was cutting himself, living in a cemetery, and rarely wore clothes. Psychiatrists would have had a heyday diagnosing him with the DSM-5-TR. When Jesus asked him his name, he answered, "My name is Legion, for we are many."[6] No way that's the name his parents gave him! He was doing what we do—identifying himself by his issues.

During the reign of Caesar Augustus, a Roman legion consisted of 6,100 foot soldiers and 726 cavalry.[7] If you add it up, this man was pulled in 6,826 different directions. He heard 6,826 different voices in his head. "My name is Legion" is the plight of us all.[8]

If you want to hear the still small voice of the Spirit, you have to turn down the volume on those other voices. That includes self-talk. How do you do that? Try a social media fast. Do a twenty-four-hour silent retreat. Begin your day with five minutes of meditation. Download a Bible reading plan. If you want to over-write negative narratives and rewrite false narratives, you have to ground yourself in God's Word.

"The great irony of our time," said anthropologist Mary Catherine Bateson, "is that even as we are living longer, we are thinking shorter."[9] It's the tyranny of the urgent. It's a cognitive bias called hyperbolic discounting—we prefer smaller rewards sooner over larger rewards later.[10] That's why we make shortsighted decisions that undermine gradually then suddenly.

In psychology, there is a three-second hack called grounding that helps defuse anxiety. By articulating specific facts out loud, like *when* and *where* you are, you can refocus on the present moment—"It's 12:17 P.M. and I'm at my writing desk." Studies have found grounding techniques to be quite effective at reducing inflammation, alleviating pain,[11] and enhancing mood.[12] Even more effective than verbalizing time and place? Ground yourself in God's Word by reciting chapter and verse!

I certainly believe in being present in the present—be where your feet are. But we also have to exercise our God-given imagination. The average person only spends 14 percent of their time thinking about the future.[13] And only 14 percent of that 14 percent is spent thinking a year ahead.[14] In my opinion, that is too little time! We are overdriving our headlights—the faster you go, the further ahead you need to look. There is no magic number, but long vision requires deep thought. And deep thought takes large chunks of time.

Most of us spend more time planning a three-day vacation than we do planning the next five years. Have you ever done a vision retreat? You don't have to go to an exotic location or stay at a five-star hotel. For more than a decade, Lora and I have done an annual retreat in December. We kick it off by counting our blessings. After reviewing our gratitude journals, we review our budget and calendar for the upcoming year. That's how we guard against going legion!

We've been married more than three decades, and the number one source of conflict has been the calendar. More specifically, overscheduling! If you overcrowd your calendar, life starts to feel like a chore. You feel like you're playing catch-up all the time. That's why you shouldn't just schedule work—schedule play! All work and no play makes Jack a dull boy.

THE POWER OF PLAY

In the early 2000s, Ivy Ross was the senior vice president for design and development of girls' toys at Mattel. She launched an initiative called Project Platypus where twelve employees from different backgrounds—with different skill sets and varying levels of education—worked together for three months in a two-thousand-square-foot building set up like a playground.[5]

A playground? That doesn't sound like work, does it? But if you're making toys for kids, you can't approach it as work, now can you? That team of twelve checked their titles at the door when they joined the team. It's sandbox rules all over again—share and share alike.

Why three months? That was the typical maternity leave at the time. The team of twelve had co-workers who picked up the slack while they birthed new ideas, just like they would if someone were birthing a baby. But Ivy Ross also made this acute observation: "If you want to get milk out of a cow, you have to give it time to graze. These days, no one has time to graze."[16]

Mattel gave their employees three months to graze new ideas. Ross brought in outside speakers who lectured on everything from improv comedy to Jungian psychology to architectural design. When the team got stuck, they took field trips to zoos and museums. They even had a sound chair that vibrated at a frequency that fused the two hemispheres of the brain, creating a theta state where creativity is catalyzed.[17] Sign me up!

Their goal was a new product, complete with business plan and product packaging. So it wasn't all fun and games! Creativity isn't stress-free. But there is a healthy stress called eustress. It's work, but it's playful work! When the three months were up, the team returned to their regular routines, but they brought back a playfulness that promoted creativity and productivity.[18]

One of the most spiritual things you can do is play more! Every year our team does a Play and Pray retreat. The name of the retreat is self-explanatory, but I think the playing is as important as the praying. The team that plays together stays together!

THE ACORN BRAIN

The Long Now Foundation coined a concept called the acorn brain—it's the part of the brain that focuses on long-term planning. More specifically, it's a function of the dorsolateral prefrontal cortex. "In the early Neolithic period, one of our ancestors did something extraordinary," wrote Roman Krznaric. "Instead of eating a seed, she decided to save it to plant the next season."[19]

For the record, we actually know that ancestor's name. It was

Cain, as in Cain and Abel, the first farmer. "This moment—the beginning of the agricultural revolution—marks a turning point in the evolution of the human mind and is the symbolic birth of long-term thinking."[20]

Since we're on the subject of early civilization, there is an eruption of creativity just four chapters into Genesis. It starts with Jubal, "the first of all who play the harp and flute."[21] Jubal makes music, and the rest is reverb. The Grammys trace their origin back to Genesis 4:21, as do the Country Music Association Awards. Jubal was the prime mover. Yes, music has evolved into lots of different genres—everything from hip-hop to heavy metal. But whether we're talking jazz, funk, or rock and roll, the first domino was the first chord that Jubal played.

Along with Jubal, Tubal-Cain is identified as an innovator. He was an artist, alchemist, and engineer who made tools.[22] Only four chapters into human history and there is a genesis of genius. Why this explosion of creativity? The obvious answer is that we are created in the image of our Creator, but there is a second, more subtle reason.

SUPERLINEAR SCALING

In 1932, a Swiss biologist named Max Kleiber published an offbeat academic paper in an obscure Danish journal. Kleiber was fascinated with the metabolic rate of animals, large and small. Plotting mass versus metabolism across a broad spectrum of animals from mice to elephants, Kleiber discovered something called negative quarter-power scaling.[23] As organisms get larger, their metabolisms get slower.

Seventy years after Kleiber discovered negative quarter-power scaling, Geoffrey West wanted to see if Kleiber's law held true for human-made organisms, namely cities. West discovered that transportation systems and energy delivery were governed by the negative-quarter-power-scaling ratio—bigger mass equals slower metabolism. But there was one curious exception. The quarter-power law governing innovation wasn't negative; it was positive.[24]

If you live in a city of ten thousand people and move to a city of one hundred thousand, that city is ten times larger, but it isn't ten times more innovative. When you measure key creativity data points—patents, research and development budgets, number of new inventions—the city that is ten times larger is seventeen times more innovative! And if you moved to a city that was fifty times larger, it would be 130 times more innovative.[25] It's called superlinear scaling, and that principle applies to any and every organization.

What does superlinear scaling have to do with Cain? His original intent was building a place to live for him and his family. He even named the city after his son, Enoch. Catalyzing creativity wasn't even on his radar, but that's what cities do. Without even knowing it, Cain was creating an innovation incubator.

A few chapters later, in a place called Babel, we see the true potential of quarter-power scaling. God Himself says, "There will be nothing they cannot accomplish."[26] We interpret this story negatively, but it reveals positive potential if harnessed the right way. In the case of Cain, city building led to an artistic renaissance and a scientific revolution.

SLOW PRODUCTIVITY

In the day and age of ever-evolving artificial intelligence, Georgetown professor Cal Newport advocates for an approach to work called "slow productivity." An offshoot of cathedral thinking, slow productivity is slowing your pace to increase productivity. I know that sounds as counterintuitive as it is countercultural, but it's the law of diminishing return. Sometimes less is more and more is less!

Productivity is often the enemy of creativity. Why? Because ideas have to ruminate before they germinate! The most prodigious inventors in history have one thing in common—they found a time and a place to daydream. Alexander Graham Bell had a dreaming place overlooking the Grand River. Thomas Edison sat in a thinking chair. Carl Jung built his Bellingen Tower for the purposes of meditation. Henry David Thoreau skipped stones on Walden Pond. And George Washington Carver took prayer walks through the woods at four o'clock in the morning.

Slow productivity is anything that happens gradually then suddenly, and that includes everything from Bell's telephone to Edison's lightbulb. I certainly don't belong in the same sentence as any of those inventors, but my dreaming place is the rooftop of Ebenezers Coffeehouse. I dream bigger and think longer when I'm on top of a miracle!

How do you practice slow productivity? That's up to you, but Cal Newport offers three ways to start. One, do fewer things. Two, work at a natural pace. And three, obsess over quality.[27] It's not as easy as one, two, three. But that's not a bad place to start.

There's nothing wrong with a side hustle, but buyer beware. If you work seven days a week, it will come back to bite you. Why? Because you cannot break spiritual laws—spiritual laws will make or break you. And one of them is the Sabbath. The seventh day is a gift from God—a day of rest and recovery. It's a day to recreate. It's not only one of the Ten Commandments; in terms of words, it's the longest. The Sabbath is God's way of reminding us that we don't keep the planets in orbit. The Sabbath is a day for daydreaming.

Permission to speak frankly? Many people take pride in breaking this commandment, but busyness is not a virtue. Patience is a virtue! How's your pace? Is it sustainable? What are your daily, weekly, monthly, and yearly rhythms?

Letting the ground lie fallow is not laziness; it's holiness. It's a biblical principle that takes tremendous discipline. Just as the seventh day is holy, so is the seventh year.

> For six years you are to sow your fields and harvest the crops, but during the seventh year let the land lie unplowed and unused. Then the poor among your people may get food from it, and the wild animals may eat what is left. Do the same with your vineyard and your olive grove.[28]

I know the old axiom—idle hands are the devil's workshop. And I'm certainly not advocating for the abdication of duty. But I also know that fallow ground becomes the fertile ground where God ideas take root and bear fruit. My advice? The ruthless elimination of hurry![29]

I get more requests for meetings than I can take, and it's hard saying *no*. But if I took every request, I'd have no margin for dreaming. And that's my job as lead visionary of National Community Church. Tuesdays and Thursdays are meeting days, and they often get scheduled wall to wall. But that buys me Wednesdays and Fridays as dreaming days. You may not have that flexibility built into your schedule, but you still have to prioritize dreaming personally and professionally. If you don't, you'll stop creating the future and start repeating the past. That's the way, that's the day, you stop dreaming and start dying!

HALF-FORMED IMAGINATION

Some of us don't let the ground lie fallow unless we find ourselves flat on our backs. That's certainly true of John Ronald Reuel Tolkien, the man who imagined Middle-earth. His magnum opus, *The Lord of the Rings*, has captivated generations of readers, selling more than 150 million copies.

Few authors had a more fertile imagination, but where did those fantastical ideas come from? It wasn't sitting at a writing desk from dawn until dusk. After fighting on the front lines in World War I, Tolkien was convalescing from trench fever at a British hospital. It wasn't where he wanted to be, but that downtime proved to be a gift, granting time for his imagination to run wild.[30] It was a brachistochrone curve, of sorts.

Tolkien's legacy isn't just his books. It's another author named Clive Staples Lewis. An ardent agnostic, Lewis once referred to himself as the most reluctant convert in all of Christendom. What won him over? Tolkien stopped trying to debate Lewis into the kingdom with logical arguments. "Your inability to understand," Tolkien said to his friend, "stems from a failure of imagination on your part."[31]

A failure of imagination? It's hard to imagine saying that of the man who created the Chronicles of Narnia, isn't it? But the conversion of C. S. Lewis demonstrates what a sanctified imagination is capable of. Tolkien and Lewis were part of a literary group called the Inklings, which met in the infamous Rabbit Room—a back room at The Eagle and Child pub in Oxford, England. Talk about iron sharpening iron! That's when and where ideas became books—gradually then suddenly.

"Too many Christians today," said Ian Bradley, "brought up on the penny plain prose favored by Rome and even more by the Reformers, have half-formed imaginations."[32] That may be our greatest spiritual shortcoming. A half-formed imagination results in a deformed soul. Without imagination, long vision loses its purpose.

THE GREAT VISION

We don't always think of Jesus in these terms, but there is no greater visionary in the history of humankind. In a day and age when the average person never traveled thirty miles beyond their birthplace, Jesus cast a long vision called the Great Commission.

Go into all the world and preach the gospel to all creation.[33]

Go into all the world? This was fifteen centuries before the age of exploration!

The Great Commission echoes the Genesis Commission: "Fill the earth and subdue it."[34] We mistakenly think Adam and Eve would have stayed in the Garden of Eden if they had not eaten from the tree of the knowledge of good and evil, but God's original intent was for them to explore, to redeem, and to enjoy every square inch of His creation. Our mission is to establish outposts of Eden in a fallen world. Our vision is the redemption of all things. What does that look like? The short answer is shalom, which is four dimensional—right relationship with God, with ourselves, with others, and with creation.

If we're going to be great at anything, we ought to be great at the Great Commission. No vision is bigger or better than the good news called the gospel. It's the fulfillment of our deepest desires. It's the answer to our hardest questions. It's the solution to our biggest problems.

There is a little line from the movie *Up* that has become a life motto: "Adventure is out there."[35] In my opinion—and my experience—there is no greater adventure than following Jesus! You'll go unanticipated places and do inconceivable things with unexpected people—never a dull moment.

Most of the disciples grew up within a stone's throw of the Sea of Galilee, and that's where they would have lived out the rest of their days if they hadn't crossed paths with Jesus. The vision Jesus cast was so compelling that eleven of twelve disciples were martyred for their faith. Many of them were crucified on Roman crosses, just like Jesus. They were stoned to death, hung from trees, beheaded by swords, executed with arrows, and burned as human torches. Only an encounter with a resurrected Christ could have commanded that kind of devotion. The amazing thing? They counted it a privilege!

The persecution of the church didn't extinguish passion for the mission; it added fuel to the fire. "The blood of the martyrs," said the second-century theologian Tertullian, "is the seed of the church." According to Eusebius of Caesarea, a third-century historian, John traveled as far as Asia while Andrew went to modern-day Russia. James, the son of Zebedee, traveled to Spain. Even Doubting Thomas is believed to have gone to Syria, Iran, and India.

CAESAR IS A SALAD

Two thousand years ago, Rome was the most powerful empire on Earth. It numbered around sixty million people, about one-quarter of the planet's population.[36] Rome built a network of military highways—372 major and minor roads that measured 250,000 miles. They connected three continents, reaching as far north as Britain, as far south as Egypt, as far east as Iraq, as far west as Portugal.[37] All roads led to Rome!

At the peak of Rome's power, Caesar Augustus declared himself *pontifex maximus,* chief priest of Rome. He renovated eighty-two Roman temples and reinstituted sacrifice to the Roman gods. It was upon his death—August 19, A.D. 14—that Rome declared his divinity, "Caesar is Lord."[38] The inscription on Roman coinage identified Caesar as the "Son of God."[39]

If you were placing bets on Caesars Sportsbook in the first century on what would last the longest—the Roman Empire or this thing called Christianity—and on who would have the greatest influence—Caesar Augustus or Jesus—you'd bet the farm on Rome.

Two thousand years later, Caesar is a salad. I don't know any-body who worships Augustus or Julius or Marcus Aurelius. The Roman Empire is long gone while 2.3 billion people from every nation, tribe, people, and language follow a Nazarene named Jesus.

How does that happen? You guessed it—gradually then sud-denly! Before the Day of Pentecost, the church numbered 120 people. But that's all it takes for God to turn the world upside down if we're willing to pray the price. After ten days in an upper room, God poured out His Spirit like a flash flood. In one day, three thousand people from fourteen nations were baptized. And we feel the domino effect two thousand years later.

The growth curve of Christianity is tough to model because estimates are all over the map. But one graph of church growth estimates 40,500 Christians by A.D. 150, which would represent 0.07 percent of the Roman Empire. By A.D. 200, Christians num-bered 218,000 or 0.36 percent. That is less than a minority, let alone a majority. But by A.D. 250, those who claimed to follow Christ had spiked to 1.2 million or 1.9 percent of the Roman Empire.[40] In the eighteen centuries since then, Christianity has grown exponen-tially from 1.2 million to 2.3 billion.[41]

TRIUMPHAL PROCESSION

In A.D. 82, the Arch of Titus was built on the Via Sacra as a conse-cration of Rome's victory over the rebels in the province of Judea. The fall of Jerusalem is depicted on that arch as a symbol of Rome's triumph.[42] But who got the last laugh? The apostle Paul said:

> Thanks be to God, who always leads us as captives in Christ's triumphal procession and uses us to spread the aroma of the knowledge of him everywhere.[43]

That phrase—"triumphal procession"—painted a poignant picture. It was a reference to Roman armies, led by Roman generals, who returned to Rome with the spoils of war. The parade route began at Campus Martius, outside the city's sacred boundary. Troops would enter Rome through the Porta Triumphalis—the Triumphal Gate. They would march down the Via Sacra past the Forum, past the Circus Maximus. The procession ended at the temple of Jupiter on Capitoline Hill where a bull was ceremoniously sacrificed to the gods.

Paul borrows the embodiment of Roman arrogance, the symbol of Roman power, and flips the script. Caesar isn't Lord; Jesus is. And we are more than conquerors because of Christ. The earliest creed of the church—"Jesus is Lord"—was a coup d'état against the Roman Empire. The kingdoms of this world are becoming the kingdom of our Lord and of His Christ, and He will reign forever and ever.

Rome thought it was the overstory, but it was just the understory. Rome was the greatest show on earth, but the good news of the gospel is the overstory.

Are you fixated on the news?

Or are you focused on the good news?

We are inundated with information overload every day. There are algorithms designed to keep us in our echo chambers. There are advertisements designed to hijack our attention. If we aren't careful, we start living outside in rather than inside out. We start reacting instead of proacting. We stop living out of imagination and we start living out of logic.

"When [a] crisis occurs," said Milton Friedman, "the actions that are taken depend on the ideas that are lying around."[44] Beware of the recency bias! It's putting too much weight on the understories that are happening in real time. You have to stay focused on the overstory. You have to discern what's really happening when what's happening is happening!

God is always writing a bigger story!

God is always writing a better story!

As this chapter ends, a new chapter of your life begins. Jesus invites you into the "unforced rhythms of grace."[45] That sounds like slow productivity, doesn't it? "He is no fool who gives what he cannot keep," said martyred missionary Jim Elliot, "to gain what he cannot lose."[46] That's the essence of cathedral thinking—my utmost for His highest. His will, His way—nothing more, nothing less, nothing else!

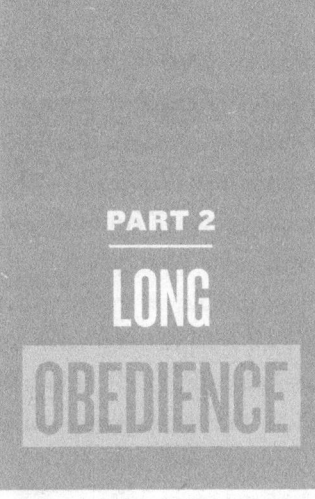

PART 2

LONG
OBEDIENCE

n 1849, a French immigrant named Isidore Boudin established Boudin Bakery—the oldest continuously operating business in the city of San Francisco. If you've never been there, I recommend the sourdough bread bowl with Fisherman's Wharf clam chowder. Trust me, it's the best of both worlds—San Francisco's most iconic meal. Boudin combined his French mother dough with yeast from the Bay Area whose foggy microclimate produced its inimitable taste.[1]

I'm neither a baker nor the son of a baker. So when I discovered that sourdough starter lives forever—yeast begetting yeast begetting yeast—it was news to me. What I found even more fascinating than that was this: When a baker kneads the dough, traces of their DNA get baked into the bread.[2] That's kinda gross and kinda awesome at the same time. Scientifically speaking, those DNA traces remain fertile forever. Long after the baker is long gone, their DNA lives on in that starter. It's baked into every loaf of bread ever after.

I have no idea how many millions of loaves Boudin Bakery has baked, but every loaf has Isidore Boudin's fingerprints on it. Every

loaf contains more than 166 years of double-helix DNA from anyone and everyone who has kneaded that mother dough.

What's true of bread is true of people. All of us are born into
somebody else's story. Their understories get baked into our overstories. That's true of tragedy and triumph and everything in between.

There are countless people—parents, coaches, teachers, and
friends—who left their fingerprints on your soul. You wouldn't be
who you are without their influence in your life, but they wouldn't
be who they are without the people who influenced them. And we
could play that game all day, ad infinitum.

MULTIVARIABLE CALCULUS

Long obedience is multivariable calculus. It's the big decisions and
little decisions that have a domino effect. We only make a few
major decisions in life—where to live, what career path to pursue,
who to marry or not marry. Then we spend the rest of our lives
managing those major decisions. But it's small acts of obedience—
words of encouragement and acts of kindness—that get baked into
other people's lives. "While survival of the fittest may lead to
short-term gain," said neurosurgeon James Doty, "research clearly
shows it is survival of the kindest that leads to the long-term survival of a species."[3]

There are countless people who have helped me differentiate
and individuate into the person I am. My mom and dad top the
list. My wife and children rank up there too. So do the teachers
and coaches who have influenced my life in the classroom and on
the court. I wouldn't be who I am or where I am without them.

I have a spiritual father, Dick Foth, who has mentored me for
more than three decades now. A former pastor and college president, he took me under his wing when I started pastoring. And I'll

just put this out there—his wife, Ruth, can bake a pie like nobody's business. Dick and Ruth were part of our original core group of nineteen people that got National Community Church off the ground. The fact that I was coming off a failed church plant made their vote of confidence all the more meaningful.

Who has left their fingerprints on your soul? Not only is that a question I learned to ask from Foth; he is my answer to that question! I'm at least 17.2 percent Dick Foth. Yes, that percentage is totally fabricated. You can't quantify influence, but Dick Foth is at least 17.2 percent Roy Blakeley—his spiritual father. Whether we know it or not, all of us are the beneficiaries of someone else's long obedience in the same direction.

> Abraham was the father of Isaac,
> Isaac the father of Jacob,
> Jacob the father of Judah and his brothers.[4]

You can read that one verse in two seconds, but it represents 502 years of collective history. It's full of overstories and understories. The genealogies—those laundry lists of hard-to-pronounce names—teach us many life lessons. Can I rapid fire a few of them?

One, it's not about us! Two, you never know who is in your womb. Three, all of us are born into somebody else's story. Four, we drink from wells we did not dig. Five, God is bigger than generational curses. Six, we overestimate what we can accomplish in one generation, but we underestimate what God can accomplish in three or four. Seven, God is always writing a bigger story!

EPIGENETICS

The idea of epigenetics is as old as Moses. When God inscribed two tablets with ten commandments on Mount Sinai, He made no

bones about the fact that obedience and disobedience have consequences.

> I, the LORD your God, am a jealous God, visiting the iniquity
> of the fathers on their children to the third and fourth gen-
> erations of those who hate Me, but showing loving devotion
> to a thousand generations of those who love Me and keep
> My commandments.[5]

There is a cause-and-effect to our actions and inactions that is
irreversible. Even when God forgives us—and the penalty for sin
is pardoned—there are still real-world consequences. For better or
for worse, our decisions have a domino effect.

Rats have large litters, up to twenty pups. Would you like to
know the difference between good rat moms and bad rat moms?
In one word, licking. That's how good moms nurture their babies.
Researchers have discovered that rat babies who are licked, in turn,
lick their babies. So what? Licking is a learned trait, which is where
it gets scientifically interesting. The rats who were licked more
frequently showed a spike in the protein that activates maternal
instincts. More specifically, there is a subset of proteins called transcription factors that regulate gene expression by binding to certain DNA sequences.[6] That study is rewriting the rules of genetics.

The prevailing assumption among geneticists was that you cannot alter DNA behaviorally, but this study called that age-old assumption into question. When rat pups are licked, it releases
adrenaline and noradrenaline. Those hormones flip a switch in the
thyroid, activating a neurotransmitter called serotonin, which
functions as an antidepressant. But it doesn't just alter a rat pup's
mood. It actually has an epigenetic effect that alters the genetic
code of the next generation.[7]

This is where nature meets nurture—the holy grail. The proteins that regulate gene expression—transcription factors—have a domino effect on DNA by altering the genetic code. In simple terms, behavior alters our genetics. I'm not minimizing the impact of hereditary traits, but you can break genetic curses that are generational. We don't just think our way into behaving differently; we also behave our way into thinking differently. Genetics is a two-way highway.

Your actions and inactions impact the next generation. If you have an addiction, breaking it for the next generation is a more powerful motivator than doing it for yourself. Your bravery is someone else's breakthrough. Your obedience is someone else's blessing.

PLANT A TREE

In the book of Genesis, a man named Terah set out on an epic journey from Ur of the Chaldeans to a land called Canaan. But Terah and his family stopped short of their ultimate destination. When they got to Haran, Terah settled there.[8]

The journey from Ur of the Chaldeans to Haran—if they took the route along the Euphrates River—was 641 miles, as the crow flies.[9] I have no idea why they stopped in Haran, but it begs the question: Did Terah fail? If you think in terms of one generation, the answer is *yes*. He fell 426 miles short of Canaan. But if you think intergenerationally, Terah got Abram more than halfway there.

Remember the monarch butterfly? It takes four generations for a kaleidoscope of butterflies to complete their three-thousand-mile migration cycle. We could learn a thing or two from their intergenerational journey. Terah may not have been a super generation, but he set up his son, Abram, for the next leg of the journey.

When Abram finally got to Canaan, after a five-year holding

pattern in Haran, he made a few grand gestures. He built an altar to the Lord.[10] He walked the length and breadth of the land God was giving him.[11] He did one more thing that is quite curious— Abram planted a tree. So what? Planting a tree was a statement of faith. Why? Because the land didn't belong to him yet.

> Abraham planted a tamarisk tree in Beersheba, and there he called on the name of the LORD, the Eternal God. And Abraham resided in the land of the Philistines for a long time.[12]

At the time, the land belonged to the Philistines. But Abraham was putting a stake in the ground. It's almost like he was saying, *This ground belongs to God—this is holy ground.* That tree was a down payment for future generations.

Abraham was putting down roots, literally. And not just any roots but deep roots. Beersheba bordered the Negev desert, which meant the soil was inhospitable. But tamarisk trees are incredibly resilient because they shoot their roots all the way down to the water table. Tamarisks are also slow-growth trees. You don't plant tamarisk trees for yourself. You plant them for future generations. You plant them because you have long vision. Tamarisk trees, and their deep roots, symbolize long obedience in the same direction.

STAKE YOUR CLAIM

For more than two decades, Lora and I had the joy of pastoring in the same city as our friends, Dennis and Donna Pisani. They epitomized long obedience by pastoring Capital City Church for a quarter century. They plowed the ground that many of us planted in!

Like many urban churches, Capital City Church met in rented facilities because the price of real estate was cost prohibitive. Of course, that didn't keep them from praying for property. One Sunday, just a few years into their pastorate, someone handed them a small wooden stake that looked like a tent peg. It was a strange offering, to say the least. But the prophetic words he shared carried weight.

> I believe God told me to give this to you. Pray over where He wants to establish His church. Then drive this stake into the ground as a declaration of faith.[13]

A few weeks later, Dennis and Donna started circling a city block in prayer. It was a design warehouse a few blocks off the National Mall. For many months they prayed circles around that building. "We believed. We prayed. We waited. And then—*nothing happened.*"

Ever been there? It can shake your faith! "The building never became ours," said Donna. "And honestly? It stung. Had we heard wrong? Had we wasted the stake?" Year after year, Capital City Church continued meeting in rented locations. "It felt like a forgotten prayer," Donna recalls. Then one day, many years later, they visited the newly opened Museum of the Bible. That's when they connected the dots. "This was it," said Donna. "This was the exact block where we had placed that stake."

Did the Museum of the Bible get that property because Dennis and Donna Pisani staked their claim? I have no idea and neither do they. That's past our pay grade! "I do know this," notes Donna. "When you stake your claim in faith, God writes a story far bigger than you could imagine." Yes and amen!

FUTURE GENERATIONS WILL THANK YOU

In 1837, a slave named Robert Laws was born on Wood Farm Plantation in Middlesex County, Virginia. In 1863, the same year the

Emancipation Proclamation was signed, he somehow managed to escape. He made the trek from southern Virginia to Washington, DC—a distance of more than three hundred miles—while evading capture. That's where he met and married his wife, Patsey A. Williams.

In 1865, Congress established Freedman's Village for former slaves on the site of Robert E. Lee's estate—what is now Arlington National Cemetery. The most recognizable resident was Sojourner Truth, but no one left a longer legacy than Robert Laws. He not only oversaw the first school; he also pastored the first church. And his wife, Patsey, worked as a nurse at the hospital.[14] What a power couple!

In 1875, just a decade removed from the shackles of slavery, Robert Laws graduated from the Preparatory Department at Howard University. That same year, he planted Friendship Baptist Church.[15] In 1886, that congregation purchased property a few blocks from the Capitol and built their first church building. I can only imagine the way they worshipped that first Sunday!

Why am I sharing that story? Because National Community Church purchased that 1886 church in 2025. But we didn't just buy a building; we inherited long obedience in the same direction. When you walk into the sanctuary, you can almost hear the worship in the walls.

In the 1950s, the federal government executed an urban renewal plan that razed an entire quadrant of the nation's capital to the ground. Thirteen churches in southwest DC were demolished to make room for redevelopment. The only church to survive the wrecking ball was Friendship Baptist Church because of its historic importance to the community—one of the oldest Black churches in the city.

At the turn of the twenty-first century, that building had become a zombie property. That's when some visionaries, Steve and

Sophia Tanner, reimagined it and repurposed it as the Culturehouse.[16] Not unlike Michelangelo who painted the ceiling of the Sistine Chapel, they hired muralists to paint the inside and outside of that church. It may be the most colorful building in the nation's capital. The Culturehouse has served as an art gallery and event venue for two decades, and we get to write the next chapter.

Here's the catch—we have a church campus a few blocks away that is ten times the size. So why did we buy it? Because we're tired of church buildings being turned into condos! Plus, as we prayed about it, the Holy Spirit whispered these words: "Future generations will thank you."

Over a span of fifteen years, from 2008 to 2023, the population of DC increased 11 percent while houses of worship decreased by 33 percent.[17] We can't save every historic church in DC, but we want to change that trend. I should probably add this little footnote: The former Friendship Baptist Church-turned-Culturehouse sits on the 4.7-mile prayer circle that I prayed in 1996.

We aren't sure what the future holds for that piece of property, but purchasing it was our way of planting a tamarisk tree. We decided to put a stake in the ground. Why? Why not. We aren't just trying to build a church. We're trying to bless a city to the third and fourth generation. And, for us, it's not just about the name above the church door. It's about the name above all names!

"There are those who look at things the way they are, and ask why?" said George Bernard Shaw. "I dream of things that never were, and ask why not?"[18]

Why not you?

Why not now?

CHAPTER 5

THE POWER OF SAME

I n 1890, a thirteen-year-old boy named Pablo was wandering the streets of Barcelona. He popped into a secondhand music store where he found a tattered copy of six cello suites by Johann Sebastian Bach. Pablo was already a musical virtuoso—he played the piano, flute, and violin by age four. But when Pablo discovered Bach's cello suites, the door opened and let the future in. Pablo Casals fell in love with the cello.[1]

The fact that a secondhand music store in Barcelona was selling sheet music that Bach composed between 1717 and 1723 is musical serendipity, but serendipity means nothing without blood, sweat, and tears. Pablo Casals would practice those pieces in private every single day for twelve years before performing them publicly.[2] It wasn't until 1936, nearly half a century after finding those cello suites, that Pablo Casals recorded them at Abbey Road Studios in London.

Pablo Casals is considered by many "the greatest man who ever drew the bow."[3] He played a private concert for Queen Victoria at her summer residence when he was twenty-three. Six decades later, he played for President John F. Kennedy at the White House, where he was later awarded the Presidential Medal of Freedom.[4]

How did Casals become the best of the best? Two ways— gradually then suddenly. Casals lived to the age of ninety-six, and he was still practicing three hours a day. When asked why, Pablo Casals famously said, "I'm beginning to notice some improvement."[5]

Are you trying to beat the competition?

Or are you trying to become the best version of yourself?

Do you do what you do for extrinsic reasons? Or intrinsic reasons?

If you study highly successful people, very few of them see other people as their competition. The competition is in the mirror! They aren't driven by extrinsic motivation like fame or fortune. They are driven by intrinsic motivation—to become the best version of themselves. Their goal is not awards. Their goal is tapping God-given potential.

Remember Rowdy Gaines? He swam around the world for a race that lasted less than a minute! What drove him? "At every practice," said Rowdy, "I would try to beat myself."[6] That's what great athletes and artists and entrepreneurs do! And by tapping our potential, we glorify the God who gave it to us in the first place.

"What you *do* in the present," said N. T. Wright, "by painting, preaching, singing, sewing, praying, teaching, building hospitals, digging wells, campaigning for justice, writing poems, caring for the needy, loving your neighbor as yourself—*will last into God's future*."[7] What you do matters now and forever. I can't promise that someone will pick up something you write 167 years from now—like Casals did Bach—but you never know.

WILL NOT SKILL

At the 2024 Olympic Games in Paris, American swimmer Regan Smith won the silver medal in the two-hundred-meter butterfly. It wasn't the first or last time she'd win silver because of a certain

Canadian swimmer named Summer McIntosh who kept inching her out. When Regan was interviewed after missing gold by a split second, I wondered how she would respond. I honestly expected a measure of disappointment, but I didn't discern one ounce of displeasure. Regan was over the moon about her performance, as evidenced by the huge smile on her face.

"That's the fastest I've ever been," said Regan. "I beat myself, and that's what matters." Regan didn't beat Summer McIntosh, but that wasn't her competition. She beat herself by establishing a PR—personal record.[8]

Steph Curry is arguably the greatest shooter the game of basketball has ever seen. It will come as no surprise that the all-time leader in three-pointers is religious about his routines, but that doesn't mean he doesn't have fun. Fun is an underappreciated factor when it comes to success in any endeavor—do what you love and love what you do.

"There is no boring in our workouts," said his longtime trainer, Brandon Payne. "Every drill is a game."[9] The goal of those workouts? "The person you're competing with is your past self, and the bar you're raising is for your future self."[10]

In a landmark study on the roots of exceptional talent, researchers recruited a wide variety of geniuses that included Olympic athletes, internationally acclaimed pianists, Guggenheim-winning sculptors, prizewinning mathematicians, and professionally ranked tennis players. Of note, only a few of those geniuses were childhood prodigies. Researchers came to this conclusion: "What any person in the world can learn, *almost* all persons can learn."[11]

I'm not negating epigenetic factors. I believe in nature and nurture, just like I believe in mind and matter. But if you press me, I believe in mind over matter and nurture over nature. Remember the old song lyric? "Anything you can do I can do better!"[12] That's true, but it takes time and a whole lot of patience. You'll have to make sacrifices and take risks. You'll have to outwork the competition, and the competition is you.

The highest-performing athletes, artists, and musicians weren't singled out by their coaches for their skill. It was will—not skill—that set them apart. "If they were singled out by their coaches," said Adam Grant, "it was not for unusual aptitude but unusual motivation."[13]

THE DEPARTMENT OF REDUNDANCY DEPARTMENT

In 1952, Winston Churchill was serving as chancellor of the University of Bristol when he was given the honor of laying the foundation stone of a new building on campus. As he picked up the silver trowel to lay the ceremonial stone, he said, "The stone isn't level."[14]

The very embarrassed officials produced a plumb line to double-check, and sure enough, Churchill was right. That story begs the question: How did a professional politician have the eye to notice that kind of architectural detail?

A few decades earlier, Winston Churchill was under tremendous pressure as the chancellor of the exchequer—a position he held from 1924 to 1929. The prime minister at the time, Stanley Baldwin, gave Churchill a leave of absence to rest and recover. Baldwin encouraged him to "paint, write, play." Not a bad prescription for burnout still, by the way!

Churchill did those things—paint, write, play—but he also took up bricklaying. By the end of his sabbatical, he had built a cottage for his daughter. That change of pace proved to be just what the doctor ordered: "I have had a delightful month building a cottage and dictating a book: 200 bricks and 2000 words a day."[15]

Whether you're building a cottage or writing a book, the name of the game is gradually then suddenly. If you keep laying two hundred bricks and writing two thousand words, you'll eventually have a cottage or a book to show for it. It's all about cultivating consistency—the department of redundancy department.

MAKING MAGIC

In her groundbreaking book on grit, Angela Duckworth made this observation: "We prefer mystery to mundanity."[16] If someone is more successful than we are, it's easier to assume they won the talent lottery or the luck lottery. Why? It makes us feel better about maintaining the status quo. "We prefer our excellence fully formed," said Duckworth. But there are no cheat codes when it comes to excellence.[17]

"Do you know what moviemaking is?" asked the Swedish filmmaker Ingmar Bergman. "Eight hours of hard work each day to get three minutes of film."[18] It takes eight hours of gradually to get three minutes of suddenly! And that's true whether you're making music like Pablo Casals, making cottages like Winston Churchill, making movies like Ingmar Bergman, or making magic like David Blaine.

In 2010, David Blaine delivered a TED Talk that has been watched more than 29 million times. The title—"How I Held My Breath for 17 Minutes"—is self-explanatory. How did Blaine do it? It wasn't magic, that's for sure! "Magic, whether I'm holding my breath or shuffling a deck of cards, is pretty simple. It's practice."

As he uttered those words, David Blaine started crying on stage! After regaining his composure, he picked up where he left off: "It's practice, it's training and experimenting, while pushing through the pain to be the best that I can be. And that's what magic is to me."[19] If I'm hearing him correctly, magic is anything but magical. Like everything else, magic happens gradually then suddenly!

LITTLE BY LITTLE

There is a little phrase in Scripture that I have a love-hate relationship with—"little by little."[20] I'll explain the mixed emotions, but let me set the scene. When the Israelites finally cross the Jordan River, God tells them that He will drive out their enemies. But He adds this little addendum: "I will not drive them out in a single year."[21] And that is where mixed emotions enter the equation.

I love nonstop flights. Anyone else? The nonstop from Egypt to the Promised Land should have taken eleven days, but it turned into a forty-year flight with forty-two stops called the stations of the exodus.

Remember the brachistochrone curve? This is that. If you map the Israelites wandering in the wilderness, it's all over the map! They were walking in circles, but that's because they weren't learning the lessons God was trying to teach them. God loves us too much to graduate us to the next grade if He knows we'll fail all over again. If you want the testimony, you have to pass the test.

Little by little I will drive them out before you, until you have increased enough to take possession of the land.[22]

Maturity is not a mystery—it's mundanity. It's doing little things like they're big things. It's doing the right things day in and day out. If you do that long enough, sooner or later, you will possess the Promised Land.

God delivers us little by little.

God promotes us little by little.

God grows us little by little.

In this instance, the reasons are more ecological than theological. If God delivered the land in one fell swoop, "the land would become desolate and the wild animals too numerous for you."[23] In the same vein, I never want my gifts to take me where my character cannot sustain me. And character is cultivated like everything else. "I now see character less as a matter of will," said Adam Grant, "and more as a set of skills."[24]

The only ceiling on your intimacy with God and impact on the world is daily spiritual disciplines. What disciplines? Journaling, meditating, praying, and studying Scripture to name a few. How do you put them into practice? One day at a time! "Anyone who has mastered a golf swing or a Bach fugue," said professor and author James K. A. Smith, "is a ritual animal."[25] That not only includes gym rats; it also includes Bible geeks.

Robert and Taylor Madu launched Social Dallas in 2021, and from the outside looking in, it sure seemed like an overnight success. That church was impacting thousands of people, almost out of the gate. But before their launch, Robert felt challenged to up his game with a twenty-one-day water-only fast. Why? He felt like the Spirit said, "Your current level of discipline will not sustain the leader I'm calling you to be."[26]

What discipline do you need to develop to go to the next level? What are you waiting for?

RITUAL ANIMAL

When Phil Mickelson was a young golfer, his coach challenged him to make 100 three-foot putts in a row. Once, he made ninety-nine putts in a row but missed his one hundredth attempt. Let's be honest, most of us would have rounded up! But Phil Mickelson started all over again.[27] Why? That's what ritual animals do!

"One simply doesn't achieve such excellence otherwise," said James K. A. Smith. "Ritual is marked by *embodied repetition*. Ritual recruits our will through our body: the cellist's fingers become habituated by moving through scale after scale; the golfer's whole body is trained by a million practice swings. Because we are embodied creatures of habit—God *created* us that way—we are profoundly shaped by ritual."[28]

Are there any rituals you need to make or break?

I have a variety of sacred rituals that are part of my daily, weekly, and annual rhythms. When I write, I take my shoes off because it's holy ground. I always kneel before preaching and pray, "Lord, help me help people." And when I eat chocolate, I put some on my front teeth and smile real big. That last one may not be a *sacred* ritual, but the Bible does say that laughter doeth good like a medicine![29]

Why are rituals so important? Because consistency beats intensity seven days a week and twice on Sunday! Of course, sometimes you have to add a little variety to your consistency. One of my sacred rituals is a daily Bible reading plan, but I try to read a different translation every year. Why? Because the NIV and NLT read a little differently. And the KJV reads a lot differently—the Shakespearean English slows me down. It makes me process what I'm reading a little more carefully and consciously.

Whatever goal you're going after, you possess that promised land "little by little"! You win the Masters, like Phil Mickelson, one putt at a time. You win the Grammy Lifetime Achievement Award, like Pablo Casals, one scale at a time. You win an Academy Award, like Ingmar Bergman, one shoot at a time.

USE IT OR LOSE IT

Katie Ledecky is widely regarded as the greatest female swimmer in history. Along with fourteen Olympic medals, she has set sixteen world records and thirty-seven American records. How has she done it? Two ways—gradually then suddenly!

Katie Ledecky's training regimen is legendary. She spends two hours in the pool ten times a week. She does an hour of strength training five days a week. Then she does a dryland workout that includes battle ropes, prowler sleds, and bike sprints.[30]

All of us would love to win a gold medal, would we not? But very few of us are willing to dive into a freezing cold pool at five o'clock in the morning, then rinse and repeat for years on end. We want success without sacrifice, but it doesn't work that way. You cannot break the law of measures—"with the measure you use, it will be measured to you."[31] The law of measures will make or break you. And that's true financially, relationally, spiritually, and professionally. Whatever you're trying to achieve excellence at, it's going to take maniacal effort.

Katie Ledecky has swum more than twenty-three thousand miles over the course of her career—that's the equivalent of one lap all the way around the world.[32] But Katie doesn't see the gym or the pool as work. "I see it as playtime."

Like all great performers, her motivation is intrinsic. She's not trying to beat the swimmer in the lane next to her; she's trying to beat herself. That's how she's broken her own world records fourteen times! "I love the sport more and more every year, and I think, more than anything, that's what contributes to longevity in the sport."[33]

Are you trying to achieve excellence for extrinsic reasons? Extrinsic motivations always evaporate. Using your gifts to glorify the God who gave them to you? That's a quest that never ends. Intrinsic motivation has no expiration date. If you do what you love, you'll love what you do—and God will too!

Remember the name Eric Liddell? He was the sprinter featured in the movie *Chariots of Fire*. "When I run," the Olympic gold medalist said, "I feel His pleasure." God is not a cosmic killjoy. He is the opposite of that—our joy fuels His joy!

During the peak of his NBA career, Michael Jordan had a love-of-the-game clause written into his contract that allowed him to play pickup basketball whenever and wherever he wanted to. I grew up in Chicago during the Jordan era, so I'll admit implicit bias. But Jordan became the GOAT—greatest of all time—because no one loved the game more than he did.

It's time for a gut check.

Are you focused on inputs or outcomes?

Are you driven by intrinsic or extrinsic motivations?

Do you love gradually as much as suddenly?

If you're going to achieve your goals, you have to count the cost. It's going to take longer than you like and be harder than you hoped for. So be it. Harder is better! And sometimes, slower is faster!

AS LONG AS IT TAKES

In standardized math tests, Japanese children consistently score higher than their American counterparts. Some have assumed that a natural proclivity for numbers is the primary difference—nature over nurture. But researchers would argue that it has more to do with effort than ability.[34]

In a study involving first graders, students were given a difficult puzzle to solve. The researchers weren't interested in whether the children could solve the puzzle. They wanted to see how long the kids would try before giving up.

American children lasted, on average, 9.47 minutes. Japanese children lasted 13.93 minutes. In other words, the Japanese children tried 47 percent longer.[35] Is it any wonder they scored higher on standardized math exams? The difference in math scores has less to do with intelligence quotient and more to do with persistence quotient.

In 1978, Warren Willingham, the director of the Personal Qualities Project, attempted to identify the common denominators that determine success in young adulthood. The key to success? It wasn't GPA or test scores. Out of more than one hundred different characteristics, one rose to the top—*follow-through*.[36] What is it? It's a person's ability to "muscle through, press on, get to the finish line."[37] That sounds a lot like gradually then suddenly, does it not?

It's the old adage: *If at first you don't succeed, try, try again.*

Or how about this one? *Slow and steady wins the race.*

"Success is stumbling from failure to failure," Winston Churchill is credited with saying, "with no loss of enthusiasm."[38] And he should know. Churchill had his fair share of setbacks and shortcomings. But his ability to bounce back was legendary: "Churchill . . . was incredibly persistent in the face of long odds and often took actions that were unpopular."[39]

In one of his most famous speeches, Churchill cited the English poet Rudyard Kipling. "Meet with Triumph and Disaster," said Kipling. "And treat those two imposters just the same." Then Churchill added a twist. "Never give in, never, never, never—in nothing, great or small, large or petty—never give in except to convictions of honour and good sense."[40]

If you're like me, you want things to happen yesterday. I'm as ASAP as anyone—*as soon as possible.* But when it comes to long obedience, ALAT is the name of the game—*as long as it takes.*

HOW LONG, O LORD?

Thousands of years ago, King David asked a question: "How long, O LORD, how long?"[41] That question echoes across the centuries.

I've asked God that question a time or two or ten. Few things are harder to trust than God's timing!

David utters those words during a season of distress while fleeing for his life. His own flesh and blood, Absalom, was trying to kill him. David used to sing his son to sleep, and now his son was trying to steal his crown. David was living in the ellipsis. It's a painful punctuation mark, especially when you aren't sure how long it will last.

Those are difficult seasons to survive. Just getting out of bed is a major accomplishment. There are seasons when it feels like the dream has died, but this is a word for someone—it's not buried; it's planted.[42] Sometimes *no* means *not yet*. Well, *when* then? I can't answer that question, but God is still in the resurrection business.

"It is not for you to know," Jesus said to His disciples right before His ascension, "the times or dates the Father has set by his own authority."[43] We fixate on timelines. But do you remember what Jesus told them to do? "Wait [in Jerusalem] for the gift my Father promised."[44] Notice that He didn't tell them how long.

We live our lives forward, but God is working in our lives backward. We count up, but God is counting down. Those disciples climbed the stairs to the upper room for ten days. They were counting up, but God was counting down—10, 9, 8, 7, 6, 5, 4, 3, 2, 1. Pentecost is the power of same—it's climbing the stairs to the upper room day after day after day. The outpouring of the Spirit happened "suddenly,"[45] but it was preceded by gradually!

When we started our House of Prayer on Thursday nights, I asked Al and Chrissy Toledo for some advice. They pastor Chicago Tabernacle, and their Tuesday night prayer meeting is fire! What advice did they give me? "Do three hundred prayer meetings, then let's talk." Really? That's almost six years! And that was the point. Play the long game! Or maybe I should say, pray the long game.

If God has put a dream in your heart, don't take *no* for an answer! Try, try again. As long as it takes! Remember the Japanese schoolchildren who tried a little longer? Four minutes may not seem like much, but extrapolated over time, it makes all the difference.

KEEP CIRCLING

More than a decade ago, I wrote two books on prayer—*The Circle Maker* and *Draw the Circle*. I honestly didn't think the world needed another book on prayer, but both of those books have sold millions of copies. I should point out, however, that neither one sold a high volume of copies year one or two or three. Those books became bestsellers gradually then suddenly via word of mouth.

In *The Circle Maker*, I share the story of the 4.7-mile prayer walk I felt prompted to pray around Capitol Hill on August 16, 1996. I wasn't praying for property. I was praying for people. I was praying the Lord's Prayer: "May Your kingdom come, Your will be done, on Capitol Hill as it is in heaven."

Three decades later, we own seven properties on that prayer circle worth more than $100 million, and we own them debt-free. I can hardly believe it, even as I write it. There is nothing magical about praying circles, but there is something biblical about it. Like the Israelites who marched around Jericho for seven days, you need to circle your dreams in prayer. Then what? Keep circling!

I've received thousands of letters and emails from people who have prayed circles around their dreams, and their stories have inspired me to draw even bigger circles. There are coaches who circle football fields and chaplains who circle basketball courts in prayer. There are realtors who circle homes. There are teachers who circle classrooms, lawyers who circle courthouses, and doctors who circle hospitals. I've met with members of Congress who circle the Capitol on the regular. Then there's the guy who circled his bank in prayer believing God for a financial miracle until the cops came. He had to explain to them that he wasn't casing the bank, just circling it in prayer. Be careful what you circle!

A few years ago, an NBA chaplain started circling their home court in prayer. He gave copies of *Draw the Circle* to the team, and eleven out of twelve players read it during the playoffs. I'm not saying that's why they won the NBA championship that year, but I'm not saying it's not. My point? You have to circle your dreams the way the Israelites circled Jericho.

SIXTY-FIVE CIRCLES

When Max Calzada went to college, he set his sights on working at the World Bank. He knew the odds were against him—out of 150,000 applications each year, only 1.3 percent of applicants get hired.[46] That may not be one in a million, but one in a hundred is no joke.

Max knew it was a long shot, but God seems to love long odds! "God is not a God who asks us to ignore the facts," said Max, "but He works despite them."

Max majored in actuarial science and minored in theater, but it wasn't smooth sailing out of the gate. Like Norman Borlaug who failed his initial entrance exam, Max failed Calculus II. Of course, most of us never make it past Calculus I. After earning his undergraduate degree, Max moved to DC and started attending National Community Church. He earned his master's degree in data science with an emphasis on international economic relations.

Max landed his first job as a civilian data scientist with the Navy, but that job ended with his termination. He could have thrown in the towel on his dream, but he kept circling. He participated in the World Bank Data Dive hackathon on December 18,

2024. Max and his team won that competition, and the door opened an inch. That's when Max started circling the World Bank in prayer. He circled that building sixty-five times over the course of sixty-five days.

On March 11, 2025, Max got an email offering him a consultant role at the World Bank.

Sixty-five circles are enough to make you dizzy! "But God was up to something," said Max. "He is always writing a much larger story."[47]

That's the power of same.

That's the power of prayer.

That's the power of long obedience in the same direction.

CHAPTER 6

DARE TO BE DIFFERENT

n 1894, the city of London faced an impending crisis—an imminent threat to civilization itself. What was this potential apocalypse? In a word, manure! The population of London had topped four million people, and more people meant more horses. Fifty thousand, to be exact. The average horse poops about thirty pounds per day, which added up to 1.5 million pounds of poop per day. London, we have a problem!

One London newspaper is purported to have estimated that London would be buried under nine feet of manure in fifty years.[1] And New York City was even worse. There were vacant lots with manure piled sixty feet high. Forecasters predicted that the Big Apple would be up to its third-story windows in manure by 1930.[2]

Just before the turn of the twentieth century, urban planners gathered in London to try to solve the poop problem. The conference was scheduled to last ten days, but they called it quits after three days with no solution in sight.[3] Why? They made the classic mistake—attempting to solve present-tense problems with past-tense solutions.

If you keep doing what you've always done, you'll keep getting what you've always gotten—same ole, same ole. If you want to do something that hasn't been done before, you have to dare to be different. That's what Henry Ford did. The solution to the manure problem wasn't better sanitation. It was a better form of transportation—a horseless carriage.

"The greatest danger in times of turbulence is not the turbulence," said Peter Drucker. "It is to act with yesterday's logic."[4] If you try to solve today's problems with yesterday's solutions, the net result is the status quo.

Remember the island of Visingsö? The Swedish parliament had long vision by planting an oak forest for the third and fourth generation, but there is a fun footnote. When the Swedish parliament approved that plan, there was a lone objector, the bishop of Strangnas. Why did he object? "He had no doubt that there would still be war in the late twentieth century," said Stewart Brand, "but that ships might be built of other materials by then."[5]

The bishop of Strangnas wasn't just thinking long. He was thinking different. At critical junctures in history, long obedience is daring to be different.

"When we come to the place where everything can be predicted and nobody expects anything unusual from God," said A. W. Tozer, "we are in a rut."[6] How do you get out of a rut? Most of us try harder, but that's like spinning your wheels in the mud. Maybe, just maybe, you should *try different*. If you want God to do something new, you can't keep doing the same old thing. Jesus said it this way: "New wine is poured into new wineskins."[7]

FOSBURY FLOP

In 1964, a high school high jumper named Dick Fosbury revolutionized the sport of track and field. Of course, no one knew it at the time. The conventional methods of clearing the bar—the straddle, the Western roll, and the scissors jump—didn't fit his 6'5"-inch body type. Fosbury innovated a face up, shoulders-first technique that looked so awkward one reporter described it as "a fish flopping in a boat."

Four years and hundreds of awkward attempts later, Dick Fosbury represented Team USA at the 1968 Olympic Games. Not only did Fosbury win the gold medal, he set a new Olympic record, jumping 7 feet, 4¼ inches. By the next Olympic Games, twenty-eight out of forty Olympians had adopted the technique named after the man who dared to be different—the Fosbury flop.[8] Can I tell you what usually precedes awesome? Awkward.

If you want to repeat history, do it the same.

If you want to make history, dare to be different.

I know the last chapter was all about the power of same, so daring to be different might sound like a contradiction in terms. But it's equally important when it comes to long obedience in the same direction. Most people eventually conform to the world around them—giving in to peer pressure, popular opinion, and political correctness. Daring to be different requires moral courage, but the only other option is moral compromise.

Are you taking your cues from trending hashtags?

Or are you living for the applause of nail-scarred hands?

In the age of political polarization, it takes courage to stand in the gap as a peacemaker, grace giver, truth teller, and tone-setter. The Sermon on the Mount is about defying the spirit of the age by operating in the opposite spirit—love your enemies, pray for those who persecute you, and bless those who curse you. That's how we shift the atmosphere. We double down on faith, hope, and love!

In the age of algorithms designed to keep us in our echo chambers, groupthink is harder and harder to overcome. It takes courage not to conform, but Ralph Waldo Emerson was right: "Imitation is suicide."[9] Do a Fosbury flop! How? That's for you to figure out.

Is there a courageous choice you need to make? Maybe it's time for a grand gesture—make the call or make the move, submit the application or schedule the appointment.

When I gave up a full-ride scholarship to the University of Chicago to transfer to Central Bible College, it seemed nonsensical. When Lora and I made the move to DC with no place to live and no salary, it seemed illogical. When National Community Church gave its first check to missions, it seemed irresponsible because we weren't even self-supporting as a church. Those defining decisions proved to be turning points—those are the days when decades happen. And the stakes only get higher!

THE INFINITE GAME

In 1986, a professor of religion named James P. Carse coined a concept called "the infinite game." A finite game is played for the purpose of winning, but that is a zero-sum game. An infinite game is played for the purpose of continuing the game.[10] That's a very different endgame because there is no finish line. Which way are you living your life?

If you approach life like a zero-sum game where someone wins and someone loses, you're playing the wrong way. News flash: All the toys go back in the box at the end of the game.[11] The infinite game is intergenerational. "They are not dead who live in hearts they leave behind," said Hugh Robert Orr. "In those whom they have blessed, they live a life again."[12]

If you lead something long enough, you haven't led the same thing that whole time. I've led the same church for thirty years, but it's gone through more iterations than you can imagine. So have I, and I'm not just talking about clothing styles.

For many years, National Community Church was known as the church at Union Station. That's where we gathered for thirteen magical years before the movie theaters at Union Station shut down. During those years, our call sign was theaterchurch.com. Our vision was meeting in movie theaters at metro stops throughout the DC area because we felt like that was the most organic way to reach our city. And truth be told, we never thought we'd own property! When God gave us a city block after two decades of doing church in rented facilities, it was a game changer.

There are critical junctures in the life cycle of an organization—the sigmoid curve—when the organization must jump the curve. Of course, it's true of individuals too! It's a leap of faith, but the only other option is a slow death. Simon Sinek calls it an existential flex. "To infinite-minded players," says Sinek, "staying on the current path is the bigger risk."[13] Settling for the status quo usually seems like the safe play, but playing it safe is risky.

"When an infinite-minded leader with a clear sense of Cause looks to the future and sees that the path they are on will significantly restrict their ability to advance their Just Cause," said Simon Sinek, "they flex."[14] Go ahead and flex. Seriously! Just as we flex our muscles, we have to flex our imaginations. But how we do that is counterintuitive. Long vision involves long memory, so this may sound like a contradiction, but it also involves forgetting.

Forget the former things;
    do not dwell on the past.
See, I am doing a new thing!
    Now it springs up; do you not perceive it?[15]

It's so easy to learn *how* and forget *why!* That's when you stop creating the future and start repeating the past. "The greatest opposition to what God is doing today," said R. T. Kendall, "comes from those who were on the cutting edge of what God was doing yesterday."[16]

IT'S TIME

For more than two decades, multisite was our model as a church. We were one church with eight campuses. Then I went on a silent retreat, and I felt like the Lord said in no uncertain terms, "Do more things that don't have your name on it." We have since shifted from a campus model to a network model, which felt like a Fosbury flop. We've launched our campuses as network churches, and we started something called the Dream Collective on our twenty-sixth anniversary—January 14, 2022.

Launching those campuses was a grand gesture—relationally, financially, and philosophically. We had to reimagine ourselves as a church. We had to repurpose our staff. We had to reorient our congregation with a new vision. Like any and every existential shift, it came at a cost.

It felt a little like walking my daughter down the aisle on her wedding day. Ironically, it was walking her down the aisle that gave us the courage and clarity to do what we did. I had this eureka moment on her wedding day that I wasn't losing a daughter—we were gaining a son-in-law. And that's how you get grandchildren!

Life is lived in stages, and not all stages are created equal. You need to know the stage you're coming out of and the stage you're going into. For National Community Church, we are intent on giving a birthright and a blessing to as many dreamers as we can. The Dream Collective is how we turned NCC inside out. We don't want control or credit. We just want to see His kingdom come, His will be done. That's gonna take every church in our city! That's one reason we've invested in more than forty church plants in our city. If a church is preaching and practicing the gospel, we're on the same team.

We see ourselves as a dream factory—an incubator for poets

and prophets, entrepreneurs and artists, dreamers and doers. Our vision? Revival in the church, reformation in the kingdom, and renaissance in culture. If you've got a God-sized dream, we want to be shareholders in it. We want you to know two things: You're not crazy and you're not alone.

YESTERDAY'S ANOINTING

I've been profoundly impacted by the writing of R. T. Kendall. So impacted I once did a round-trip day trip from DC to NYC to have lunch with him. Along with pastoring Westminster Chapel in London for twenty-five years, R. T. has written more than fifty books. My personal favorite is *The Anointing: Yesterday, Today, and Tomorrow.* In that book, R. T. warns of something he calls "yesterday's anointing."

> A person who had a tremendous anointing yesterday can continue to see the momentum of that anointing continuing to manifest itself. He or she may hastily conclude that "the anointing is still with us" when it is but the momentum of yesterday's anointing.[17]

That's a sobering statement, is it not? That should keep us on our knees in daily dependence on God. In the words of Moses, "If your Presence does not go with us, do not send us up from here."[18] Long vision is about going after God-sized dreams, but it takes long obedience to get there.

By definition, a God-sized dream will always be beyond your ability, beyond your education, beyond your resources. You can't do it, but God can. At some point, most of us stop playing to win. We hedge our bets. We start playing not to lose by burying our talent in the ground. My advice? Go after a dream that is destined to fail without divine intervention. But that God-sized dream is going to take God's anointing!

Even more dangerous than employing yesterday's logic is living off yesterday's anointing. Neither one will get you where God wants you to go. That takes a new anointing, a fresh anointing, a greater anointing. Every new season demands a new anointing! The good news? The anointing is for everyone. And I might add, for everything.

> The anointing you received from Him remains in you, and you do not need anyone to teach you. But just as His true and genuine anointing teaches you about all things, so remain in Him.[19]

The anointing doesn't make you any better than anyone else. It makes you better than you. It brings out the best version of yourself. The anointing is the difference between the best you can do and the best God can do, and that's a big difference! The anointing is your JND—just noticeable difference. It intensifies and amplifies the gifts God has given you. The anointing is the multiplier that turns you into an outlier. The anointing is the difference between the natural and the supernatural.

Make no mistake, the anointing is not a cheat code. It can compensate for your weaknesses, but you're still subject to the ten-thousand-hour rule. I like the way Annie F. Downs says it—"If you don't practice, God can't put you in the game!" You've got to work like it depends on you, but the anointing is the X factor, the It factor.

Without the Holy Spirit, I'm below average! Anybody else? My best isn't good enough. "Accepting our limitations," said R. T. Kendall, "is essential to accepting our anointing."[20] It's when we come to the end of our abilities that we discover how important the anointing is.

THE MULTIPLICATION ANOINTING

Three days before the release of my first book, *In a Pit with a Lion on a Snowy Day*, I was at a conference in Baltimore, Maryland. After speaking, I sat in on a session with Tommy Barnett, who co-founded the LA Dream Center with his son, Matthew. Tommy epitomizes long vision, long obedience, and long legacy. He shared about going after a God-sized dream—the 360,000-square-foot Queen of Angels Hospital that sits on 8.8 acres overlooking Highway 101 in Los Angeles. It took millions of dollars and more than a few miracles, but the LA Dream Center has impacted millions of people over thirty years. It also inspired our Dream Center in DC—Tommy and Matthew both get partial credit.

After sharing about God's miraculous provision, Tommy invited anyone who wanted what he called a "multiplication anointing" to come to the altar. I think I was the first one at the altar—if the altar is open, I'm there!

As a first-time author, I knew the sobering statistic that 98 percent of books don't sell five thousand copies in their lifetime. I mustered all the faith I had and prayed that mine would sell twenty-five thousand copies. That was my magic number, but I also had a whisper number that I didn't have enough faith to verbalize. I only had enough faith to *think it*. My whisper number— my faith ceiling—was one hundred thousand copies. Nearly two decades later, that book has 20xed my magic number and 5xed my whisper number. How? I don't want to discount the entire team at my publishing house, WaterBrook & Multnomah. They all deserve partial credit, but I also believe that multiplication anointing has been the X factor. And I might add, a prayer team that asked God to put my books in the right hands at the right time. God has answered those prayers ten million times!

I don't write for numbers. To me, a book sold is a prayer answered. Nothing is more gratifying than hearing stories about how one sentence on one page gave someone the courage to *Chase the Lion, Draw the Circle,* or *Win the Day.* That's what the anointing does—it turns our natural into the supernatural.

I have no idea what you do, but God wants to anoint it. I need His anointing for pastoring and writing, but I also need it for parenting! When I bike a century[21], I need His anointing too—right around mile ninety-three! How do you get the anointing? You ask for it.

On February 2, 2013, I wrote these words in my prayer journal: "a new anointing for a new address." Honestly, I wasn't even sure what I was asking for. But that little phrase kept echoing in my spirit. I wasn't sure what it meant until August 16, 2014—that's the day we signed the letter of intent on a $29.3 million city block that would become the Capital Turnaround. When we started gathering at that new address—700 M Street, SE—God gave us a new anointing. That's where we do House of Prayer, and God has turned us into a House of Miracles, House of Healing, and House of Dreams.

SHOW UP DIFFERENT

Remember the twelve spies who did reconnaissance in the Promised Land for forty days? All of them spied the same cities and saw the same giants. They all sampled the same charcuterie board, but those twelve spies came back with very different reports. Two of them—Caleb and Joshua—came back singing Queen, "We are the champions." But they were outnumbered by ten spies who came back singings the blues.

What was the difference? The negative spies had forgotten the overstory. They were focused on the understory. Instead of putting their faith in the God who made the promise, they let fear dictate their decisions.

Negativity may not be the unpardonable sin, but it can keep you out of the Promised Land. Ten negative people cost Israel forty years! Not only is negativity toxic; it's highly contagious. Nothing short-circuits long obedience in the same direction like the negativity bias, and the net result is sideways energy.

Long obedience is staying focused on the end goal.

Long obedience is staying tethered to core convictions.

I was forty years old when Moses the servant of the LORD sent me from Kadesh Barnea to explore the land. And I brought him back a report according to my convictions.[22]

Did you catch the key phrase? "According to my convictions." Caleb was a conviction-driven leader. He didn't take his cues from opinion polls. His moral compass was his convictions, and the promises of God were true north.

Is it frustrating when negative people oppose the vision God gave you? Of course it is, but that's par for the course. Even if your name is Moses and you come down from Mount Sinai with stone tablets inscribed by the finger of God, you should expect 16 percent opposition. It's called the diffusion of innovation curve. On one end of that bell curve is the 16 percent of people called laggards, or late adopters. On the other end is the 16 percent of people called innovators and early adopters.[23] As leaders, we love early adopters! But I've come to appreciate late adopters, also called resisters. Why? They force you to become a better vision caster!

There will always be naysayers. Prove them wrong! That doesn't mean you dismiss them out of pocket. As hard as it is, listen to them and learn from them. Then cast an even more compelling vision.

THE MOMENT OF TRUTH

According to Jewish tradition, when Caleb entered the Promised Land with the other spies, there was a moment when he broke off from the group. "They went up through the Negev," it says in the third person plural. Then it switches to the third person singular, "And he came to Hebron."[24] Who is he? Caleb is him!

That nuance is easily overlooked, but this was the day when decades happen. This was the moment—a moment of truth— when Caleb did a Fosbury flop. He swore on his ancestors' graves that he would be back to stake claim to that promised land.[25] For more than four decades, his conviction neither waxed nor waned.

I don't need to be a prophet to know that there will come a moment—a moment of truth—when you will have to make a difficult decision, a defining decision. When and where, I have no idea! Either you will go with the flow and give in to groupthink. Or you will disassociate yourself from popular opinion, peer pressure, and political correctness.

Caleb dared to be different by disassociating from the ten spies who had lost faith. Caleb made a vow: "My fathers, pray on my behalf, that I may be delivered from the plan of the spies." It's hard not to listen to loud voices, but that is when and where the still small voice of the Holy Spirit needs to be the loudest voice in your life!

How did Caleb hold on to that promise? How did Caleb conquer the hill country called Hebron? Two ways—gradually then suddenly! The genesis was a grand gesture—kneeling on the graves of his ancestors. But the differentiating factor was a "different spirit."

Because My servant Caleb has a different spirit and has followed Me wholeheartedly, I will bring him into the land he has entered, and his descendants will inherit it.[26]

This predates Pentecost by more than a millennia, but that "different spirit" was the Spirit of God. The same Spirit that raised Christ from the dead dwells in us.[27] That is our JND—just noticeable difference. It's also my TOE—theory of everything: *The answer to every prayer is more of the Holy Spirit.* But what about love, joy, or peace? Those are fruit of the Spirit, so what we really need is more of the Spirit that produces more of that fruit. And the same goes for the gifts of the Spirit.

It's not easy staying positive when everyone gets negative. It's not easy living according to convictions that might get you canceled either. But who said long obedience in the same direction was going to be easy? Long obedience is holding on to the promise God has given you for forty years! It's holding out for the high ground called Hebron.

I had severe asthma for more than forty years. There weren't forty days in forty years that I didn't have to take multiple puffs of a rescue inhaler. I slept with an inhaler under my pillow. I played basketball with an inhaler in my sock. But I never stopped believing that God was able. I prayed a bold prayer on July 2, 2016, and I have not touched an inhaler from that day to this day!

GIVE ME THE HILL COUNTRY

When the Israelites finally entered the Promised Land, Caleb was an old man. "Here I am today, eighty-five years old" said Caleb. "I am still as strong today as the day Moses sent me out."[28] If I'm reading this right, Caleb could still squat five hundred pounds. He was still doing eight reps with six plates on the bench press. How is that even possible? Because nothing keeps us young—keeps us energized—like a God-sized dream.

The writer of Proverbs said, "Where there is no vision, the people perish."[29] The word *perish* refers to fruit that is past its prime— it's not ripening, it's rotting. But the opposite is true too. If you have vision, you're never past your prime! Your vision gets bigger as your faith gets stronger.

Then Caleb throws down the gauntlet: "Now give me this hill country that the LORD promised me that day."[30] What day? The day he swore on the graves of his great-great-great-great-grandparents.

You don't have to be a military major to know that the high country is the hardest to conquer, but Caleb wouldn't have it any other way. Go big or go home! Caleb conquered Hebron, but let me add an endnote. Caleb didn't just conquer Hebron for himself. The domino effect of his decision to disassociate from the other spies was felt generations later.

Caleb had no way of knowing this, but Hebron is where David would be crowned king hundreds of years later. Your choices matter, more than you know! And I might add, long after you are long gone!

Remember the 1886 church, a few blocks from the Capitol, that we purchased? We didn't need that building, but we were uniquely positioned to purchase it and preserve it for future generations. Our original intent is to use that building as an incubator for artists and entrepreneurs and church planters. But whatever God does in and through the Culturehouse—every dream inspired in that space—is a tribute to the former slaves who built that church. And that building belongs to future generations. We're just one link of the rope—*whakapapa*!

When you persist in pursuing God-sized dreams, you aren't just claiming the promise for yourself. You're doing it to honor the generations who came before and the generations who will come after. You owe it to your ancestors and you owe it to your descendants to play the long game, and the name of the game is long obedience in the same direction.

DO THINGS TWICE YOUR SIZE

As you get older, one of two things will happen. Either your theology conforms to your reality or your reality conforms to your theology. And the choice is yours! Remember the ten spies who gave up on God? They let fear dictate their decisions instead of faith. The irony is that their negativity became a self-defeating, self-fulfilling prophecy. Caleb, on the other hand, eventually conquered Hebron. How? Forty years of gradually followed by one day of suddenly!

Longitudinal studies show a neurological shift in the cognitive center of gravity from the creative right-brain to the logical left-brain as we age. At some point, we stop living out of imagination and start living out of memory. Most of us stop creating the future and start repeating the past, but it doesn't have to be that way. It's never too late to be who you might have been.

Is there a hill you need to take? Maybe it's a dream that seemed so daunting you gave up on it before you even began. If God is in it, it's never too little and it's never too late. Will you have to dare to be different? No doubt. Will it take a multiplication anointing? You can take it to the bank, pun intended. Don't stop believin'. Hold on to that feelin'.[31]

Three decades ago, I was at a leadership conference and five words changed the trajectory of my life—"Do things twice your size." At the time, National Community Church wasn't even a hundred people, but we put that principle into practice by hosting a Convoy of Hope outreach that would require four hundred volunteers. That doesn't add up, does it? It wasn't twice our size, it was four times our size with 100 percent participation! By faith, we cast a vision for that outreach, and area churches rallied around us. We ended up giving fifty thousand pounds of free groceries to five thousand people, and we kept putting that principle into practice by doing things twice our size.

When God gave us the vision to turn a crackhouse into Ebenezers Coffeehouse, our annual income as a church was right around $100,000. That doesn't add up, which is how the little boy with five loaves and two fish must have felt. But if you put what's in your hands into the hands of God, it doesn't add up anymore—it multiplies. The multiplication anointing turned those five loaves and two fish into a miracle for five thousand.

Is there a defining decision you need to make? Since we're on the subject of giving, maybe it's giving God the tithe—the first 10 percent of your income. I know people who say, "I'll give more when I make more." With all due respect, I'm not buying what you're selling. If you aren't generous with a little, you won't be generous with a lot. Don't let what you cannot do keep you from doing what you can.

Let me close this chapter with a challenge, because that's how you start a new chapter in your life. You don't have to finish it, but I'd challenge you to start it. What? Whatever God is stirring in your spirit. If it's running a marathon, download the training plan. If it's getting a degree, submit the application. If it's writing a book, pen a paragraph. If it's getting counseling, make the call.

Will it happen overnight? You should know by now, it'll happen two ways—gradually then suddenly! But you can't finish what you don't start.

CHAPTER 7

THE CREATIVE MINORITY

In the eighteenth century, a visionary named Count Nikolaus Ludwig von Zinzendorf founded something called the Order of the Mustard Seed. It was an eclectic group that eventually included the king of Denmark, the archbishop of Canterbury, Scotland's secretary of state, and the eighty-seven-year-old chief of the Creek Nation, Tomochichi.

Each member wore a ring with this inscription: *None of us lives to himself.* Each member pledged their wealth, pledged their influence, to the cause of Christ. Each member of that order took a vow that involved three simple yet radical commitments.

One, *be true to Christ.*
Two, *be kind to people.*
Three, *take the gospel to the nations.*

In 1727, Count Zinzendorf started what many believe to be the first 24-7 prayer movement. The Moravian church would pray around the clock—around the calendar—for more than a hundred years![1] If that's not long obedience in the same direction, I'm not sure what is.

When you pray that way, your heart begins to break for the things that break the heart of God. Your heart begins to beat for things that make the heart of God skip a beat. There is actually a scientific name for it—physiological synchrony.

When horses travel in herds, their heartbeats sync up. It actually helps the herd sense danger. And that phenomenon happens with other animal species. Birds of a feather don't just flock together; they synchronize the flapping of their wings.[2] The same thing happens when we practice sacred rituals in community.

What's *really* happening when we pray? We're getting in sync with the good, pleasing, and perfect will of God. It's not about outlining our agenda to God. It's about God outlining His agenda to us! It's in prayer that God can conceive new desires within us— a supernatural synchronization. The same thing happens when we worship—we're harmonizing with heaven. And that's what happens when we get into God's Word—God's Word gets into us! Nothing primes faith like the promises of God. I need a daily dose of God's Word to keep me focused on the overstory God is writing in and through my life.

AMAZING THINGS

Long before the abolition of slavery, two members of the Order of the Mustard Seed—Johann Leonhard Dober and David Nitschmann—sold themselves into slavery as a way of sharing the gospel with slaves on the island of St. Thomas. As their ship sailed from the docks, they yelled to the family and friends they left behind, "May the Lamb that was slain receive the reward of His suffering."[3]

Sometimes long obedience involves long suffering! It's making sacrifices for the greater good. It's taking up your cross for the cause of Christ. It's consecrating yourself to God—time, talent, treasure. Why? Because it's all from Him and all for Him.

Consecrate yourselves, for tomorrow the LORD will do amazing things among you.[4]

We want to do amazing things for God, but that isn't our job. God is the one who does amazing things for us! Our job? To consecrate ourselves to God. It's submitting your past, present, and future to God. It's loving God with your heart, soul, mind, and strength. Consecration is going all in with God.

Few people have left a more lasting legacy on the church in America than Dwight L. Moody. Moody Church has impacted hundreds of thousands of people since its inception in 1864. Moody Bible Institute has probably trained more ministers than any other organization or university. Then there's Moody Radio and Moody Publishers, whose spoken words and written words are felt far and wide. On a personal note, it was a D. L. Moody biography that inspired my early-morning prayer habit. Moody made it a habit to be up praying before the blacksmiths started hammering.

In the 1860s, there wasn't a city with more than a million inhabitants in America. Chicago had just cracked the top ten with a population of 112,172.[5] But Moody saw the future: "Cities are centers of influence. Water runs downhill and the highest hills in America are the great cities. If we can stir them up, we can stir the whole country."[6]

Moody had long vision, and it was backed up by long obedience in the same direction.

But it started with a moment of consecration. A British revivalist named Henry Varley challenged Moody with these words: "The world has yet to see what God can do with a man fully consecrated to him."[7] That exhortation sent shock waves through his soul. "By God's help," said Moody, "I aim to be that man."[8]

Why not you?

Why not now?

If you reverse engineer any revival or reformation or renaissance, the genesis is someone saying, "Here am I. Send me!"[9] You don't have to sell yourself into slavery like Dober and Nitschmann, but it will take courage.

UNSUNG HEROES

A shoemaker named George Robert Twelves Hewes. A homemaker named Lydia Darragh. An army physician named William Gorgas. And a slave named Anna "Ann" Williams. Those are not household names we learn in history class, but without the sacrifices they made, history would read very differently. They are the unsung heroes.

George Robert Twelves Hewes led one of the boarding parties during the Boston Tea Party because of his "whistling talent."[10] Lydia Darragh uncovered a British plot to attack American troops at Whitemarsh and risked her life to warn General George Washington.[11] William Gorgas, the chief sanitation officer during the building of the Panama Canal, made the work possible by creatively combating mosquito-borne diseases.[12] That leaves a slave named Ann Williams, but her story takes a little more time to tell.

There is a statue that sits outside the National Archives with an inscription that reads, "What is Past is Prologue." It's taken from Act II of *The Tempest* by William Shakespeare.[13] The irony is that most people do not know the history of the city block that the National Archives now occupies.

In L' Enfant's original plan, the block was actually designated for a National Church halfway between the White House and the Capitol. That idea was vetoed by those who believed it might hamper the freedom of religion by establishing a "state" church. So in 1797, President George Washington designated that two-acre plot to serve as a public marketplace.

Center Market opened its doors in 1801. Farmers, fishers, and bakers sold their goods at that market. At its peak, there were as many as seven hundred vendors! Artesian wells provided fresh water. Cold storage rooms kept food refrigerated. Center Market was the economic hub of the nation's capital, but it didn't just sell goods and groceries. It sold slaves to the highest bidder. Those slaves were held in slave pens near what is now the National Mall. Once they were auctioned off, they were coffled with chains and marched hundreds of miles on foot as far south as Georgia.

In November 1815, Ann Williams was sold to Georgia slave traders. The night before her march south, she was held at George Miller's tavern at 13th and F Street, NW. She could not bear the thought of being separated from her family, so Ann attempted to escape by jumping from the third-story window of Miller's tavern. The fall broke both of her arms and shattered her lower spine.[14]

Ann survived long enough to tell her plight to a young Pennsylvania doctor named Jesse Torrey who happened to be visiting the capital city. When he heard her story, he said it "pervaded my *full* heart and agitated mind."[15] Torrey couldn't believe slaves were being sold in the shadow of the Capitol. He canceled his congressional visit and took up the abolitionist cause. Torrey published a ninety-four-page volume titled *A Portraiture of Domestic Slavery* in 1817. Included in that volume was an artist's rendering of Ann's jump. That picture pricked the conscience of some and inspired the courage of others to ban slave trade in the capital city.

For two hundred years, she was known only by her first name, Anna. Then in 2015, researchers at the National Archives—the very place where so many slaves had been sold when it was Center Market—discovered her full name. In 1828, Anna Williams had filed a petition for freedom that went unrequited for two centuries. Upon discovering her true identity, that petition was granted posthumously by the circuit court of DC—two hundred years too late.

From 1934 to 1961, a British historian named Arnold Toynbee published a twelve-volume history that traces the rise and fall of nineteen civilizations.[16] Civilizations go through life cycles from birth to death, but Toynbee believed that civilizations could experience a rebirth. The key is something Toynbee called the creative minority. It's any minority that responds to crisis creatively, and Toynbee cites the church as exhibit A.

The church has taken some hits in recent years because of high-profile failings or fallings; and to be blunt, it's inexcusable. The level of skepticism and cynicism is pretty high, and in all too many instances, it's the result of self-inflicted wounds. If you let celebrity culture creep into the church and put people on pedestals, you turn them into Humpty Dumpty. Sooner or later, it leads to a great fall.

The church has made plenty of mistakes because it's led by imperfect people, but those shortcomings don't negate all the good the church has done. For all its faults and foibles, no organization on earth, no government in the history of humankind, has done as much collective good as the church. And there is no close second. The church is still the bride of Christ. The church is still the body of Christ. The church is still the hope of the world.

One of our core convictions is that the church belongs in the middle of the marketplace. A church that stays within its four walls isn't a church at all. We are called to be salt and light. We are a company of prophets called to compete for the truth in the marketplace of ideas.

Almost a century ago, an executive at 20th Century Fox sent letters to Christian college presidents asking them to send him screenwriters. "Did the church capture this opportunity? No. One college president wrote back saying he'd sooner send their young people to hell itself than send them to Hollywood."[17] That's how things go to hell. Salt that stays in the shaker isn't fulfilling its purpose. Faithfulness is not holding the fort—it's incarnating the gospel, which certainly includes movies and music and media. Yes, even social media. Remember the chapter on opportunity cost? This is that. I can't help but consider the counterfactual—what if those presidents had sent their best and brightest to make movies?

In his book *Roaring Lambs*, Bob Briner reflects on missionary conventions he went to as a kid where he was challenged to commit himself to missions. We certainly need to follow in the footsteps of Johann Leonhard Dober and David Nitschmann. But culture-shaping professions—entertainment and education, politics and journalism—are mission fields too!

"The church needs writers, performers, artists, speakers, politicians, businessmen, and workers in every craft and trade," exhorted Briner. "I envision a whole generation of roaring lambs who will lay claim to these careers with the same vigor and commitment that sent men like Hudson Taylor to China."[18]

> Why not believe that one day the most critically acclaimed director in Hollywood could be an active Christian layman in his church? Why not hope that the Pulitzer Prize for investigative reporting could go to a Christian journalist on staff at a major daily newspaper? Is it really too much of a stretch to think that a major exhibit at the Museum of Modern Art could feature the works of an artist on staff at one of our fine Christian colleges? Am I out of my mind to suggest that your son or daughter could be the principle dancer for the Joffrey Ballet Company, leading a weekly Bible study for other dancers in what was once considered a profession that was morally bankrupt?

"I don't think so," said Bob Briner.[19] Neither do I.

That mindset—pursuing callings rather than careers—is vitally important for such a time as this. This cultural moment is daring us to be different. Instead of making a living, make a life! We are called to invade hellholes with the light and love of Jesus. We are called to create outposts of Eden where heaven invades earth. We're not just believing for revival in the church. We're believing for renaissance in culture—the redemption of all things.

The church is not only a creative minority, it is also a moral minority. We should be more known for what we're *for* than for what we're against. That said, we live in a culture where it's wrong to say something is wrong, and I think that's wrong. "The church has its greatest relevance to the world," says Timothy Gombis, "when it is most unlike the world in its corrupted forms."[20]

INTERREGNUM

When I was in seminary, I read a book titled *Resident Aliens* by Stanley Hauerwas and Will Willimon. They said, "The world needs the church, not to help the world run more smoothly or to make the world a better and safer place for Christians to live. Rather, the world needs the church because, without the church, the world does not know who it is."[21]

There are no perfect churches because there are no perfect people, but the church plays a critical role in culture by offering an alternate narrative, alternate identity, alternate reality. At critical junctures in human history, we hold our moral ground. If we don't, moral relativism leads to moral nihilism. The net result is a loss of principle and purpose, and eventually the bottom falls out.

Joseph Daniel Unwin earned his PhD in anthropology from the University of Cambridge. Two years before his untimely death at age forty, he published his magnum opus titled *Sex and Culture*.

Unwin studied eighty tribes and six civilizations across five thousand years of human history, identifying the keystones that made civilizations rise and fall. What did he discover? According to Unwin, the single most influential factor in a civilization's longevity is prenuptial chastity coupled with postnuptial monogamy.[22]

Let me put it in simple terms. When sex is treated with dignity as something holy—a sacred covenant between a husband and a wife—it doesn't just hold marriages together. It holds civilizations together. You can dismiss Unwin's opinion as archaic, but sexual ethics isn't just about sexual ethics. It's part of the fabric of society called morality. And without morality, democracy doesn't even work. Those aren't my words. That's what John Adams said.[23] And every generation serves as guardians of the galaxy, I mean theology.

According to Toynbee, the collapse of civilizations doesn't happen outside in. It happens inside out. The disintegration of civilization is caused by the deterioration of the creative minority. How does that happen? When the creative minority starts worshipping its *former self.* The creative minority has to keep imagining new tomorrows and innovating new ideas. Why? Because you never arrive! Remember what R. T. Kendall said? Sometimes the greatest opposition to what God wants to do next comes from those who were on the cutting edge of what God did last.[24]

In political science, there is a concept called an interregnum. It's the discontinuity between political regimes. Those interregnums are coming fast and furious these days. And they are amplified by political polarization. Hermann Hesse described it this way:

> There are times when a whole generation gets caught to such an extent between two eras, two styles of life, that nothing comes naturally to it since it has lost all sense of morality, security and innocence.[25]

Does it feel like we are living in one of those moments? The tectonic plates of culture are shifting. I live on one of those cultural fault lines called Capitol Hill, but I would proffer a little reminder. There is a hill higher than Capitol Hill—it's a hill called Calvary. That's where sin and shame met their match in the sinless Son of God. And death was defeated three days later at the empty tomb.

Spiritually speaking, interregnums are a Hebrews 12:27 moment. "All of creation will be shaken," said the writer of Hebrews, "so that only unshakable things will remain."[26] Don't let the shaking shake your confidence! God is shaking false securities and false identities, false assumptions and false narratives, false idols and false ideologies. Why? "So that what cannot be shaken may remain."[27] We don't trust in horses and chariots. We trust in the name of the Lord our God. This is our moment to rise up as a creative minority, a moral minority.

Interregnums present a clear and present danger, but they also present us with a unique opportunity to rediscover who we are and reimagine a better future. "About every five hundred years," said Phyllis Tickle in her book *The Great Emergence*, "the Church feels compelled to hold a giant rummage sale."[28] That's when and where and how reformations happen. Of course, that takes courage—the kind of moral courage embodied by two unsung heroes named Shiphrah and Puah. You may not know their names, but they delivered a boy named Moses who delivered a nation from slavery.

THE DAY THE DELIVERER WAS DELIVERED

God delivered the Israelites out of Egypt with a tour de force—ten signs and wonders. Moses led the people out of slavery, but that isn't the day when deliverance happened. Their deliverance had been in the works for eight decades. Eighty years earlier, two midwives risked their lives to deliver the deliverer.

The king of Egypt had issued an executive order that the midwives were to abort all the baby boys born to the Jews. The midwives had a choice to make—obey the law of the land or obey the law of God.

The king of Egypt said to the Hebrew midwives, whose names were Shiphrah and Puah, "When you help the Hebrew women give birth, observe them on the birthstools. If the child is a son, kill him. . . .
The midwives, however, feared God and did not do as the king of Egypt had instructed; they let the boys live.[29]

Make no mistake, this was a do-or-die decision. By defying the king of Egypt, they were putting their lives on the line. But they feared God more than they feared man! If you fear man, you will ultimately offend God. If you fear God, you will ultimately offend man. The choice is yours! The good news? If you fear God—if God's Word is the final authority, if you give the Spirit of God veto power, if you're living for the applause of nail-scarred hands—you have nothing else to fear!

God honors their obedience with compound interest. "So God was good to the midwives, and the people multiplied and became even more numerous."[30] But wait, there's more. "Because the midwives feared God, he gave them families of their own."[31]

I said it before, but I'll say it again for good measure: *You may not influence a million people, but you might influence one person who influences a million people.* It was Moses who delivered the Israelites out of Egypt, but it was Shiphrah and Puah who delivered the deliverer! They certainly get partial credit for Israel's exodus out of Egypt.

When God made a sidewalk through the sea and delivered Israel all over again, I imagine that moment through Shiphrah and

Puah's eyes. They're standing with their children and their children's children. That's when they lean over and whisper, "We cut his umbilical cord."

I love the fact that Moses, the author of Exodus, includes the names of Shiphrah and Puah. I think it was personal for him. He wanted to give credit where credit is due. Their names are mentioned very briefly, but they made it in the Bible! Put that on your LinkedIn profile!

Remember *whakapapa*—the idea that each of us is one link between our ancestors and our descendants? This is that. It may be Moses who made historical headlines, but that overstory doesn't even get written without the courage of two midwives named Shiphrah and Puah.

THE CREDITS

Does the name Silvanus ring a bell? He's not a household name, but he co-authored four books of the Bible. He also accompanied Paul on his second missionary journey. Paul was the lead actor, no doubt. But even lead actors need supporting actors. And I might add, extras. And don't forget about stunt doubles, unless you're Tom Cruise.

The last chapter of Romans is like the credits at the end of the movie. Paul thanks twenty-eight people by name. Remember Rufus? He only gets one verse, but Paul is giving partial credit to each and every person who left their fingerprints on his soul.

There is no way Paul writes half of the New Testament without some help. It was Silvanus who helped Paul write some of those epistles, and it was Epaphroditus who delivered it. "Honor men like him,"[32] said the apostle Paul. Why? "He nearly died for the work of Christ, risking his life."[33]

If the book of Philippians has ever blessed your soul, you owe

Epaphroditus a thank-you. Paul wrote that epistle in prison, so he could not deliver it himself. It was Epaphroditus who played Pony Express, which was no simple task before planes, trains, and automobiles. Epaphroditus traveled 787 miles from Rome to Philippi to deliver that letter, which included crossing the Adriatic Sea.

We read right over it, but Epaphroditus risked his life to deliver that epistle! When was the last time you risked your life for the gospel? Some of us aren't even willing to risk our reputation!

If you made it this far, can I get in your business a little bit? When was the last time you risked rejection by sharing your faith? When was the last time you risked failure by going after a God-sized dream? When was the last time you risked a promotion by refusing to compromise your convictions?

The Greek word translated "risk" is *parabouleuomai*.[34] This is the only place it appears in the entire New Testament. It's a gambling term—it's pushing your chips to the middle of the table and going all in.[35]

A MESSAGE TO GARCÍA

Many years ago, I had coffee with film director and producer Jon Erwin. One half of the Erwin Brothers, his films have grossed more than $150 million.[36] One of my dreams is to make a movie, so I asked Jon a pretty straightforward question: How do you make it in the movie industry? "When you get a foot in the door," he said, "you've got to be a Rowan." I had no earthly idea what he meant, but Jon explained with a story.

When the Spanish-American War broke out just before the turn of the twentieth century, President William McKinley needed to get a message to General García, the leader of the Cuban insurgents. There was one problem—no one knew where he was. The island of Cuba is 42,426 square miles, which is comparable in size to the state of Virginia. So finding General García was like finding a needle in a haystack! That's when someone said to President McKinley, "A fellow by the name of Rowan will find García for you, if anybody can."[37]

Andrew S. Rowan was a first lieutenant in the U.S. Army. He was a graduate of West Point. He was trained in topography and barometric hypsometry. At the time, he was serving as head of the Military Information Division Map Section in Washington, DC.[38]

Upon his commission, Rowan put the top-secret letter from President McKinley in an oilskin pouch and strapped it around his shoulder. He sailed to Cuba, landed on the beach in the dead of night, then he disappeared into the jungle. For three weeks, no word. But when Rowan finally reappeared, mission accomplished. Rowan had hand delivered that letter to General García. Rowan was celebrated as the unsung hero of the Spanish-American War.

> There is a man whose form should be cast in deathless bronze and the statue placed in every college of the land. It is not book-learning young men need, nor instruction about this and that, but a stiffening of the vertebrae which will cause them to be loyal to a trust, to act promptly, to concentrate their energies; do the thing—"carry a message to García!"[39]

A hundred years ago, "getting a letter to García" was synonymous with doing something difficult and dangerous without making any excuses. Where there's a will, there's a way. It's doing what needs to be done, come hell or high water.

A Rowan was someone willing to risk life and limb for a noble cause. A Rowan was someone who did what they said and said what they did—no ifs, ands, or buts about it. A Rowan was someone who embodied long obedience in the same direction.

That brings us back to Jon Erwin and making it in the movie

industry. "When you get a foot in the door," said Jon, "you've got to be a Rowan." It doesn't matter whether you're trying to make it in the entertainment industry, professional sports, or the business world. I think Jon is right: "Rowans rocket to the top."

THE GAMBLERS

Long before Rowan delivered that letter to García, Epaphroditus risked his life to deliver Paul's epistle to the church at Philippi. What if that letter had gone undelivered? The opportunity cost would have been the canon of Scripture. Philippians is one of twenty-seven books canonized by the Council of Hippo in A.D. 393.

Hundreds of millions of people have taken courage, taken comfort, from that prison epistle. It includes some of my favorite verses—verses that have changed the trajectory of my life. In a sense, you and I owe any encouragement we've drawn from that book of the Bible to a brave soul named Epaphroditus.

According to church tradition, Epaphroditus served as the first bishop of Philippi. But his most lasting legacy was a creative minority—an order of nurses—called the *parabolani*. The etymology of that name was taken from the Greek word for "risk" I mentioned earlier, *parabouleuomai*. Not unlike the Order of the Mustard Seed, the members of the *parabolani* risked their lives for the well-being of others. In A.D. 252, when a devastating plague broke out in Carthage, it was the *parabolani* who risked their lives to care for the sick and bury the dead.[40]

Stop and think about it. The risk that Epaphroditus took had a ripple effect—the standard he set was still inspiring the *parabolani* in A.D. 252. And it's still impacting people two millennia later.

Every decision we make, every risk we take, has a domino effect. After our failed church plant in Chicago, it took a little more courage to try again. Why? If you fail once, it might be an anomaly. If you fail twice, it might be saying something about you.

After planting National Community Church, there were a few moments when we were tempted to throw in the towel. If we had folded up shop and called it quits, our original core of nineteen could have found another church to attend. But we wouldn't have been quitting on nineteen people present tense. We would have been quitting on tens of thousands of people future tense.

We would have been quitting on Ebenezers Coffeehouse. We would have been quitting on the DC Dream Center, the Capital Turnaround, and the Culturehouse. We would have been quitting on every mission trip we've taken, every person who's been baptized, every couple who have met and married at NCC.

You never quit on present-tense circumstances. You're always quitting on future-tense possibilities. My advice? Be a Rowan!

Keep playing offense.

Keep taking risks.

Keep going after God-sized dreams.

CHAPTER 8

THE BUTTERFLY EFFECT

I n 1960, an MIT meteorologist named Edward Lorenz made an accidental discovery while attempting to code a computer program that could simulate and forecast weather systems. Lorenz was in a hurry on the day of said discovery, so instead of entering the number he had used in an earlier simulation—0.506127—he rounded down to 0.506. Lorenz didn't think that tiny difference—one hundredth of 1 percent—would make a difference. Lorenz thought wrong.

When Edward Lorenz returned to his lab an hour later, he discovered a significant change in simulated weather conditions. How significant? Lorenz equated it to a tornado in Texas! The amazing thing? That cataclysmic change in weather conditions was caused by a miniscule modification that Lorenz likened to "a puff of wind created by a butterfly's wing." That is when and where and how the "butterfly effect" was born.[1]

In 1972, Lorenz gave a speech to the American Association for the Advancement of Science titled "Predictability: Does the Flap of a Butterfly's Wing in Brazil Set Off a Tornado in Texas?" The title is fanciful yet tangible. And I might add, unforgettable.

The butterfly effect is the idea that small changes to a complex system can have big consequences. Simply put, little things make a big difference over time. And time is the key exponent in that equation. The butterfly effect happens two ways—gradually then suddenly!

I'm writing this book at my writing desk—a seven-foot cross section from an oak tree that was felled near Green Bay, Wisconsin. Based on the number of rings, that tree was older than America. Maybe twice as old, which is pretty incredible given the harsh winters in Wisconsin. Think of all the windstorms and snowstorms that tree survived over hundreds of years. Even more amazing than that? That oak tree, more than a hundred feet tall, was once a two-inch acorn!

Nature is replete with amazing transformations that defy imagination—an acorn turning into an oak tree is certainly one of them. Then why do we take it for granted? Because it's a slow-growth tree. Slow growth is what gives the oak tree its density, which enables it to reach full maturity. But it's also why we tend to take it for granted—its growth isn't perceptible.

Every oak tree was once an acorn, but let me flip that script. Every oak tree produces as many as ten million acorns during its lifetime! Every acorn is endowed by its Creator with that kind of potential, and so are you.

"Do not despise these small beginnings," the Lord said to Zechariah. Why? Big things always start out as little things! Then it says, "For the LORD rejoices to see the work begin."[2] Is that as encouraging to you as it is to me? God doesn't rejoice when we finish. God gives us a standing ovation when we start.

There is a picture of our first Easter service that hangs in our church offices. As I already mentioned, forty-three people showed up that Sunday. Three decades later, we have the joy and privilege of hosting the Easter Sunrise at the Lincoln Memorial. A few more than forty-three show up—a few thousand more! How does that happen? The same way an acorn turns into an oak tree—gradually then suddenly. The same goes for the first $50 check we gave to missions. It was an acorn, but it has turned into an amazing giving tree! Because of the generosity of our congregation, National Community Church will give $4 million to kingdom causes that don't have our name on it this year.

Don't despise the day of small beginnings!

Most of us get paralyzed by *outcomes* when all we can control are *inputs*. Reading the Bible cover to cover is impossible if you try to do it in one sitting. Break it into 365 days, and it's very doable. The same goes for a six-pack—abs, not beer! Do a two-minute plank every day for thirty days and see what happens. Want to write a book? All you have to do is write "two crappy pages a day," according to Tim Ferriss.[3]

Whatever dream you have, it's going to happen "little by little." Want to increase flexibility? Stretch every day! Want to control blood sugar? Try intermittent fasting. Want to regain work-life balance? Turn your phone off on your day off. Want to increase creativity and decrease stress? Take ten thousand steps per day.

A PUFF OF WIND

When I was in high school, I wanted to be a history teacher. I love ancient history, political history, and church history. But my favorite branch of history is called counterfactual theory. It explores how history might have changed by asking *what-if* questions.

What if Teddy Roosevelt hadn't had his fifty-page speech manuscript in his pocket when he was shot by a would-be assassin on October 14, 1912? True story, by the way. Or what if George Washington had been shot in the head rather than the hat during the French and Indian War? The one-dollar bill would look very different, that's for sure. And I wouldn't live in a city named after him.

The Battle of Long Island is one of the worst military defeats George Washington ever experienced. His ten thousand troops were crushed by the British and their armada of four hundred ships. But it could have been worse, much worse. If the British had sailed up the East River, they could have cornered Washington's troops, which would have been game, set, match. The American Revolution would have ended then and there. That did not happen. Why? Because the wind was blowing in a direction that made sailing upriver impossible!

"If the wind had been in the other direction on the night of August twenty-eighth [1776]," said historian David McCullough in an interview with Charlie Rose, "it would have all been over."

"No United States of America if that had happened?" Rose asked.

"I don't think so," said McCullough.

"Just because of the wind, history was changed?" asked Rose.

"Absolutely," said McCullough.[4]

"The wind blows where it wishes," Jesus said. "You hear its sound, but you do not know where it comes from or where it is going. So it is with everyone born of the Spirit."[5]

Long obedience in the same direction sounds linear, but it's full of twists and turns. The Holy Spirit is not only the X factor, He is the "wind factor." A single puff of wind can change your trajectory forever! Remember when Paul was sailing to Rome? "When a gentle south wind began to blow, they thought they had their opportunity."[6] Of course, that's when a northeaster blew them off course and resulted in a shipwreck. That sounds like a detour to me, but it turned into a divine appointment.

That shipwreck landed them on the island of Malta, where Paul was bitten by a poisonous snake. At that point, Paul had to be questioning God's good, pleasing, and perfect will. *Why would You let me survive a shipwreck only to be bitten by a venomous snake?* But when Paul was miraculously healed, it allowed him an audience with Publius, the chief official on the island. Publius' father was dying of dysentery. Paul laid hands on him and prayed for him, and he was healed.

Who wrote that script? Not Paul, that's for sure. All of us want a miracle. Of course, none of us wants to be in a situation that necessitates one. But you can't have one without the other. Just as you can't have a comeback without a setback, God can't heal you if you don't get sick. I'm not trying to play mind games. Honestly, all of this is past my pay grade. But it's not lost on me that "a puff of wind" resulted in a revival on the island of Malta.

Wind factor doesn't just affect sailors and field goal kickers. The winds of doctrine are blowing every which way these days. Be careful when and where you set your sail. Like good doctrine, bad doctrine has a butterfly effect. "You gotta challenge all assumptions," said John Boyd. "If you don't, what is doctrine on day one becomes dogma forever after."[7]

THE HUMMINGBIRD EFFECT

The butterfly effect is more than a meteorological phenomenon. It holds true physically, financially, relationally, and spiritually. Small changes in input make a big difference in outcome. If you do little things like they're big things, God has a way of doing big things like they're little things.

I recently did a protocol that involved no sugar, no dairy, and no carbs for six weeks. No fun, right? But I felt like a totally different person six weeks later. I wasn't even trying to lose weight, but I dropped ten pounds in the first ten days. Of course, that may say more about my diet pre-protocol than anything else.

The butterfly effect is common knowledge, but the humming-bird effect is not. In simple terms, innovation tends to happen in clusters. Remember the idea of superlinear scaling? This is related to that. If you chart the dots, innovation doesn't happen in a forty-five-degree angle. It's more like a shot chart in basketball. Innovation tends to happen in clusters.

Remember Warby Parker? Their billion-dollar business has nothing to do with Gutenberg's printing press, right? Wrong. "Johannes Gutenberg's printing press created a surge in demand for spectacles," said Steven Johnson in his book *How We Got to Now.* "The new practice of reading made Europeans across the continent suddenly realize that they were farsighted."[8]

Of course, that's the tip of the iceberg.

"The market demand for spectacles encouraged a growing number of people to produce and experiment with lenses, which led to the invention of the microscope."[9] And don't forget the telescope! Gutenberg isn't the father of a single science. A multitude of occupations ranging from microbiology to astrophysics owe their origin, to one degree or another, to Gutenberg's printing press!

That sudden explosion of innovation is called the hummingbird effect—breakthroughs in one field often trigger completely unexpected results in very different domains. The invention of the printing press didn't create the multibillion-dollar eyewear business, but it did set up something called the adjacent possible.

When Jack Kilby and Robert Noyce invented the first microchip, that singular invention made a wide variety of applications possible. The adjacent possible included the personal computer, which spawned new companies like Apple. Apple, in turn, spawned new applications. Like what? Applications called apps. Hard to imagine your life without them, isn't it? Especially Google Maps, if you're geographically challenged! All those industries and innovations were once impossible until the microchip made them possible—the adjacent possible.

That's precisely what long obedience does. Don't underestimate the way one act of obedience can change your life or change the world. "The history of life and human culture," said Steven Johnson, "can be told as the story of a gradual but relentless probing of the adjacent possible."[10]

BACK TO THE FUTURE

Remember *Back to the Future*? Before Marty McFly travels back in time to November 5, 1955, Dr. Emmett Brown offers a timeless warning: "This could affect the entire future of the space-time continuum."[11] That makes intuitive sense when we look in the rearview mirror, but the same is true when we look ahead. It's just harder to imagine because it hasn't happened yet.

"If you went back in time before your birth you'd be terrified to do anything," observed Tim Urban, "because you'd know that even the smallest nudges to the present can have major impacts on the future."[12] We nod in agreement to that assessment, but then we fail to apply it to the future.

When we die, we look like our decisions. The age spots I see in the mirror are evidence of that truth. I wish I had applied a little more sunscreen thirty years ago! The good news? You are one decision away from a totally different life. That decision, which is often a difficult decision, could have a domino chain reaction on your life. Good decisions bring us one step closer to the adjacent possible we're dreaming of. Of course, that's true of difficult circumstances too! When our church plant in Chicago failed, we didn't know what to do or where to go. By faith, we moved to Washington, DC. That one step of faith was the magic carpet in *Aladdin* that opened up a whole new world.

If you change your trajectory by one degree, it doesn't make much of a difference at first. A mile later, you're less than a hundred feet off course. But if you're flying from Washington, DC, to San Francisco, you miss the mark by forty-two miles.

"Human beings cannot comprehend very large or very small numbers," said the Nobel Prize–winning economist Daniel Kahneman. "It would be useful for us to acknowledge that fact."[13] While we are acknowledging that reality, here's another one: Human beings cannot comprehend very short or very long time-frames either, but perhaps a thought experiment will help.

Given the fact that there are eight billion people on the planet, a one-in-a-million miracle ought to happen to eight thousand people every single day. "In the course of any normal person's life," said Freeman Dyson, "miracles happen at a rate of roughly one per month."[14] What kind of miracles? Honestly, almost anything. How is that possible? If the sample size is large enough, anomalies are bound to happen.

Two thousand years ago, geographical and chronological horizons were incredibly small. News was almost always local, rarely global. With the advent of social media—thanks to the microchip—the opposite is true. Most of us have no idea what's happening locally, but we're all aware of the latest global tragedy. Globally speaking, "the odds of something terrible happening in any given moment are 100 percent."[15] Why? The sample size is so large.

"We shouldn't be surprised that the world feels historically broken in recent years," observed Morgan Housel. "It's not—we just see more of the bad stuff that's always happened than we ever saw before."[16]

On April 10, 1953, the *Boston Globe* ran a rather curious story: "Predicts Telephone of the Future Will Be Carried Like Watch." At the time, household telephones were rented from telephone companies and they had a rotary dial. Touch-tone phones were still a decade away! But that didn't keep Mark Sullivan, the president and director of Pacific Telephone and Telegraph Company, from making the following prediction:

> Just what form the future telephone will take is, of course, pure speculation. Here is my prophecy:
>
> In its final development the telephone will be carried about by the individual, perhaps as we carry a watch today. It probably will require no dial or equivalent, and I think the users will be able to see each other, if they want, as they talk.
>
> Who knows but what it may actually translate from one language to another?[17]

That's pretty incredible foresight, is it not? Mark Sullivan predicted the far-distant future with incredible accuracy. Of course, for every accurate prediction there are a thousand infamously inaccurate ones. Why? Because the future isn't linear. It's more like a brachistochrone curve!

"If you were to say to a physicist in 1899 that in 1999, a hundred years later, moving images would be transmitted into homes all over the world from satellites in the sky; that bombs of unimaginable power would threaten the species; that antibiotics would abolish infectious disease but that disease would fight back," said Michael Crichton, "that humankind would travel to the moon, and then lose interest; that microscopes would be able to see individual atoms; that people would carry telephones weighing a few ounces, and speak anywhere in the world without wires; or that most of these miracles depended on devices the size of a postage stamp, which utilized a new theory called quantum mechanics—if you said all this, the physicist would almost certainly pronounce you mad."[18]

In less than one hundred years, we went from telegrams to telephones, from smoke signals to satellite signals, from horses to horseless carriages called cars. Each of those innovations involved a quantum leap in technology and psychology, and each one enabled the adjacent possible. But if you zoom out and look at the big picture, all of them happened gradually then suddenly!

Can I have a little fun with our infamously poor prognostications?

"The horse is here to stay," said Henry Ford's lawyer, Horace Rackham. "But the automobile is only a novelty, a fad."[19] Film producer and studio executive, Darryl Zanuck, scoffed at the "idiot boxes" called television—"People will soon get tired of staring at a plywood box every night."[20] Henry Warner, as in Warner Brothers, said in 1927, "Who the hell wants to hear actors talk?"[21] Then there's Simon Newcomb, professor of mathematics and astronomy, who said, "Flight by machines heavier than air is unpractical and insignificant, if not utterly impossible." Less than eighteen months later—December 17, 1903—the Wright brothers took flight at Kitty Hawk, North Carolina.[22]

Last, but not least, is the founder of 3Com, Robert Metcalfe: "I predict the internet will soon go spectacularly supernova and in 1996 catastrophically collapse." In his keynote address to the International World Wide Web Conference in 1999, Metcalfe literally ate his words. He cut up a copy of the printed article where he had predicted the end of the internet, put it in a blender with some liquid, and drank said smoothie.[23]

Those shortsighted predictions were made by really smart people. How could they be so wrong? "Reasonable people," said George Friedman, "are incapable of anticipating the future."[24] That's why it's unreasonable people—people who dare to be different—who usually change history. A. W. Tozer said it this way:

In every field of human endeavor, progress has been made by those who stood up and said, "I will not adjust to the world." The classical composers, poets and architects were people who would not adjust.

Then Tozer said this: *"Jesus was among the most maladjusted people of his generation."*[25] If that sounds like an insult, you're reading it wrong. Normal is overrated. Jesus walked to the beat of His own drum, and that's who we follow.

We revere the prophets of old, but most of them were written off as one card short of a full deck. Why? Because they refused to compromise their convictions based on circumstances. As the writer of Hebrews said, "The world was not worthy of them."[26] Then this ageless challenge is leveled: "We do not belong to those who shrink back."[27]

Maybe this is your moment to step up and step in? Don't let what you cannot do keep you from doing what you can. Long obedience in the same direction always starts with the first step.

RECENCY BIAS

When I started pastoring in my mid-twenties, I lacked life experience, so I borrowed it from books. I came across a statistic claiming that the average author put about two years of life experience into the average book. Some books are worth more and some less, no doubt. But I did the math—if I read two hundred books a year, I figured I'd gain four hundred years of life experience! And I'd only be one year older!

I was thirty-five years old when I wrote my first book, but I was six thousand in book years. How so? I read three thousand books before writing one. Some people have a hard time believing I read that many books, but that was before smartphones. Did you know that the average person spends two hours and twenty-four minutes a day on social media? You can read a lot of books in that same amount of time—at least two hundred per year!

"Books," said Carl Sagan, "permit us to voyage through time."[28] Books are one way we borrow life experience, especially biographies. A good book is an out-of-body experience. It's a window through which we view someone else's experience, but it's also a mirror that helps us see ourselves differently. Books inspire long obedience by giving us a big-picture perspective.

Permission to speak frankly? I have grown a little weary, even leery, of the latest and greatest. I'm all for innovation, but the recency bias is real. It's a cognitive bias that weights recent events as more important than historic ones.[29] Maybe that's why C. S. Lewis warned against something he called "chronological snobbery."

"It's a good rule after reading a new book never to allow yourself another new one till you have read an old one in between," said Lewis.[30] Citing Lewis, John Piper observed that following this principle "has freed me from the tyranny of novelty and opened for me the wisdom of the ages."[31] Why is that so important?

> Every age has its own outlook. It is especially good at seeing certain truths and especially liable to make certain mistakes. We all therefore need the books that will correct the characteristic mistakes of our own period.... None of us can fully escape this blindness, but we shall certainly increase it, and weaken our guard against it, if we read only modern books....

The only palliative is to keep the clean sea breeze of the centuries blowing through our minds and this can only be done by reading old books.[32]

"If you want a new idea," Ivan Pavlov is credited with saying, "read an old book."[33] I would start with the oldest book of all, the Bible. It's the longest longitudinal study in human history. It also represents the widest cross section of humanity. Written in three languages on three continents over fifteen hundred years, the Bible puts things in perspective. What things? All things!

Old books don't just help us see the big picture; they also inspire more patience. "It's gonna take time," sang the Beatles' legend George Harrison. "It's gonna take patience and time, to do it, to do it, to do it, to do it, to do it, to do it right."[34]

STRATEGIC PATIENCE

In her book *The Long Game,* Dorie Clark advocates for something she calls "strategic patience."[35] What is it? It's persistence in the face of resistance. It's showing up when others are giving up. Strategic patience is remaining vigilant while waiting for the expected outcome.[36]

No one embodies strategic patience better than an octogenarian named Anna. When her husband died, she devoted herself to serving God at the temple. "She never left the temple but worshiped night and day, fasting and praying."[37] For how long? Eighty-four years!

That's long obedience in the same direction, and that's how divine appointments happen. Because she kept showing up, Anna was at the temple the day Mary and Joseph dedicated Jesus. She had the distinct joy and privilege of prophesying over the Messiah.

Anna isn't the only widow celebrated in Scripture. Jesus told a parable about a persistent widow who may have violated cultural norms and sidestepped a few protocols, but her persistence paid off. Where do you need some patience? If you're a parent, I can take a wild guess! Can I tell you how Lora and I have cultivated it? We have a therapist who has taught us how to foster non-anxious curiosity. About what? About everyone and everything, including our kids.

We are quick to judge others based on our experience—or is that just me? Non-anxious curiosity asks questions. Then it says, "Tell me more." Remember—everyone you meet is a thousand-piece jigsaw puzzle! Everyone is fighting a battle we know nothing about. A little curiosity often leads to a lot of empathy!

DEFINING MOMENTS

On the morning of March 25, 1911, a fire broke out in a garment factory where hundreds of immigrants were employed. The workers, most of them under the age of twenty-two, could not escape because the doors had been locked by employers who didn't want them taking breaks. The firefighters who arrived on the scene were unable to help those trapped on the eighth, ninth, and tenth floors because their ladders only reached as high as the sixth floor. Not unlike the terrorist attack on the Twin Towers, many workers jumped to their deaths to escape the flames.

The tragedy at Triangle Shirtwaist Factory is one of the deadliest in history—146 workers lost their lives. A woman who witnessed the fire, Frances Perkins, described the scene to a reporter later that day:

> They came down in twos and threes, jumping together in a kind of desperate hope. The life nets were broken. The firemen kept shouting for them not to jump. But they had no choice; the flames were right behind them.[38]

Frances Perkins was marked by that moment. It had a butterfly effect on her personal and professional life. Thirty years later, she was appointed by President Franklin D. Roosevelt as secretary of labor—the first woman in American history to hold a cabinet-level position.

Remember Henry Wallace? The man who appointed Norman Borlaug to his research post in Mexico? Wallace and Perkins served on the same Cabinet.

"There is always one moment in childhood," said the novelist Graham Greene, "when the door opens and lets the future in."[39] Those defining moments are the days when decades happen. They shape our psyches in subtle yet significant ways. They change the trajectories of our lives like the flap of a butterfly's wing!

I did a life plan with a life coach many years ago, and one of the exercises was identifying defining moments—the turning points and tipping points that changed the trajectory of my life. All of us are a complex combination of adaptive strategies. Simply put, our behaviors and beliefs are the byproduct of our upbringing. The more self-aware you are, the more likely you are to rise above those conditioned reflexes. You may even discover that your destiny is hidden in your history, just like Frances Perkins.

DECISION TREE

Have you ever had to make a difficult decision—the kind of decision you absolutely agonize over because of its wide-ranging ramifications? One helpful tool, when weighing a welter of factors, is something called a decision tree. While it's impossible to account for every conceivable outcome to our choices, a decision tree enables us to envision different scenarios.

Hold that thought.

I recently had one of the hardest phone calls of my life—I cried before, during, and after that call. Imagine the emotional anguish of losing a nine-year-old daughter to a natural disaster. The only way you survive something like that is by the grace of God. *But couldn't God have kept it from happening?* That's the question that haunts us and taunts us when an unexplainable tragedy occurs. Honestly, it's a question that can't be fully answered on this side of eternity.

I'll never forget something this grieving father said: "This unspeakable tragedy has distilled my faith journey into the clearest decision tree I could ever imagine." Tragedy has a way of doing that, doesn't it? Important things become way more important and unimportant things become way less important. "It forces a choice: either I back away, I fold, I give up on God because of this horrific, senseless loss of my perfect angel." The other option? "I triple down on my faith."

What did he decide to do? "For me, the answer is unwavering. The only way I will ever be reunited with my daughter is to lean into my faith. Losing my faith now is logically equivalent to losing her again. I cannot, and will not, stand for that."[40]

The last thing I want you to hear when it comes to the most painful moments of our lives? I hope you hear it loud and clear: You can overcome! Overcome what? Anything and everything life throws at you. Will life be the same? No, it will not. You have to find a new normal. But there is a God who gives beauty for ashes, the oil of joy for mourning, and the garment of praise for a spirit of heaviness.

Like everything else, you have to work your way through the stages of grief gradually then suddenly! And I might add, grieve at *your* pace. Like an old injury, there will be scar tissue. And the grief never goes away completely, but neither does joy. "Those who sow with tears," said the psalmist, "will reap with songs of joy."[41]

You can bounce back from pain and suffering. You can rise above the naysayers and doomsdayers. You can turn setbacks into comebacks. How do I know this? I've witnessed it too many times not to believe it. In the process, I would challenge you to heed a grieving father's advice: "Prioritize what really matters."

That's when and where and how long obedience turns into long legacy.

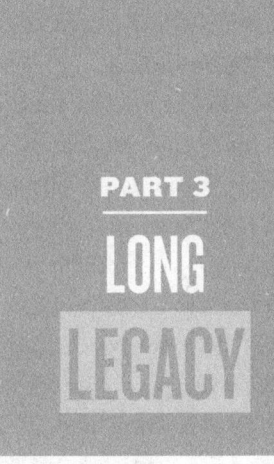

At the entrance to the Rhone Valley in southern Switzerland sits the picturesque town of Saint-Maurice. The Rhone River runs through it, but its most prominent feature is a limestone cliff that forms a 1,362-foot rock wall on the east side of the city. If you're feeling brave, you can climb 484 steps to the chapel of Notre-Dame du Scex, which sits above the Abbey of Saint-Maurice—the oldest monastery in Europe.

That town was the site of a Roman outpost during the reign of Emperor Maximian, which is when and where the plot thickens. A Roman military commander named Maurice led the legendary Theban Legion that consisted of 6,666 soldiers. In A.D. 286, the emperor issued an order to kill the Christians who lived there, but Maurice refused to obey said order. An inscription on an altar at the Chapel of the Martyrs explains why.

We are your soldiers, O Emperor, but above all servants of God. We owe you military obedience, we owe him innocence.[1]

According to one legend, Maurice made this declaration in defiance of the emperor: "We'd rather die innocent than live guilty."[2] When Maurice refused to kill innocents, the emperor ordered that every tenth soldier in his legion be killed. After refusing once again, a second decimation was ordered. Ultimately, Maurice willingly and sacrificially handed over his insignia and joined his fellow Christians as a martyr for his faith.[3]

In subsequent centuries, the sword and spurs of Saint Maurice were part of the regalia used during the coronation of Austro-Hungarian emperors. He is the patron saint of soldiers and swordsmiths. No less than fifty-two towns and villages in France have been named in his honor. He's even depicted on manhole covers in the town of Coburg in Bavaria, Germany.[4]

Unless your area of expertise is third-century Roman history, I bet you've never heard of the Roman military commander-turned-Christian-turned-martyr. But his singular sacrifice—one act of courage—is long remembered. In A.D. 1003, that Roman outpost was renamed in honor of the man who chose to die rather than kill his fellow Christians—Saint-Maurice, Switzerland. More than seventeen centuries after his death, his legacy lives on.

Legacy is difficult to measure because it can't be quantified by the dash between life and death. Only eternity will tell. Or as Maximus Decimus Meridius put it, "What we do in life echoes in eternity."[5]

Are you living for time?

Or are you living for eternity?

Only one of them is forever!

MEMENTO MORI

In 1994, Robert Fulghum spent New Year's Day sitting in a lawn chair on his gravesite. What a way to ring in the new year, right?

But Fulghum refers to that "ritual of reckoning" as one of the "most affirmative," and "potent" experiences of his life.[6]

There is a Latin phrase—*memento mori*—that means "remember you will die." We all know it's true—none of us are getting out of here alive! But we don't spend much time really meditating on it. Why? It seems kind of morbid. I'm certainly not suggesting you fixate on death, but thinking about death makes for a better life.

Fifty-six years old at the time, Fulghum confronted his finitude. "More than a grave, the site has become a workshop and a laboratory. I go there when the muddy springs of my mind need cleaning."[7]

The best way to prepare for the day of reckoning is a ritual of reckoning. "It ought to be the business of every day," said Matthew Henry, "to prepare for our last day."[8] Legacy always begins with the end in mind. We need rituals of reckoning where we take stock of our lives. That's how we connect the dots—we count our blessings and audit our regrets.

If you don't own a burial plot, there is a digital alternative. I occasionally visit death-clock.org. If you enter your birthday, along with your body mass index and smoking status, it will approximate your death date. My favorite feature? You can check one of the following modes: normal, pessimistic, sadistic, or optimistic. The last time I checked, I've got 1,283,147,094 seconds left. Of course, the clock is ticking.

THE TWENTY-FIVE-YEAR TIME MACHINE

My friend Derek Coburn recently released a book titled *Let's Retire Retirement*.[9] It's a reframing of retirement that aims at leaving a long legacy. "Many people take magical moments in their lives for granted every single day," says Derek. "While I am not perfect, I have discovered a way to make the most of these interactions."[10] What is it? Derek describes it as a twenty-five-year time machine.

When his children were young, Derek would tuck them into bed. "Those snuggles were magical—their small bodies curled against mine, their hair still damp from the bath, smelling of shampoo." But eventually Derek did what most parents do—he would keep one eye on the clock because there were emails to answer and shows to watch. Then one night it dawned on him that those magical moments wouldn't last forever. "I imagined myself 25 years in the future," said Derek. "A company had invented a time machine that could send me back to relive a single moment from my past."

"How much would you pay," they asked me, "to go back and experience one more bedtime with your 10-year-old son?"

Before I could answer, they named their price: $50,000.

The truth? I would have emptied my retirement account. I would have mortgaged my house. Because I knew with absolute certainty that the older version of me would give anything to feel my son's small hand in mine one more time, to hear his sleepy voice ask one more question, to watch his eyelids grow heavy as he drifted off.[11]

That night, Derek stopped watching the clock and embraced the time machine effect. He started treating that bedtime routine for what it was: a $50,000 moment that could never be replaced. "Those bedtime snuggles have long since ended," said Derek. "But the $50,000 moments haven't disappeared; they've just changed form."[12]

Are there any $50,000 moments that you're taking for granted? What are the moments that will matter most twenty-five years from now?

I've lived long enough to know that what we think is our legacy may not be our legacy at all. You can't plan your legacy, per se. You can, however, cultivate character traits like kindness, gentleness, and thoughtfulness. You can establish priorities like "family first." And I highly recommend a rule of life based on the words and ways of Jesus. But legacy is often the offbeat moments you can't script.

When I was playing basketball for the University of Chicago, my parents drove all the way from Chicago to Boston to see me play. The crazy thing? I only played five minutes in the second half. I was ticked at my coach, but it made what my parents did all the more meaningful. They drove thirty hours round-trip—through the night, no less—to see me play five minutes! That's not just a long drive; that's a long legacy.

LONG THROW LENS

There is a moment in *The Secret Life of Walter Mitty* when Walter, played by Ben Stiller, tracks down the wildlife photographer Sean O'Connell, played by Sean Penn. Walter finds him looking through a long throw lens at the so-called ghost cat—a snow leopard. After many months of searching at high altitude, O'Connell finally has it in his sights, but he never snaps the picture. When Walter asks why, O'Connell explains it this way:

> If I like a moment, I mean me, personally, I don't like to have the distraction of a camera. I just want to stay in it.[13]

Some of us are so consumed with taking selfies that we lose ourselves along the way. We start living our lives for public consumption. Neil Postman put it this way in his prescient book *Amusing Ourselves to Death:* "Americans no longer talk to each other, they entertain each other. They do not exchange ideas; they exchange images."[14]

If that was true forty years ago, it's even truer now. If we aren't careful, we start living our lives vicariously or virtually. My advice? Live your life in a way that is worth telling stories about. Time may be measured in minutes, but life is measured in moments. Like the lens that Sean O'Connell used to spot the all-elusive snow leopard, legacy is looking at life through a long throw lens.

What do you want people to say about you at your funeral? Can I tell you what I'd want to hear people say? "Look, he's moving!" If that doesn't happen, there are character traits I'm aiming at— humility, curiosity, and generosity. I also want one last laugh. When I eat chocolate, as you may remember, I have a habit of putting some on my front teeth and flashing a big smile. When they put me in a casket someday, I've asked Lora to put chocolate on my front teeth. I doubt she'll do it, but I'd love one last laugh!

What contributions are you making that matter most?

What convictions are you aspiring to embody?

Writing your own eulogy might be a good place to start—a ritual of reckoning.

THE OLD MAN

In 1994, I had the joy of sharing a meal with the Senate chaplain, Richard Halverson, in the Senate dining room. I'll never forget it, in part, because Muhammad Ali was having lunch at the table next to us!

We have a benediction at National Community Church that I adapted from Dr. Halverson. It's actually taped in the back page of my Bible: "When you leave this place, you do not leave the presence of God. The presence of God goes with you wherever you go."

Richard Halverson was an incredible storyteller, and one of my favorites is a memento mori of sorts. It's a second-person story called "The Old Man."

You're going to meet an old man someday down the road—
ten, thirty, fifty years from now—waiting there for you. . . .
That old man will be you. He'll be the composite of everything you do, say, and think—today and tomorrow. . . . His
heart will be turning out what you've been putting into it.
Every little thought, every deed goes into this old man.[15]

Remember what Crawford Loritts said? "When you're born,
you look like your parents. When you die, you look like your decisions."[16] I am a decision tree and so are you!

Every day in every way you are becoming more and more like
yourself. Amazing but true. You're beginning to look more
like yourself, think more like yourself, and talk more like
yourself. You're becoming yourself more and more.[17]

Do you like who you're becoming?
If you do, double down. If you don't, it's never too late to be who
you might have been. How do you change your story? You start a
new chapter! How do you leave a legacy? Two ways—gradually
then suddenly!

CHAPTER 9

GOOD ANCESTORS

---

arriet Beecher Stowe was born June 14, 1811—the seventh of thirteen children. Her father, Lyman Beecher, was one of the most respected pastors in America. Her brother, Henry Ward Beecher, was one of the most famous preachers in America. But it was Harriet who would radically alter the course of American history.[1]

On a Sunday morning in 1851—during a church service, during communion—Harriet had a vision of a slave being beaten to death. That vision left her so shaken she could hardly stop crying. She went home that day and started writing *Uncle Tom's Cabin*.[2]

Released on March 20, 1852, the initial print run was only five thousand copies. As I already mentioned, only 2 percent of books sell more than five thousand copies in their lifetime? And that's with the help of online retailers like Amazon! That first print run sold out within ten days! The novel sold more than 300,000 copies in nine months.[3] It would eventually sell millions of copies worldwide.

It could be argued that no book, save the Bible, changed the course of American history more than *Uncle Tom's Cabin*. When Harriet Beecher Stowe met President Abraham Lincoln many years later, he is purported to have said, "So you are the little woman who wrote the book that started this great war!"[4] The conviction with which she wrote—the passion in her prose—pricked the conscience of a nation.

Legacy is almost impossible to measure because history is still being written. For better or for worse, our influence is felt long after we are long gone. Harriet suffered from Alzheimer's at the end of her life, so she wasn't even cognizant of what she had accomplished. But her legacy is freedom for four million slaves and their descendants. Of course, it's partial credit—like everyone and everything else.

STILL MULTIPLYING

A few years ago, I had one of the most memorable phone calls of my life with one of the most remarkable people I've ever met. It was many years before that call that Stanley Tam spoke at National Community Church. He was ninety-four at the time, which makes him the oldest preacher we've ever had. For the record, I'd love to break that record if I can pull it off.

Stanley was the founder of the United States Plastic Corporation, but he wasn't just an innovative entrepreneur. Stanley Tam epitomized long vision, long obedience, and long legacy.

He made a defining decision on January 15, 1955—that's the day he legally transferred all the shares of his company to his Senior Partner, his name for God. Stanley's generosity is legendary. The butterfly effect of that one predecision is the $120 million he gave to kingdom causes. I'll never forget something he said over dinner. "God cannot reward Abraham yet because his seed is still multiplying."

Remember the multiplication anointing? This is that. Legacy is the gift that keeps on giving after we are long gone. It's compound interest on generosity. It's deeds done that have a domino effect. It's words that echo into eternity.

On his 107th birthday, I had the joy of wishing Stanley a happy birthday. That twenty-minute phone call was a gift. I prayed for him and he prayed for me. Have you ever had a centenarian pray for you? Have you ever had someone pray for you who prays three hours a day? I could feel the compound interest of long obedience in the same direction. That prayer packed a powerful punch!

What's true of Abraham is true of us: The seeds we plant never stop multiplying. In the counterintuitive kingdom of God, the way we reap a harvest in our garden is by planting seeds in someone else's. "Let us not become weary in doing good," said the apostle Paul, "for at the proper time we will reap a harvest."[5]

GOOD SAMARITAN

In 1955, Jonas Salk and his team of researchers developed the first safe and successful polio vaccine. At the time, polio was killing or debilitating half a million people every year. Salk was hailed as a hero, but he refused the fame and fortune that could have been his. He even refused to patent the vaccine he invented. Why? Salk's philosophy of life was captured by a rhetorical question: "Are we being good ancestors?"[6]

"If we want to be good ancestors," said Salk, "we should show future generations how we coped with an age of great change and great crises."[7] We have no shortage of crises these days, which means plenty of opportunity to rise to the occasion.

"In the critical periods of history it is the national soul which counts," said Evelyn Underhill. "No nation is truly defeated which retains its spiritual self-possession."[8] Underhill spoke of conferring on the next generation "an unconquerable hope." Then she tipped the cap to poet Gerard Manley Hopkins. "Nature is never spent," said Hopkins. "There lives the dearest freshness deep down things."[9]

"Deep down things"—that phrase is a century old. But it's a

timeless depiction of conviction. It's the truest truth—what you know that you know that you know. In the words of Nikolai Vavilov, "We shall not retreat from our convictions."[10] Remember Caleb? He had the courage of conviction. Ten spies brought back a negative report, but Caleb stayed true to his true north. "I brought . . . back a report according to my convictions."[11]

I don't know what opportunities the future holds for you, but if anything requires you to compromise your convictions, it's not an opportunity. That's called temptation. If you compromise your convictions, you lose your legacy with it.

"The old biblical aspiration to be a Good Samaritan," said Roman Krznaric, "is no longer enough. It's time for a twenty-first-century update: to be a Good Ancestor."[12] *Good Samaritan* and *good ancestor* are synonyms. It's the greatest good for the greatest number of people. It's doing things that will make a difference seventy years from now.

LIKE THOSE WHO DREAM

More than a decade ago, I wrote a book titled *The Circle Maker*. It's based on a story in the Talmud about a Jewish sage named Honi who lived during a drought that threatened to destroy a generation of Jews. When asked to pray, Honi did something curious and courageous. He took his staff and drew a circle in the sand. Then he knelt in that circle and prayed this prayer: "Lord of the universe, I swear before Your great name that I will not move from this circle until You have shown mercy upon your children."

The Sanhedrin wanted to excommunicate Honi for his prayer because it was too audacious for their taste, but it's hard to argue with answered prayer! When Honi started praying, it started raining. Honi was ultimately honored for "the prayer that saved a generation."

There is another story, not as famous, about Honi. He was taking a walk one day when he encountered a man who was planting a carob tree. Honi knew it took seventy years for carob trees to bear fruit, so he asked the man the obvious question: "Do you think you'll live long enough to eat of that tree?"

"I myself found fully grown carob trees in the world," said the man. "As my forebears planted for me, so am I planting for my children."[13]

Honi had a life verse: "When the LORD restored the fortunes of Zion, we were like those who dream."[14] It's an allusion to Israel's seventy-year captivity in Babylon. They were prisoners of war, but God refers to them as "prisoners of hope."[15] How is that possible? They never stopped dreaming!

The phrase "like those who dream" captured the imagination of Honi the Circle Maker. It catalyzed a question that became the driving motivation of his life: Can a person dream continuously for seventy years? I don't know about you, but I want to keep dreaming until the day I die! And I want to dream dreams that will outlive me.

I don't know what circumstances you find yourself in. Maybe you're walking through a personal crisis, profound disappointment, or a difficult diagnosis. Without knowing the specifics, can I issue an exhortation? It's time to dream again!

ORTHODOX SEED

In 1963, Israeli archaeologists were excavating Herod the Great's palace at Masada. As they dug, they found the usual suspects— ancient artifacts, artistic fragments, even some skeletal remains. But the most curious discovery was a sealed jar with seeds perfectly preserved inside. Radiocarbon dating gave them an age of roughly two thousand years old—somewhere between 155 B.C. and A.D. 64.

And DNA testing revealed that those seeds belonged to an extinct species of trees called the Judean date palm.

Those seeds were put in storage for forty years at Bar-Ilan University in Israel. In 2005, three seeds were planted in the Arabah desert. Eight weeks later, one of those two-thousand-year-old seeds sprouted, making it the oldest seed to ever be germinated. So, they named it Methuselah. By 2008, that single seed had grown into a five-foot palm tree with a dozen leaves. It flowered for the first time in 2011.[16] And at last measurement, in 2015, Methuselah was a ten-foot tall, pollen-producing palm tree.[17]

In the field of botany there are two types of seed—orthodox and unorthodox. What differentiates those two types of seed is survivability. Unorthodox seeds are unable to survive a deep freeze or a drought. Orthodox seeds, on the other hand, can survive glaciers and famines and fires. Orthodox seeds can survive centuries, even twenty centuries, like Methuselah.

Legacy is an orthodox seed.

In recent years, I've encountered lots of leaders struggling with discouragement. Circumstances beyond their control have taken their toll. Can I tell you what I've told them? Even if you feel like your leadership has taken a downturn, don't discount the difference you've already made! Leadership is playing the long game— long vision, long obedience, and long legacy. Don't overinflate last week's meeting, this month's sales, or next quarter's financials. Leadership is measured by your body of work.

THE POWER OF A SINGLE SEED

The kingdom of God is like . . . a mustard seed, which is the smallest of all seeds on earth. Yet when planted, it grows and becomes the largest of all garden plants, with such big branches that the birds can perch in its shade.[18]

A mustard seed measures less than two millimeters in diameter. Yet in a matter of months, that seed can turn into a twenty-foot tall tree with a twenty-foot span. If you didn't know what kind of seed it was, you would never imagine what it could become. That little seed is packed with Vitamins B6, B12, C, E, and K. It contains calcium, magnesium, potassium, iron, and zinc.[19] And it's the key ingredient in one of my favorite condiments—mustard. Where are my classic yellow people? Spicy brown? Grey Poupon?

Let me ask the obvious question: Why did the farmer plant the mustard seed? Don't overthink it—the farmer wanted mustard on his kosher hot dog! But God had ulterior motives. God was writing a bigger story—"so that the birds of the air nest in its shade."[20] Mustard is the understory, but nesting is the overstory.

When we were planting National Community Church, our name felt like a misnomer. Nineteen people meeting in a DC public school didn't feel national, but that name proved to be prophetic. We've had the privilege of impacting tens of thousands of people from across the country and around the world.

A few years ago, Dick Foth was speaking on an ordinary Sunday. That morning, he met a family that had emigrated from China; a woman from Mongolia who had won a green card; and the German wife of an American diplomat who had been appointed consul general in Hamburg, Germany. That same morning, at another campus, I happened to meet a member of Finland's parliament. That afternoon, Dick called me and he sounded like a kid in a candy store: "Mark, don't go anywhere. You can reach the nations!"

National Community Church represents more than a hundred nationalities, and that's just our immediate family. Our extended family—those who are part of our online campus—dot the globe.

Did we plant NCC to reach the nations? We weren't dreaming that big! We had a hard time believing God for our city. But God's vision is bigger and better and longer than ours! "Ask of me, and I will give you the nations."[21]

God has turned us into a nest for all nations. During our House of Prayer on Thursday nights, we'll sometimes have people pray in different languages. It's a beautiful thing to behold. It sounds heavenly—every nation, tribe, people, and language. Like the farmer who wanted mustard on his hot dog, we had no clue what God was up to when we first got started. And it didn't happen overnight. It happened gradually then suddenly!

LONG RELATIONSHIPS

I have a friend, Kevin Warren, who is the president and CEO of the Chicago Bears. We met more than a decade ago when Kevin was the chief operating officer for the Minnesota Vikings. In between, Kevin served as commissioner of the Big Ten.

Kevin is a high-level leader, to the say the least. He helped lead the building of U.S. Bank Stadium in Minneapolis, which was no small task. Kevin is the kind of person, when you're with him, who is fully present. He makes people feel seen, heard, and loved. He makes each person feel like they are the only one in the room.

Many years ago, I was doing a chapel service for the Vikings and Kevin gave me a field pass. We were down on the field before the game and we took a picture with a woman named Millie who was celebrating her ninety-ninth birthday at the game. The last time I saw Kevin, I asked him whether he remembered Millie. Internally, I'm thinking, *There is no way! Kevin meets so many people!* Kevin said, "Yes, I do. Millie passed a few years ago and I stay in touch with the family. I check in every now and then to see how they're doing." Are you kidding me? You're the president of the

Chicago Bears now. Why would you do that? Because Kevin knows that his legacy isn't U.S. Bank Stadium. His legacy is people, and so is yours!

I recently did a chapel for the Chicago Bears, and Kevin made an offhanded comment I will long remember: "I don't do meetings. I do relationships."

That's a totally different posture.

That's a totally different objective.

Honestly, I think that's how Kevin has risen through the ranks. As president and CEO of the Chicago Bears, he has to make un-popular decisions. And in the world of sports, you're only as good as your last game! But it's Kevin's likability factor that has opened doors of opportunity.

That conversation was a game changer for me. I tend to be task oriented rather than relationship oriented. I've got places to go, things to do. But I've stopped doing meetings and started doing relationships. I try to be more fully present with people. I try to make them feel seen, heard, and loved. I try to treat them for who they are—the apple of God's eye!

What if you stopped doing meetings?

What if you started doing relationships?

One way to put this principle into practice is to pray for the people. Who? Anyone and everyone you encounter! When I pray for opportunities to show God's love, those opportunities have a way of presenting themselves! While you're at it, pray over your calendar. It'll turn some of those appointments into divine ap-pointments.

IMPLICIT BIAS

Sir Ken Robinson, the educator whose TED Talk has been watched more than seventy-eight million times, is from the same hometown as Sir Paul McCartney—Liverpool, England. One day they were swapping stories, and Sir Ken discovered that Sir Paul got poor scores in his music class in high school. As an educator, that piqued his curiosity. Paul McCartney has written no less than thirty-seven UK Top 40 songs as a solo artist—not to mention fifty Top 40 hits with the Beatles! McCartney has sold more than 500 million records, and *Rolling Stone* dubbed him the second-greatest songwriter of all time.[22] How in the world did McCartney's teacher not notice his talent?

But it gets even better. Or maybe I should say, worse. George Harrison, lead guitarist for the Beatles, had the same teacher and he didn't fare any better. "Let me get this straight," said Sir Ken to Sir Paul. "This teacher had half the Beatles in his classes and didn't notice anything out of the ordinary?"

In the first chapter of John's gospel, Jesus is starting to work on His draft board. He drafts Peter and Andrew in His first round of recruits. Then He drafts Philip in the third round, and Philip invites his friend Nathanael to the after-party.

Philip found Nathanael and told him, "We have found the One Moses wrote about in the Law, the One the prophets foretold—Jesus of Nazareth, the son of Joseph."

"Can anything good come from Nazareth?" Nathanael asked.[23]

Nathanael is sus, to say the least. He writes Jesus off before he even meets Him. Why? Because Jesus was from the wrong side of the tracks. This amounts to an ethnic slur back in the day. This goes without saying, but you've got a pretty bad case of implicit bias if you're stereotyping Jesus. Of course, we would never do that. Or would we?

We tend to politicize, demonize, and dehumanize anyone who

doesn't look like us, think like us, or vote like us. We fill the gaps with negative assumptions. We judge the book by its cover, but Jesus does the exact opposite.

Are you seeing people for who they really are?

Or are you seeing in stereotypes?

Are you filling the gaps with negative or positive assumptions?

Are you writing people off or writing people in?

NO ORDINARY PEOPLE

Several years ago, I heard Erwin McManus tell a story about speaking at a TED conference in Tanzania. Erwin is an introvert, so he did what introverts do—he found another introvert to eat lunch with. He had a wonderful conversation with a woman named Jane, with one quirk. Have you ever met someone who always steers the conversation back to a topic they love to talk about? Regardless of the subject matter, Jane kept talking about chimpanzees. That's kind of weird, unless you're the foremost primatologist on the planet. After about an hour, it finally dawned on Erwin who he was talking with. "Jane, can I ask you a question?" said Erwin. "Is your last name Goodall?"

Initially, he had no idea who he was talking to, and neither do we. "There are no *ordinary* people," said C. S. Lewis. "You have never talked to a mere mortal."[24] I have a rule of life: *Everyone is my superior in some way, in that I learn of them.* If you want to understand people, you have to stand under.

Can I make a confession? For many years, I struggled with low-grade social anxiety. In social settings, I felt tremendous pressure to be Jonathan Goldsmith—"the Most Interesting Man in the World." Then something shifted inside me, like tectonic plates. Instead of trying to be *interesting,* I tried to be *interested.* That's a very different posture, very different objective. I started cultivating a non-anxious curiosity toward everyone I met.

Are you trying to be interesting?

Or are you trying to be interested?

Nathanael stereotyped Jesus, but Jesus does the exact opposite. Remember Kevin Warren? This moment turns into a divine appointment because Jesus didn't do meetings. Jesus did relationships. No one could spot potential like Jesus. Why? Because He's the one who gave it to us in the first place!

> When Jesus saw Nathanael approaching, He said of him, "Here is a true Israelite, in whom there is no deceit."
>
> "How do You know me?" Nathanael asked.
>
> Jesus replied, "Before Philip called you, I saw you under the fig tree."
>
> "Rabbi," Nathanael answered, "You are the Son of God! You are the King of Israel!"[25]

Nathanael goes from skeptic to convert in one sentence. Why? Because Jesus saw him for who he was! He called out his true identity. This meeting turns into a three-year relationship, apprenticeship, and discipleship. Nathanael becomes one of the twelve apostles and takes the gospel all the way to India. Then he circled back to Armenia and Azerbaijan before being martyred for his faith.

THE GRANDMOTHER OF US ALL

In the summer of 1937, Henrietta Mears was serving as the director of Christian education at First Presbyterian Church in Hollywood, California. Under her leadership, average attendance grew from four hundred to more than six thousand students. Henrietta believed that catalytic change happened best in a camp setting, so she was looking for a place to do retreats with her students. "If you place people in an atmosphere where they feel close to God and then challenge them with the Word, they will make decisions."[26]

Henrietta learned of a campground in the San Bernardino Mountains called Forest Home whose owner was dying of cancer. When Henrietta did a driving tour of the property, it was love at first sight, but she also saw dollar signs! "Don't even bother to stop," she said to the friend who was driving the car. "Go on back down the highway. I know we can't afford all of this." Henrietta added, "This is just ridiculous!"[27]

Have you ever been there? Ever said that? Your vision is too big—no way, no how. To be honest, we never thought we'd own property, but God owns the cattle on a thousand hills—and that includes Capitol Hill. The Forest Home property was valued at $350,000 in 1937 dollars, but the owner was willing to entertain a $50,000 offer. While that was one-seventh of the estimated value, it was still way beyond reach.

What happened next seems awfully apocalyptic, but it started to storm like no tomorrow. Three cabins that sat by the stream running through the property were washed away by flash floods. The damage caused by that storm resulted in a 40 percent discount. The owner offered to sell for $30,000, and the rest is history.[28]

Over many decades, Forest Home became a place where tens of thousands of lives were powerfully impacted by God. Perhaps none more than a young Billy Graham. It was there, during a crisis of faith, that Billy made a defining decision. Four words got into his gut—"Thus sayeth the Lord."[29] Billy Graham made a solemn vow to trust the Word of God and preach the Word of God.

"A major bridge had been crossed," said Billy Graham in his autobiography.[30] He started preaching crusades with a newfound conviction—"deep down things." But it was Henrietta Mears who discipled Billy Graham through those days of doubt. She also discipled Bill Bright, the founder of Cru, and Jim Rayburn, the founder of Young Life. That's an awfully long legacy!

If Etta May Budd, George Washington Carver, and Henry Wallace get partial credit for Norman Borlaug's Nobel Prize, Henrietta Mears certainly gets partial credit for each of those ministries. Maybe that's why *Christianity Today* famously dubbed her "the grandmother of us all."[31] Henrietta Mears never had biological children, but she was a spiritual mother to thousands and a spiritual grandmother to millions. That's a good ancestor!

THE SPEED OF A SEED

The Moso bamboo is the fastest-growing plant on earth, but it happens gradually then suddenly. When planted, there is no discernible growth for five years. The seed disappears beneath the soil. To the naked eye, nothing is happening. But the Moso is a category of bamboo called running bamboo—its extensive and aggressive root system form a vast underground network of horizontal roots that support its eventual growth spurt. When it finally breaks through the surface of the soil, the Moso bamboo can grow up to three feet per day! That's like Jack and the beanstalk. Within six weeks, it can grow ninety feet tall.

We want things to happen at the speed of light, but in the kingdom of God, things generally happen at the speed of a seed. News flash: Seeds still grow at the speed of Eden. They have to take root before they can bear fruit.

Maybe you're frustrated because it's been five long years of planting but you have nothing to show for it. You've been going to counseling. You've been paying off your debt. You've been exercising and dieting. You've been praying for a prodigal. You've been planting mustard seeds, but the mountain hasn't moved. It might seem like nothing is happening, but is it possible that God is growing your root system?

God is always working beneath the surface.

God is always working behind the scenes.

During our first five years of church planting, there wasn't much visible growth. Can I share a lesson learned? The first five years weren't about growing the church. They were about God growing me! If you're growing as a leader, I'm not worried about whatever it is you're leading. Growth will happen organically. If you focus on the roots, God will take care of the shoots.

It took National Community Church five years to grow from our original core group of nineteen people into a church of 250. That's when a reporter from *The Washington Post* asked for an interview—not because of our size but because of our makeup. NCC was 80 percent single twenty-somethings, which the reporter found newsworthy.

After the interview, she told me the article would be in the religion section of the Sunday edition—if it made the editor's cut. At the time, NCC was meeting in the movie theaters at Union Station, so I made a beeline to the newsstand that Sunday! I picked up the paper, leafed through the religion section, and we weren't in it—total letdown! I refolded the newspaper and put it back on the newsstand. If we weren't in it, I wasn't going to buy it. That's when I saw the article—on the front page!

I'll never forget August 12, 2001—it was a day when decades happen. We doubled in size the next year, and we never looked back. I used to jokingly say that it must have been a slow news day, but I have since repented of that misattribution. It was God's favor! It was God's time! It was God's way of putting us on the map.

I don't know how big your dreams are, but they aren't big enough. How do I know? Because God is bigger still. God "is able to do immeasurably more than all we ask or imagine, according to his power that is at work within us."[32] It may take longer than you like and be harder than you hoped. So be it. If you're going to dream big, you have to think long. That's what good ancestors do—they do what they do for the third and fourth generation.

CHAPTER 10

THE DAY WHEN DECADES HAPPEN

On December 2, 1942, a select group of forty-nine scientists were working on a secret assignment called the Manhattan Project. In the world of physics, it's been called "the day tomorrow began." Led by Enrico Fermi, they built the world's first nuclear reactor in a squash court beneath Stagg Field at the University of Chicago. It was there—at precisely 3:53 P.M., CST—that they split the first atom.[1]

Since its founding in 1892, the University of Chicago has 101 Nobel laureates to its credit. That ranks third among all universities. The winners include Enrico Fermi for physics, James D. Watson for medicine, Milton Friedman for economics, Bertrand Russell for literature, and Barack Obama for peace.[2]

My undergraduate education began at the University of Chicago, and I am *not* one of those Nobel laureates, just in case you were wondering. I do, however, remember a class where our professor informed us that we were sitting a few feet from the squash court where that first nuclear chain reaction happened. The U of C has produced some academic illuminati, but I'm not sure any of them has left as large or as long a legacy as its famed football coach—Amos Alonzo Stagg.

Amos Alonzo Stagg coached the original Monsters of the Midway from 1892 to 1932, winning seven Big Ten titles and two national championships in 1905 and 1913. It was Stagg who invented modern football as we know it—the huddle, T formation, onside kick, and forward pass are his brainchildren.

It should come as no surprise that Amos Alonzo Stagg was inducted into the College Football Hall of Fame—he coached until he was ninety-eight years old. But he wasn't just inducted as a coach, he was also inducted as a player. He was also inducted into the Basketball Hall of Fame! Believe it or not, Amos Alonzo Stagg coached three sports at the U of C: football, basketball, and baseball. Did I mention that he turned down six offers to play professional baseball? But he did help a lot of future major leaguers with one of his inventions—the batting cage![3]

Can you say legacy? But his greatest legacy wasn't making the Hall of Fame or winning two national championships—his legacy was his players! Even more than a football coach, Amos Alonzo Stagg was a life coach.

After one of his winning seasons, a beat reporter congratulated the coach on a job well done. Instead of simply accepting that compliment, Stagg coached that young reporter. "I won't know how good a job I did for twenty years," said Stagg. "That's when I'll see how my boys turned out."[4]

Legacy isn't measured by what we accomplish in our lifetimes. Legacy is measured by our coaching tree, our mentoring chain. It's measured by the investments we make in others that are still earning compound interest twenty years later. It's measured by every act of kindness, every word of encouragement.

RANDOM ACTS OF KINDNESS

October 19, 1987, ranks as the largest one-day percentage drop of the Dow Jones Industrial Average in history. Black Monday destroyed many an investor, but not Paul Tudor Jones. He managed to triple his investment value by shorting his portfolio. Jones is a Wall Street legend, but that's not his legacy.

The venture philanthropist has given more than $3 billion to causes he cares about through his Robin Hood foundation. *Fortune* magazine has called that foundation "one of the most innovative and influential philanthropic organizations of our time."[5]

Whenever I'm inspired by someone's story, I always wonder about their backstory. Who left their fingerprints on that person's soul? Almost without exception, anyone who is kind or generous or hospitable was on the receiving end of someone else's kindness, generosity, and hospitality. Paul Tudor Jones is no exception.

Paul Tudor Jones is a fighter, as evidenced by the welterweight boxing championship he won in his twenties. But the defining moment and driving engine of his life is one act of kindness. When he was a young boy, Jones was at an outdoor vegetable market with his mother when he got lost. He still remembers the feeling of fear, but he also remembers a Black man he describes as very old, very tall, and extraordinarily kind. "Don't worry. We're going to find your momma," the man said. "Don't cry, we're going to find her. You're going to be happy in a minute."[6]

That was the day the door opened and let the future in. That was the day when decades happen. What was the man's name? Paul Tudor Jones has no idea! Amazing, isn't it? Yet that one act of kindness changed the trajectory of his life and inspired a lifetime of philanthropy.

You never forget stuff like that. God's every action, those little actions become so much bigger, and then they become multiplicative. We forget how important the smallest action can be. For me, I think, it kind of spawned a lifetime of trying to always repay that kindness.[7]

The Bible is full of heroes and heroines—Abraham and Moses, Esther and Nehemiah, David and Deborah and Daniel. Those lead actors make headlines, but I'm drawn to the unsung heroes who act as extras. In many cases, we don't even know their names—the little boy with five loaves and two fish, the widow who gave two mites, the woman who broke open her alabaster jar of perfume. They may be nameless, but their selfless sacrifices are celebrated in Scripture.

They remind us that our actions and inactions, our decisions and indecisions, matter more than we know. Don't let anyone tell you differently! Your kindness may inspire a venture philanthropist.

PREPARE A TABLE

Toward the end of King David's reign, his son rebelled against him. David fled Jerusalem under the cover of night, and he did so barefoot.[8] Why that detail is included in Scripture I'm not sure, but crossing the Kidron Valley, climbing the Mount of Olives, and disappearing into the Judean wilderness would be hard enough in hiking boots.

David ends up in a small town, east of the Jordan River, called Mahanaim. That geography has an interesting genealogy. That is where Jacob wrestled with God—the place where God changed his name from Jacob to Israel. This is where the king of Israel flees, and by the time they arrive, his body is tired and his feet are bloodied. He and his entourage are also starving. That's when a man named Barzillai shows up with his food truck.

They brought beds and basins and pottery. They also brought wheat and barley, flour and roasted grain, beans and lentils—

but wait, there's more—honey, curds, sheep, and cheese from the herd for David and his people to eat.[9]

This is radical hospitality, is it not? Even more, it's courageous generosity. If Barzillai gets caught aiding and abetting a fugitive, Absalom will have his head. But that doesn't keep Barzillai from putting on a Thanksgiving feast. And I love the fact that every morsel of food is acknowledged. When you're starving, every bite is sacred.

This represents a low point in David's life—his own flesh and blood, Absalom, is trying to kill him. But this is when and where David wrote his most famous psalm, Psalm 23. As David penned these words—"Thou preparest a table before me in the presence of mine enemies"[10]—he's not thinking of any old table. He's picturing the table that Barzillai set for him. It's no wonder, when David returned to Jerusalem, that he invited Barzillai to stay with him at the palace. Barzillai declined the offer, but David never forgot his kindness. Barzillai is part of David's last will and testament:

> Show kindness to the sons of Barzillai of Gilead and let them be among those who eat at your table.[11]

Barzillai's children had an OpenTable reservation at the king's table! Why? Because of the legacy left by their father.

We live in a cultural moment where people throw stones at anyone and everyone they disagree with. What if we threw parties instead? What if we set a table in the presence of our enemies? What if we sat around the table and said, "Tell me your story." And followed it up with "Tell me more!"

You don't have to compromise your convictions to show compassion. Jesus knew Judas was going to betray Him, but He invited him to the table anyway. He didn't just eat with sinners; He set a table for those who would deny Him and desert Him.

Go thou and do likewise!

TELEOLOGICALLY PRESCRIBED UTOPIA

Unless you patent an invention or hold public office, there is a good chance that your greatest legacy won't have anything to do with what you do forty hours a week. Your greatest legacy will be family and friends—the people whose lives you influence. There are those who devalue the high calling of being a homemaker because it doesn't come with a paycheck. Why would we dishonor the most important profession on the planet?

When he was a professor at the University of Pennsylvania, Tony Campolo and his wife, Peggy, would often attend faculty functions. During the course of conversation, the question would come up—"What do you do for a living?" When Peggy revealed that she was a stay-at-home mom, she often felt patronized by the intelligentsia, so she decided to redefine her role. The next person who asked got this answer:

> I am socializing two homo sapiens in the dominant values of the Judeo-Christian tradition in order that they might be instruments for the transformation of the social order into the kind of teleologically prescribed utopia inherent in the eschaton!

Peggy would pause, then ask, "And what is it that you do?"[12]

Your greatest legacy won't be the things you accomplish or acquire. Sure, two national championships look awfully good in the trophy case! But like Amos Alonzo Stagg, your legacy will be people, not trophies! And the true test is twenty years from now! We often think of legacy as impacting millions of people, but sometimes legacy is impacting one person who impacts millions.

Many years ago, I came up with a personal definition of success. It has nothing to do with pastoring or writing. I love both of those callings, but success is when those who know me best respect me most. That's my wife and my kids. Success is being a better person in private than I am in public, or at least the same person.

Legacy has nothing to do with fame or fortune. Legacy has much more to do with hospitality and generosity. When everything is said and done, legacy is integrity!

DOUBLE BACK

Elijah is famous for beating the odds by defeating the 450 prophets of Baal on Mount Carmel. He's also famous for ending a drought by praying for rain seven times. Elijah's LinkedIn profile listed no less than fourteen miracles, but his legacy was Elisha.

After Elijah wins the Super Bowl, so to speak, Queen Jezebel threatens to kill him. Elijah runs all the way to Jezreel like Forrest Gump, which was more than a marathon. It was more like the Barkley Marathons because he had to double back all the way to Beersheba.[13] He ends up under a broom tree feeling totally depressed and defeated.

> "I have had enough, LORD," he said. "Take my life; I am no better than my ancestors."[14]

When you're physically or emotionally depleted, beware of negative narratives. Have you heard of the old acronym HALT? It stands for hungry, angry, lonely, and tired. Elijah is all four. Even prophets called by God to do great things get discouraged. Even prophets wrestle with imposter syndrome, inferiority complexes, and suicidal ideation. If you find yourself in that situation, the first step is to seek help. But notice that God's prescription seems less spiritual than physical. God doesn't tell him to fast and pray. He tells him to take a nap! If you're not getting enough sleep, cognitive impairment is par for the course. So is physical and emotional fatigue.

When I created a life plan with the help of a life coach many years ago, I complained about feeling fatigued. That retreat was revelatory, but one of the insights my coach made was pretty comical. "Mark, I couldn't help but notice that you didn't eat breakfast this morning. Then you went running. Then we started our session." I nodded in agreement, having no idea where this was going. He said, "Could it be that your mental and physical fatigue is because you're *not* eating breakfast?" Aye, aye, Captain Obvious! That never even crossed my mind.

After Elijah takes a nap, he wakes up to the smell of freshly baked bread. Can I get a hallelujah? You gotta love a God who bakes bread and grills out. Then God makes some halftime adjustments that help Elijah rediscover, reimagine, and repurpose his life.

> Go back the way you came, and go to the Desert of Damascus. When you get there, anoint Hazael king over Aram. Also, anoint Jehu . . . king over Israel, and anoint Elisha . . . to succeed you as prophet.[15]

Sometimes the way forward is backward. Why? Because our destiny is buried in our history. You have to connect the dots between God's past-tense faithfulness and present-tense circumstances. Winston Churchill is often credited with saying, "The farther backward you look, the farther forward you are likely to see." Sometimes you have to go back and redig the ancient wells.

Dr. J. Edwin Orr took a group of Wheaton College students to study abroad in England in 1940. They visited the Epworth Rectory, which is now a Methodist museum. But it was once the home of a young John Wesley, the founder of the Methodist movement.

> In one of the bedrooms, there are two impressions where it is believed that John Wesley regularly knelt in prayer. As the students were getting back on the bus, Dr. Orr noticed that one student was missing. Going back upstairs, Dr. Orr found a young Billy Graham kneeling in those kneeholes and praying, "O Lord, do it again!"[16]

If Henrietta Mears gets partial credit for Billy Graham's crusades, so does John Wesley. You never know who your obedience will impact. But testimony is prophecy—the God who did it before can do it again. A. W. Tozer said it this way:

> Anything God promised or did at any time in any place for anybody, God will do for us here if we will meet His conditions. . . . If it is truth, it is true for anybody who could believe it anywhere, anytime. Two times two equals four whether it's 400 BC or AD 1963, whether in Russia, in China or in Canada. . . . Two times two equals four. No one can get around it; anybody can trust it.[17]

"I walk backwards into the future," says a Māori proverb, "with my eyes fixed on the past."

Isn't that what David did before fighting Goliath? When lions and bears attacked the sheep he was shepherding, David killed them with a slingshot. Where you have victory, you have authority!

"The same God who helped me defeat the Detroit Lions and Chicago Bears," said David, "will help me defeat the New York Giants." He didn't say it quite that way, but David did connect the dots.

The God who did it before will do it again.

The God who did it for me will do it for you.

The way you steward a miracle is by believing God for the next one. You believe God for even bigger, even better miracles. But sometimes it helps if you go back to Mount Carmel—the place where God has already done one! It renews long vision by jogging old memories! That's why I love praying on the rooftop of Ebenezers Coffeehouse.

If destiny is buried in history, then you have to go back and rebuild those ancient altars. That's why I retrace my steps and do a 4.7-mile prayer walk around Capitol Hill on August 16 every year. It reminds me of the miracles God has already done, and it helps me believe God for the next one. We overcome by the blood of the Lamb and the word of our testimony.

Have you ever written out your testimony? I highly recommend it. As you recollect the defining moments of your life, it'll stretch your faith to believe God all over again.

Do it again, Lord.

DOUBLE ANOINTING

A few years ago, Jon Tyson spoke at our annual revival. Jon pastors Church of the City in New York City, but he hails from down under. As a teenager in Australia, he worked in a butcher's shop. That wasn't Jon's dream job, but he made the most of it. He knelt at the beginning of the workday, held up his knives, and consecrated himself to God.

One day, Jon's boss said something that changed the trajectory of his life: "You're a leader." Three words! Or does the apostrophe make it four? Either way, Jon said that his boss was the first person to "cast a vision for my life."[18]

That's what Elijah did for Elisha, isn't it?

> So Elijah went from there and found Elisha son of Shaphat.
> He was plowing with twelve yoke of oxen. . . . Elijah went up
> to him and threw his cloak around him.[19]

Elisha was a farmer, the son of a farmer. He spent all day, every day, staring at the backside of oxen. He was stepping in you know what. He was breathing the fumes from their tailpipes. Elisha was going to find a wife on farmersonly.com, have a family, and grow old on that farm. Then Elijah showed up and called out his calling by casting a vision for Elisha's life.

Do you remember what Elisha did? He burned his plowing equipment and barbequed his oxen. That's on par with burning the boats or burning the bridges. Defining decisions demand grand gestures! It was a point of no return. It was a day when decades happen.

Just before Elijah was taken to heaven, he gave Elisha one last wish. "Tell me, what can I do for you before I am taken from you?"[20] Elijah had a pretty sweet ride. Elisha could have asked for the keys to his chariot. But that isn't what Elisha asked for: "Let me inherit a double portion of your spirit."[21]

After Elijah does his disappearing act, Elisha goes on to perform twenty-eight miracles. That's twice as many as Elijah, but Elijah gets partial credit. Those miracles are part of his legacy. He's the one who spotted Elisha's potential. He's the one who cast a vision for his life. He's the one who gave him his mantle.

Do you see people's problems? Or do you see their potential?

Are you throwing stones? Or are you casting vision for other people's lives?

Who are you discipling and developing and deploying?

THE JOHARI WINDOW

When I was in graduate school, I was introduced to a matrix on human personality called the Johari window. It's like a four-framed window by which we see other people. It's four angles on history, identity, personality, and destiny.

The first window is called the *open self*. This is what you know and others know about you. It's your public persona, so to speak. This is your Facebook feed, your LinkedIn profile, your Wikipedia page.

The second window is the *hidden self*. This is what you know about you but others don't know about you. This is your alter ego. This is who you are behind closed doors. It's also known as the façade quadrant.

Many years ago, our family did the back lot tour at Universal Studios Hollywood. We drove by the Cleaver home—as in, *Leave It to Beaver*—but it was nothing more than a façade with two-by-fours propping it up. Like that façade, many of us prop up our image for public consumption. But this is where loneliness lurks and shame skulks in the shadows.

"There is hardly a man or woman," said A. W. Tozer, "who dares to be just who he or she is without doctoring up the impression." He said that long before selfies and social media. Tozer called it the burden of pretense, and the problem with that is this: *If you is who you ain't, you ain't who you is.* "The rest [God] offers," said Tozer, "is the rest of meekness, the blessed relief which comes when we accept ourselves for what we are and cease to pretend."[22]

It takes tremendous courage to come out of the façade quadrant, but there are several exits. One door is called counseling, and another is called confession.

The third window is the *blind self.* It consists of those things others know about you but you don't know about you. The blind spot quadrant is where you need someone to speak the truth in love—to call out what's wrong and what's right. This is where you need someone to cast a vision for your life.

The fourth window is the *unknown self.* It consists of those things you don't know about you and others don't know about you. This is where you need a relationship with the God who knows you better than you know you. If you want to reach your full potential, get to know the God who gave it to you in the first place.

THE POWER OF PROPHECY

In her book *The Power of Positive Prophecy,* Laurie Beth Jones says that at least 40 percent of our lives are based on personal prophecies.[23] I'm not sure where that number comes from, and I'm not sure it can be substantiated by a study. But I'll go out on a limb—I think the number is too low. In my opinion, it's at least 73.2 percent!

Laurie Beth Jones tells a story in her book about a man named Michael who grew up in an abusive family with an alcoholic father. All he ever heard at home were negative words. But there was a dry cleaner in the neighborhood who kept candy on the counter, so Michael was a regular "customer." One day the dry cleaner said, "Michael, you are a very smart boy. Someday you are going to run a very big business."

"I would listen in disbelief," said Michael, "and return home only to get called a 'dog' and knocked around by my dad. . . . Jimmy the dry cleaner was the only person I can remember believing in me. . . . Today I run a multimillion-dollar health care organization, just like Jimmy predicted. I guess you could say that a dry cleaner was the prophet in my life."[24]

I don't know what you do for a living, but whether you know it or not, you are a prophet. For better or for worse, your words and actions have a butterfly effect on the people around you.

I wish that all the LORD's people were prophets.[25]

If you're a coach like Amos Alonzo Stagg, you're a prophet to your players. If you're a parent, you're a prophet to your children. If you're in business, you're a prophet to your clients and colleagues. Regardless of what you do, you are a teacher-prophet, lawyer-prophet, artist-prophet, barista-prophet, Uber driver–prophet.

FOR DAVID'S SAKE

There is a three-word phrase in Scripture that has long captured my imagination—"For David's sake." It pops up here and there, like a postscript. It's a poignant reminder that God does not forget His people and God does not forget His promises.

In 853 B.C., King Jehoram assumed the throne of Judah. He was the fifth king of the southern kingdom. This was 117 years after the death of David. King Jehoram did what is evil in the eyes of the Lord. He killed his brothers to secure the throne.

Yet for the sake of His servant David, the LORD was unwilling to destroy Judah, since He had promised to maintain a lamp for David and his descendants forever.[26]

David was long gone, but his influence was still being felt to the fifth generation. How so? The legacy David left had real-time, real-world implications for Jehoram. He wasn't fully aware of this fact, but the good decisions David made were protecting Jehoram from feeling the full effect of his bad decisions. It's six degrees of King David.

Few people have had a more profound influence on my life than my grandpa and grandma, Elmer and Alene Johnson. One of my earliest memories is overhearing my grandpa praying for me, as I already shared. When my grandma died, she left a legacy of love. She also left an inheritance that paid off my college debt in full.

My grandparents died many decades ago, but legacy lives on. Truth be told, influence is exponential. It's not easy measuring legacy, but memory is one metric. If time is measured in minutes, legacy is measured in memories. The memory of my grandpa and grandma fuels my imagination. Their long obedience left a long legacy that inspires long vision.

Remember Nathanael? One of the twelve apostles, he traveled an estimated ten thousand miles sharing the gospel. This is the same guy who dismissed Jesus out of hand—"Can anything good come from Nazareth?" How does that kind of turnaround happen? Jesus saw him under the fig tree. He spoke into his blind spot quadrant and cast a vision for his life.

Go thou and do likewise!

CHAPTER 11

DREAM FACTORY

I n 1880, a Parisian obstetrician named Stéphane Tarnier visited the Paris zoo. Tarnier was the surgeon in chief at Maternité de Paris, a hospital that served the city's poor. At the time, one out of six women died from postpartum fever caused by uterine infection. One in five babies died before learning to crawl, and the mortality rate for preemies was incredibly high because of their inability to regulate temperature.

As Tarnier wandered the zoo, it wasn't the monkeys or reptiles that caught his attention. It was an exhibit of chicken incubators. Tarnier would hire the zoo's poultry raiser, Odile Martin, to build a prototype that could incubate newborns.

Tarnier did a study of five hundred babies with low birth weight and found that 66 percent died within weeks. When those babies were put into Tarnier's incubator, the mortality rate was nearly cut in half. Only 38 percent of the incubator babies died. Within a few years, Paris passed a law requiring that incubators be installed in every maternity ward in the city. Tarnier's idea spread across Europe. It spread across the Atlantic to America. It spread all the way around the world to developing countries.[1]

It's hard to estimate how many lives Stéphane Tarnier saved, but it's quite possible your great-great-grandparents survived the neonatal period because of his field trip to the Paris zoo. That change of pace plus change of place was the change of perspective that changed history.

Legacy is incubating other people's gifts and passions, dreams and ideas. That's why we started our Dream Collective—to give dreamers a birthright and a blessing. To let dreamers know *You're not crazy and you're not alone.*

Not everyone considers themselves a dreamer. Some people are problem solvers. Either way, we have to exercise prophetic imagination. We bring supernatural solutions to the table. By faith, we do things that will make a difference long after we're long gone.

DREAMCATCHER

For nearly two decades, Ebenezers Coffeehouse has been caffeinating Capitol Hill. I know that's a little out of the ordinary for a church, but truth be told, I don't want to preach to an un-caffeinated congregation! We even came up with an equation: *the Holy Spirit + caffeine = awesome!*

When people drink our coffee, it doesn't just stimulate the central nervous system by blocking the neurotransmitter called adenosine. There is something in our coffee that causes people to dream big, pray hard, and think long. Why? Because every cup is spiked with Ebenezers' miraculous overstory. Thousands of people have made a pilgrimage to our coffeehouse because they've read the story of us circling a crackhouse for five long years.

Before we opened Ebenezers, we dedicated that building back to God. We climbed down ladders and inscribed prayers on the cement walls in the foundation. We laid hands on the walls and anointed the doors with oil. We consecrated every square inch of that coffeehouse. But there was one prayer that turned prophetic: "Lord, let this coffeehouse be a dream factory."

Dream factory? That is a strange prayer, is it not? But that combination of words—dream factory—got into our DNA. It became part of our identity, our destiny.

When I wrote the forty-day prayer challenge—*Draw the Circle*— I titled Day 9 "Dream Factory." I would have never imagined that more than a million people would take that forty-day prayer challenge. I never imagined it would make a cameo in *The Biggest Loser, American Idol,* or a Lizzo music video, but we'll save those stories for another day. When people drink our coffee, every cup comes with two shots of courage. Ebenezers is more than a coffeehouse; it inspires God-sized dreams.

TWENTY SECONDS OF INSANE COURAGE

Many years ago, I was on a transatlantic flight to Addis Ababa, the capital of Ethiopia. I usually read takeoff to touchdown, but sixteen hours is a little long. So I watched a movie called *We Bought a Zoo.* It's based on a true story about a man named Benjamin Mee, played by Matt Damon, who buys a dilapidated zoo. He had no business going into the zoo business, but he manages to reimagine, repurpose, and reopen the zoo.

There is one line in the movie that has become a rule of life: "Sometimes all you need is twenty seconds of insane courage."[2] Like Benjamin Mee, we had no business going into the coffee business. It took five years of prayer, plus twenty seconds of insane courage. In other words, it happened gradually then suddenly! Regardless of the dream God has given you, it's going to take twenty seconds of insane courage. But that's how miracles happen.

It took about twenty seconds of insane courage for David to sling a stone. It took about twenty seconds of insane courage for Benaiah to chase a lion into a pit on a snowy day. It took about twenty seconds of insane courage for Peter to get out of the boat in the middle of the Sea of Galilee. But the results speak for themselves—David defeated Goliath, Benaiah became King David's bodyguard, and Peter walked on water.

"Courage is not simply *one* of the virtues," said C. S. Lewis, "but the form of every virtue at the testing point." Lewis adds, "Pilate was merciful till it became risky."[3]

It took twenty seconds of insane courage for Zacchaeus to climb a sycamore tree, for Mary to break open the alabaster jar of perfume, for the woman with the issue of blood to touch the hem of Jesus' garment. But that's when and where breakthroughs happen.

In 1 Samuel 14, the Philistines control the pass to Michmash. Saul should have been fighting on the front lines, but he's sitting on the sidelines. He's the picture of passivity, popping pomegranate seeds, but Jonathan had a bias for action. Instead of playing defense, Jonathan plays offense. He climbs a cliff and picks a fight with the enemy.

Perhaps the LORD will act in our behalf.[4]

That's one of my favorite phrases in Scripture. But let's be honest, most people operate out of the opposite MO—perhaps the Lord *won't* act on our behalf. Instead of stepping out in faith, they let fear dictate their decisions. Part of playing the long game is playing offense. If you don't obey the promptings of the Holy Spirit, sins of omission turn into inaction regrets.

A MILLION LIVES SAVED

A few years after opening Ebenezers, I got an email from a Hill staffer named Mark Moore who would frequent our coffeehouse. One day, as he was sipping a latte, he got a God-sized vision to start a nonprofit called MANA—Mother Administered Nutritive Aid. Mark launched MANA at Ebenezers on World Food Day, and they now have factories that produce millions of RUTFs—ready-to-use therapeutic foods.

I'll never forget the email Mark sent with the subject line "A Million Lives Saved at Ebenezers." Remember the prayer we prayed on the day we dedicated Ebenezers? That it would be a dream factory? That prayer proved prophetic! "The dream of MANA," said Mark, "was formed in the dream factory of Ebenezers Coffeehouse."

Our Dream Collective recently hosted a gathering for Business as Mission leaders and one of them told me that Ebenezers had inspired his dry-cleaning business. Dry cleaning? That makes about as much sense as a coffeehouse inspiring a hunger relief organization. Those are very different visions, but they have one thing in common—twenty seconds of insane courage.

When God gives you a vision, don't expect everybody to rise up and call you blessed.[5] If your dream disrupts their status quo, there will likely be people who oppose it. Why? It convicts them of their complacency! Of course, going after your dream also gives others permission to do the same. And that's your legacy. It's not just the dreams you pursue. It's the dreams you inspire others to pursue.

We didn't start Ebenezers so Mark Moore would start MANA, but that's the net effect. Were we trying to save a million lives? Maybe sell a million lattes, but saving a million lives wasn't even on our radar. But Ebenezers is a dreamcatcher—dreams beget dreams. You never know when or where or how dreams will be conceived.

Remember Edgar Allan Poe—"Is *all* that we see or seem but a dream within a dream?"[6] Long before we got the vision to turn a crackhouse into a coffeehouse, I was reading a book by Elizabeth O'Conner. She told a story about the Church of the Savior starting a nonprofit café—the Potter's House—in 1960. There is nothing new under the sun!

Remember the film *Inception*? That movie repopularized the poem by Edgar Allan Poe, "A Dream Within a Dream." When I read about the Potter's House, a God idea seeded my subconscious. It got into my imagination—three levels down. Just as MANA is a dream within a dream that is Ebenezers, Ebenezers is a dream within a dream that was the Potter's House.

HERE COMES THE DREAMER

The story of Joseph is one of the saddest sagas in the Bible. Imagine being sold into slavery by your siblings! Why did they do it? They were offended by his dream: "Here comes that dreamer!"[7]

After being trafficked to Egypt, Joseph was falsely accused of a crime he didn't commit. He got thrown into an Egyptian dungeon, and for thirteen years, his life went from bad to worse. But dream factories come in all sizes and shapes, including prison cells. Some dreams start out as nightmares, but long suffering has a way of producing long vision. "To live is to suffer," said Gordon Allport, "to survive is to find meaning in the suffering."[8]

Joseph's life was trending in the wrong direction for thirteen years, but God was cultivating emotional intelligence in the crucible called pain and suffering. I'm certainly not suggesting that God caused that pain—that's bad theology. His brothers made a bad choice and Joseph suffered the consequences. Not unlike what happened to Joseph, Jesus warned His disciples that they would be thrown into prison on His account. But He also made a promise: "It will lead to an opportunity for your testimony."[9]

"You intended to harm me," Joseph said to his brothers. That was the understory, but God was busy writing the overstory. "But

God intended it for good to accomplish what is now being done, the saving of many lives."[10]

There is it again—"the saving of many lives." Not unlike Norman Borlaug who saved a billion lives or MANA that has saved millions of lives, Joseph would save two nations from famine. How? With one act of emotional intelligence.

EMOTIONAL INTELLIGENCE

Many years ago, I was speaking to Anglican pastors in the UK. I was scheduled to speak right after the archbishop of Canterbury, which was a little intimidating. I actually wore the same wireless mic—my claim to fame. The archbishop said something pretty profound: "Emotional intelligence is a wonderful adjunct faculty to the gifts of the Spirit."

We need the gifts of the Spirit—ministry gifts and miraculous gifts—as much as those who followed Christ in the first century. We need the gift of faith and the gift of healing. We need words of wisdom and words of knowledge. We especially need the gift of discernment, but those gifts much be exercised with emotional intelligence. How do you cultivate emotional intelligence? The short answer is pain and suffering!

When Joseph was seventeen, he had very little emotional intelligence. How do we know this? He told his brothers that they would bow down to him. Anyone with siblings knows what's going to happen next—a wet willy or worse! In this case, much worse.

Emotional intelligence is multi-dimensional, but its essence is empathy. It's an awareness of the thoughts and feelings of others. It's reading the room by picking up on emotional and relational cues. Did you know that the fusiform face area—located in the inferior temporal cortex—is capable of deciphering 10,000 facial expressions and their associated emotions?[11] Loving God with "all of your mind" includes the fusiform face area, and it's more important than we may realize.

When Joseph was thrown into prison, his fellow prisoners included a baker and a cupbearer. One morning, Joseph "noticed that they both looked upset."[12] How? With his fusiform face area! So what? It may seem like a small thing, but this single act of emotional intelligence has a butterfly effect that saves two nations from famine. Joseph interprets their dreams for them, and it leads to an opportunity, many years later, to do the same for Pharaoh.

It was long suffering that produced long vision in Joseph. He had the prophetic insight to see God's purpose in his pain. He also had the prophetic foresight to see four hundred years into the future.

> Joseph made the Israelites swear an oath before he died: "God will surely come to your aid, and then you must carry my bones up from this place."[13]

Joseph prophesied Israel's exodus out of Egypt four hundred years before it happened! That's long vision. And when the Israelites did in fact exit Egypt, they took the bones of Joseph with them as promised. That's long legacy.

In the last chapter of Joshua, after Israel has occupied the Promised Land, there is a futuristic footnote.

> Joseph's bones, which the Israelites had brought up from Egypt, were buried at Shechem in the tract of land that Jacob bought for a hundred pieces of silver from the sons of Hamor, the father of Shechem. This became the inheritance of Joseph's descendants.[14]

God does not forget His people.

God does not forget His promises.

HARD-FOUGHT HALLELUJAH

My wife, Lora, has the privilege of serving on the board of Prison Fellowship. On a recent prison visit, I got to be her plus-one. I will long remember that visit to the Prison Fellowship Academy at the Carol S. Vance correctional facility. Like the Egyptian dungeon where Joseph was incarcerated, that prison doubles as a dream factory.

Over lunch, I choked back tears as I heard testimonies of transformation from John and Bobby. Then we worshipped together. John had some pitch problems, but it was some of the purest worship I've ever heard. When we worship around the throne of God—every nation, tribe, people, and language—I definitely want my wife in close proximity. There is no one I love worshipping with more than Lora! But I also want John somewhere in proximity. For the record, glorified vocal cords will fix his pitch problems and mine!

The song we sang was "Hard Fought Hallelujah." I love the line of lyrics: "I'll bring my hard-fought, heartfelt, been-through-hell hallelujah."[15] That song hits a little different when you sing it in prison. The lyrics hit a little harder when it's led by someone in a prison jumpsuit.

There are more than a hundred Prison Fellowship academies across the country, and they double as dream factories. God has turned lots of old nightmares into new dreams. How does that happen? If you take a learning posture, long suffering turns into long vision. That's the legacy of Prison Fellowship founder Chuck Colson.

In 1974, Chuck Colson served seven months in prison for his role in the Watergate scandal. It was during his arrest and trial and imprisonment that Chuck found faith in Jesus. It radically changed his life, and he wanted to return the favor. Don't be surprised if God turns your mistakes into your ministry! That's who God is. That's what God does. He redeems and recycles and repurposes the mistakes we've made to help other people.

God did it for Joseph. God did it for Chuck Colson. And God can do it for you. But you'll have to give God some hard-fought hallelujahs along the way!

Let me double back to the axiom we explored in part 1: *Everything is created twice!* Some dreams are conceived in the imagination while others are catalyzed in the crucible called suffering. Either way, God is the Way Maker, Promise Keeper, and Dream Giver.

SHOW ME YOUR VISION

When I was twenty-one, the summer before my senior year of college, I was sitting in a stadium in Portland, Oregon, with ten thousand pastors. The speaker that night was David Yonggi Cho, pastor of the largest church in the world. He said something I'll never forget: "Show me your vision and I'll show you your future." Those words had g-force!

I was about to graduate from college, and I had no idea where to go or what to do. I ended up doing what you do when you don't know what to do—I went to graduate school. But that moment marked me. I started praying for a vision. Why? Without a vision, the people perish. But even more than a vision *from God*, we need a vision *of God*.

Our biggest problem is our small view of God. We need long vision, but that starts with knowing the heights and depths of Almighty God—His love, His power, His glory, His grace—even more!

> In the year that King Uzziah died, I saw the Lord, high and exalted, seated on a throne; and the train of his robe filled the temple.[16]

Uzziah ruled and reigned for fifty-two years—the only king most Israelites had ever known. Is it possible that the nation of Israel found their identity and security in the king rather than in God? It's also worth noting that Isaiah and Uzziah were first cousins, so this loss hit hard.

Sometimes it takes tragedy to open our eyes to spiritual reality. Sometimes it takes loss to fully lean on God's love.

SOVEREIGN SETBACKS

In 1832, Abraham Lincoln ran for the Illinois state House of Representatives and lost. He didn't finish second or third either—he finished eighth. The next year, a business venture failed. In 1835, the love of his life died from typhoid fever at the age of twenty-two. No wonder he had a nervous breakdown the next year in 1836. "I am now the most miserable man living," he wrote in a letter to a friend. "If what I feel were equally distributed to the whole human family, there would not be one cheerful face on earth."[17]

Abraham Lincoln ran for Congress in 1843 and lost. In 1849, he ran for land officer of Illinois and lost. His bid for the United States Senate in 1854 ended with a loss. And his attempt to earn the vice presidential nomination in 1856 failed.[18] His failures are infamous, but so are his successes.

Abraham Lincoln was elected the sixteenth president of the United States in 1860. He delivered one of the most memorable speeches in American history—the Gettysburg Address. He led this nation through the Civil War. He secured the necessary votes to free four million slaves. And he drafted the Emancipation Proclamation.

Long legacy is an understatement, but it came at a cost. The strongest convictions are formed in the chrysalis called crisis. I wish there was an easier way, but shortcuts tend to short-circuit God's good, pleasing, and perfect will. If you try to help a caterpillar turn into a butterfly by assisting it out of its cocoon, you aren't helping it. Your intentions are good, but you're hurting it by helping it. Without the struggle, it won't develop the wing strength necessary to fly. Such is life!

We do the same thing when we give every kid a trophy. We don't want them to feel bad about losing, but how else are they going to learn to overcome loss? In my experience, growth often begins with a setback.

There is a difference between long suffering and wrong suffering. Please don't sabotage yourself—life is hard enough as it is. Self-inflicted suffering is self-defeating. That said, suffering is par for the course. Bad things happen to good people. If you live long enough, pain and suffering will come knocking. The good news?

"After you have suffered for a little while, the God of all grace, who has called you to His eternal glory in Christ, will Himself restore you, secure you, strengthen you, and establish you."[19]

Let's be honest, "a little while" can feel like forever! If you find yourself in one of those seasons—suffering or setback—take heart. God is writing a bigger story! God is creating capacity to persevere through thick and thin. "The difference between a good life and a bad life," said Carl Jung, "is how well you walk through the fire."[20] It was suffering and setback that created capacity within Abraham Lincoln to lead through the most contentious era of American history. It steeled his convictions and produced good old-fashioned grit.

BETTER LATE THAN NEVER

Shizo Kanakuri holds the dubious distinction of being the world record holder for the longest marathon in history. The first Japanese athlete to qualify for the Olympic Games, Shizo competed in the 1912 Olympic Games in Stockholm, Sweden.

The trip by ship, followed by the Trans-Siberian Railway, took eighteen days. Shizo got so sick he could barely walk, let alone run. To make matters worse, the Olympics took place during white nights when the sun never sets, so Shizo couldn't sleep either. Plus his coach was bedridden with tuberculosis, so he had very little training. Did I mention the heat wave on the day of the marathon? One of the runners collapsed and died from heat exhaustion.

Around mile sixteen, Shizo started feeling the effects of hyperthermia. He stumbled into a Swedish garden party, delirious and defeated. Shizo Kanakuri never finished the race. He was so embarrassed by his failed effort that he never even notified Olympic officials. He caught the next train out of town and disappeared. Shizo became the laughingstock of the Sweden games for going MIA—his name was actually added to the missing persons list and kept there for fifty years.

Shizo Kanakuri returned to Japan and became a geography teacher. He got married and had six kids and ten grandkids. That's when a Swedish reporter arranged for Shizo Kanakuri—then seventy-six years old—to return to Sweden and finish what he started. This time he didn't have to travel by ship and train, he flew to Stockholm.

On March 20, 1967, Shizo Kanakuri finished the marathon he

had quit more than half a century before. His official time? 54 years, 8 months, 6 days, 5 hours, 32 minutes, and 20.3 seconds.[21]

There is an old adage: *Better late than never!* This epitomizes that. In the words of the apostle Paul, finish the race![22] Of course, you can't finish what you don't start.

Is there a dream you've given up on? A relationship you quit on? An application you never submitted? An appointment you have yet to make? Maybe it's time to finish what you started. If not now, when?

This can be the day when decades happen!

CHAPTER 12

KEEP CALM AND CARRY ON

On October 14, 1947, a B-29 bomber took off from an airstrip in Southern California. Attached to the belly of that bomber was a unique payload—an experimental aircraft called the Bell X-1. In the world of aviation, it was believed by many aeronautical engineers that the speed of sound—Mach 1—was an unbreakable barrier. A pilot named Chuck Yeager believed otherwise.[1]

Many years ago, when my oldest son was a Capitol Hill Cub Scout, we had the privilege of hearing Chuck Yeager speak at the Smithsonian's National Air and Space Museum. In that talk, he mentioned that two days before attempting to break the sound barrier, he was thrown from his horse and broke two ribs. Imagine being subjected to eight g-forces—eight times the normal pull of gravity—with broken ribs! Chuck Yeager did not tell the Air Force about the broken ribs because he didn't want to delay history.

When the B-29 bomber reached an altitude of twenty-five thousand feet, the Bell X-1 fired its engines. Every prior attempt had ended in failure or, worse, death. No airplane had even eclipsed 0.84 Mach—639 mph. As the Bell X-1 accelerated past 700 mph, Chuck Yeager felt like the plane was falling apart. At 0.965 Mach, the control panel went haywire—the dials on the dashboard started spinning like the Wheel of Fortune. At 0.995 Mach, the g-force turned his stomach in knots and blurred his vision.

Just when it felt like the plane would implode, there was a sonic boom. At 761 mph, the Bell X-1 had broken the sound barrier. At supersonic speeds, air pressure shifts from the front to the back of the plane. The perfect storm became the perfect calm. The cockpit was completely quiet, like an anechoic chamber. Why? Because the Bell X-1 was traveling faster than the sound waves it was producing!

Most of us live and love and lead at 0.965 Mach. When life goes haywire—the dials start spinning out of control—what do you do? The temptation is to kill the engine and quit trying. If you make it to 0.995 Mach, don't be surprised if your vision blurs. You'll be tempted to decelerate, but that's when you need the courage to press on—pedal to the metal.

Maybe a dream deferred has left you discouraged. Perhaps your family is falling apart and therapy isn't working. Or you're wrestling with anxiety or depression, and your stomach is in knots. Maybe, just maybe, you're closer to a breakthrough than you know. Like Chuck Yeager breaking the sound barrier, it's only impossible until it isn't.

As Henry Ford supposedly said, "Whether you think you can, or you think you can't—you're right."[2]

I CAN'T NEVER COULD

Many years ago, a fourth-grade teacher took her students on an unforgettable field trip. The irony? They didn't even leave the school grounds. The teacher asked her students to write down "I can't" statements on a piece of paper.

I can't do long division.
I can't kick the kickball past second base.
I can't get classmates to like me.
I can't do ten pushups.

After many minutes of writing down what they could not do, the teacher said, "Pencils down." She told her students to fold up their "I can't" statements and bring them to her desk. They dropped them in a shoebox, which doubled as a casket. Then their teacher marched her class out to the playground, grabbing a shovel from the custodian closet on the way.

Each student took a turn digging the grave. When they were done, the teacher had them circle the gravesite and hold hands. Then she delivered a eulogy.

> Friends, we gather today to honor the memory of "I Can't."
> While he was with us on earth, he touched the lives of everyone, some more than others. . . .
> He is survived by his brothers and sisters, "I Can," "I Will," and "I'm Going to Right Away." They are not as well known as their famous relative and are certainly not as strong and powerful yet. Perhaps someday, with your help, they will make an even bigger mark on the world. May "I Can't" rest in peace and may everyone present pick up their lives and move forward in his absence. Amen.[3]

After burying "I Can't," the teacher made a tombstone out of butcher paper. She wrote "I Can't," added an RIP, and dated it— 3/28/80. The rest of the school year, any time a student said, "I Can't," their teacher pointed to the RIP and reminded them that "I Can't" was dead and gone.

Since we're on the subject, fourth-grade teachers have long influence on their students. According to economist Raj Chetty, if they've had "even one above-average teacher" between fourth and eighth grade, the likelihood of attending college goes up, as does long-term earning potential.[4] Teachers matter, at every grade level. So do Little League coaches, music teachers, math tutors, and dance instructors.

I can't speak.[5]
I'm too young.[6]
I'm too old.[7]
I'm no better than my ancestors.[8]
I'm from the wrong side of the tracks.[9]

Those excuses are as old as Moses, Jeremiah, Sarah, Elijah, and Gideon. News flash: If you're looking for an excuse, you'll always find one. I've met plenty of people who claim they aren't creative, but I've never met anyone who isn't creative when it comes to making excuses! Redirect that creativity in a more positive direction.

THE LIFE LIE

More than a century ago, the Austrian psychotherapist Alfred Adler coined a concept called the life lie. The life lie is our guiding fiction—it's the story we tell ourselves about ourselves. For better or for worse, you are the narrator of your story. If you don't like your life, you might be telling yourself the wrong story. Maybe it's time to change your story!

The life lie is a false belief that we build our lives around. A subtle form of self-sabotage, it's the excuse we give ourselves to evade responsibility—*I'm not this. I'm not that.* Over time, that false belief turns into a false narrative that turns into a false identity that turns into a false reality. Consider this your reality check!

When God called Jeremiah to be a prophet to the nations, he was likely a teenager. No wonder he objected to God's directive. But when Jeremiah started making excuses, God gave him a gag order.

Do not say, "I am too young."[10]

Why did God give the gag order? Because it reinforced the wrong narrative! With God, age is never an issue! Neither are your abilities or inabilities. God's power is made perfect in weakness. If you are anointed and appointed by God, don't be dissuaded by your lack of education, lack of resources, or lack of ability. The greatest ability is availability—"Here am I. Send me!"[11]

Is there anything you need to stop saying?

Maybe it's a negative narrative or a false narrative. Or maybe it's someone you're *talking about* instead of *talking to*. Stop giving power to the wrong things, and start declaring the promises of God. For better or for worse, words create worlds. You have to ground yourself in God's Word. And not just read it but speak it. Why? Because faith is voice activated—"I believed; therefore I have spoken."[12]

LIVE NOT BY LIES

A few years ago, I was listening to a podcast interview with Ken Jennings, the former champion and current host of the game show *Jeopardy!* Ken is as smart as they come, as evidenced by his *Jeopardy!* winnings totaling $4,522,700.[13]

In that interview, Ken talked about the seemingly innocent lies we believe as children that end up shaping the rest of our lives. When he was a young boy, his family went camping. His sister didn't like his music, so she told Ken to turn it down because it would attract mosquitoes. That's fake news, by the way. But Ken took it as gospel truth. Many decades later, Ken and his wife went camping with his younger brother and Ken told him to turn down the music so they didn't attract mosquitoes! Ken's wife literally laughed out loud. And it would be funny if it didn't have such serious side effects. If you don't identify the lies you've long believed, those false assumptions have the power to rule your life in big ways.

Remember the man that Jesus healed by the pool of Bethesda? He almost missed the miracle because of a false assumption—only the first person into the pool after it was stirred was healed.[14] Naaman almost missed the miracle because of a false expectation—he thought Elisha would wave his hand over his leprosy.[15]

Is there a false assumption that has kept you crippled?

Is there a false expectation that has left you incapacitated?

"Wherever there is a loss of hope," says Heidi Scanlon, our longtime pastor of prayer at National Community Church, "you have believed a lie of the enemy." The enemy's tactics haven't changed since the Garden of Eden—he is the father of lies. In his brilliantly titled essay "Live Not by Lies," the Russian dissident Alexander Solzhenitsyn said that the key to liberation is "a personal non-participation in lies."[16] Those lies often take root in rather innocent ways, like a sister telling you that loud music attracts mosquitoes! We simply believe what someone says to us or about us. In the words of Lewis Carroll, "What I say three times is true."[17] My advice? Don't let anyone label you who didn't make you! Let the Author and Perfecter of faith rewrite those false narratives!

Jesus said, "The truth will set you free."[18] Any guess how it happens? Two ways—gradually then suddenly! It takes time to uproot false assumptions and false expectations that double as default settings.

Is there a life lie that has kept you from discovering your true identity in Christ?

Is there an excuse that has kept you from exercising your full authority as a child of God?

It's time to reimagine your future!

THE PERFECT STORM

The second His head hit the pillow, He was sound asleep. In His dream, He was in a boat on the Sea of Galilee. In His dream, a storm was tossing the boat like a bathtub toy. It was so full of water, the boat started to sink. That's when He heard His friends scream. That's when they woke Jesus up and He realized it wasn't a dream at all. They were in the middle of the Sea of Galilee, in the middle of the storm.

The Sea of Galilee is thirteen miles, north to south, and eight miles, east to west. In some places, it's two hundred feet deep. My point? It's not a pond. One of the lowest elevations on earth, the Sea of Galilee is seven hundred feet below sea level, but it's surrounded by mountains that are 2,500 feet above sea level. That topography makes the Sea of Galilee susceptible to very sudden, very violent storms.

> A violent windstorm came up, and the waves were breaking over the boat, so that it was being swamped. But Jesus was in the stern, sleeping on the cushion. So they woke Him and said, "Teacher, don't You care that we are perishing?"[19]

You know it's bad when the disciples, some of whom were fishermen, fear for their lives. They wake Jesus up, and it's a rude awakening to say the least. Notice the indictment: They accuse Jesus of not caring. Really? One crisis and you call His character into question? But that's what we do, isn't it?

In a crisis, we often resort to the blame game or the shame game. That tendency is as old as Eden. Eve blamed it on the serpent: *The devil made me do it.* Adam blamed it on Eve, with a passive-aggressive overtone: "The woman you put here with me—

she gave me some fruit from the tree."[20] If I'm reading that right, Adam has the audacity to indirectly blame God. Of course, we would never do that, right? Wrong! We blame it on the devil. We blame it on God. We blame it on the rain, like Milli Vanilli. No one wins the blame game or the shame game. The only way to win is by *not* playing.

This storm is a microcosm of the cultural moment that we find ourselves in. All you have to do is change news channels to discover that everybody is blaming everybody else for everything. We politicize and demonize and dehumanize like it's a sport, blood sport.

Jesus doesn't blame back, though He certainly could have. It was the disciples, after all, who row, row, rowed the boat gently into the storm. It was their fault, not His. But I love what Jesus does next. He doesn't grab a pail and bail the boat. He doesn't grab an oar and row for shore. Jesus stood up in the boat, which was quite the Karate Kid balancing act. Then Jesus rebuked the wind and the waves. Who does that? The One who spoke them into existence, that's who. And He does it with three words, no less.

He awoke and rebuked the wind and said to the sea, "Peace! Be still!" And the wind ceased, and there was a great calm.[21]

Remember Chuck Yeager breaking the sound barrier? This is that. With three words—"Peace! Be still!"—there is a sonic boom. The perfect storm turns into the perfect calm. Jesus stops this storm in its tracks, and He does it by speaking shalom.

When we find ourselves in a storm, most of us tell God all about it. We detail what's wrong, as if God is unaware. At some point, you have to flip the script. Stop talking to God about your circumstances, and start talking to your circumstances about God. You have to rebuke the wind and waves the way Jesus did.

Whatever you tolerate will eventually dominate. The good news?

Wherever you have victory, you have authority. The choice is yours: You can tolerate what's wrong or you can do something about it.

Many years ago, a Jewish rabbi named Edwin Friedman wrote a book called *A Failure of Nerve*. A student of systems theory, Friedman advocated for something called non-anxious curiosity. During crises, you can't let fear dictate your decisions.[22]

It's epitomized by a poster made popular during World War II. The UK printed thousands of posters that said, "Keep Calm and Carry On." Those posters were plastered all across the country, as a visual reminder to keep the faith.

I don't want to soft sell long legacy. There will be moments when you're tempted to toss in the towel. There will be moments when it seems like the boat is about to sink. Those are the moments you have to stand up and rebuke the wind and the waves. That is when and where you have to pronounce your faith: "Peace! Be still!"

How do you keep calm and carry on? You fix your eyes on Jesus. If Jesus is in the boat, it's going to be okay. You have to remember the future—God is writing a bigger story!

"There is no way out of a chronically painful condition," said Friedman, "except by being willing to go through a temporarily more acutely painful phase."[23] Ouch! The truth hurts, but it hurts less than untruth. The only way to end long suffering is more suffering—the suffering of the cross.

Lora and I have a family systems therapist who was trained in the same school of thought as Edwin Friedman. Ungoverned anxiety is public enemy number one. It will wreak havoc on families and teams and organizations. The only way to overcome it is to cultivate non-anxious curiosity. So many of us have so much ungoverned anxiety it's like a low-grade fever that infects everything we say and do. News flash: God is not nervous. And neither should we be! Instead of projecting anxiety, pronounce the peace that passes understanding.

"There was a time when the church was very powerful," said Dr. Martin Luther King, Jr., in his "Letter from Birmingham City Jail." "In those days the church was not merely a thermometer that recorded the ideas and principles of popular opinion; it was a thermostat that transformed the mores of society."[24]

When you walk into the room—boardroom or family room, classroom or locker room—does the anxiety level go up or down? That's a key barometer for spiritual maturity. We are not thermometers that reflect room temperature. We're called to be thermostats that shift the atmosphere with faith, hope, and love.

For better or for worse, people pick up on your energy. If you have nervous energy, even your pets pick up on it. Remember Caleb? He had a different spirit. He had to disassociate with the spies who got negative. He had to cultivate a positive energy that produces love, joy, peace, patience, kindness, goodness, faithfulness, gentleness, and self-control. Mix those nine fruits of the Spirit together like a smoothie and it spells shalom.

THE GOOD FIGHT

I cannot promise a stress-free life. That universe doesn't exist yet. I can't even promise a fair trial. Life is unfair, then we die. But I'll go on record: God is good. And He's working all things together for good to those who love Him and are called according to His purpose.[25]

The time for my departure is near. I have fought the good fight, I have finished the race, I have kept the faith.[26]

Paul is not writing these words in a vacuum. Like Dr. King, he was writing them from a prison cell. He'd been falsely accused and unjustly imprisoned. Paul was about to be beheaded, but I don't detect an ounce of regret in his words. You have to forgive reality for what it is. When life knocks you down, you get back up.

Paul took three missionary journeys, planted fourteen churches, and wrote half the New Testament. He may have logged more miles on foot than Forrest Gump. If you GPS those missionary journeys, he traveled about ten thousand miles. No Uber. No scooter. No Nikes or adidas or New Balance. Paul was the man, the myth, the legend. I would argue that he lived the good life, but the good life includes good trouble. In the words of G. K. Chesterton, "give room for good things to run wild."[27]

The good life is *not* no problems—what doesn't kill us can make us stronger! The good life is *not* no suffering—perseverance produces character; "and character, hope."[28] The good life is fighting the good fight.

"Great faith is the product of great fights," said Smith Wigglesworth, "Great testimonies are the outcome of great tests. Great triumphs can only come out of great trials."[29]

I'll say it again for good measure: Long legacy is often born of long suffering. Like the apostle Paul, you have to keep fighting the good fight.

ONE MORE ROUND

On September 7, 1892, a no-name boxer—James "Gentleman Jim" Corbett—stepped into the ring with the undefeated heavyweight champion of the world, and arguably the greatest boxer of all time, John L. Sullivan.

Sullivan was the last world champion of bare-knuckle boxing

and the first world champion of gloved boxing. In fifty fights, he was undefeated. To call Corbett an underdog would be an understatement. Somehow, someway, Gentleman Jim Corbett managed to do what no one had done. He didn't just defeat Sullivan; he knocked him out in the twenty-first round. And I love this: Corbett had a habit of giving his prize money to his church.

Knocking out John L. Sullivan ranks as one of the greatest upsets in boxing history, but in my unprofessional opinion, that's not even Corbett's most impressive fight. As of 1982, professional boxing matches are limited to twelve rounds, but there was no limit in 1891 when Gentleman Jim Corbett fought his rival and Australian champion, Peter "Black Prince" Jackson. That fight went sixty-one rounds! The crazy thing? It ended in a draw!

How did Corbett beat John L. Sullivan?

How did he become the heavyweight champion of the world?

How did he last sixty-one rounds?

The answer is his life motto—*fight one more round.*

When your arms are so tired that you can hardly lift your hands to come on guard, fight one more round. When your nose is bleeding and your eyes are black and you are so tired that you wish your opponent would crack you one on the jaw and put you to sleep, fight one more round. . . . The man who always fights one more round is never whipped.[30]

DON'T DO ANYTHING PANICKY

On the evening of January 30, 1956, Martin Luther King, Jr., was speaking at First Baptist Church in Montgomery, Alabama, when he was informed that his house had been bombed. Lots of people in that situation would respond in kind—eye for an eye. But Dr. King met crisis with calmness. He rebuked the storm, "Peace! Be still!"

Shortly after the bombing, a crowd gathered outside his house and they were mad as a mob. They wanted vengeance, but Dr. King turned his porch into a pulpit: "Don't do anything panicky."[31] If you react in circumstances like that, you lose. Why? Because we usually react in kind. Or worse, we overreact. You have to rise above the circumstances, with the help of the Holy Spirit.

Despite the personal attack, Dr. King doubled down on his nonviolent tactics. "If you have weapons, take them home. He who lives by the sword will perish by the sword," said Dr. King. "Be calm as I and my family are."

Sitting at his kitchen table later that evening, Dr. King felt like the Lord said, "Martin, do not be afraid." It was a defining moment for Dr. King. Many people would have retreated under those circumstances, but Dr. King took his stand.

You may be 38 years old, as I happen to be. And one day, some great opportunity stands before you and calls upon you to stand up for some great principle, some great issue, some great cause. And you refuse to do it because you are afraid; you refuse to do it because you want to live longer. You're afraid that you will lose your job, or you're afraid that you will be criticized or that you will lose your popularity. Or you're afraid that somebody will stab you or shoot at you or bomb your house, and so you refuse to take the stand.

Well, you may go on and live until you are 90, but you're just as dead at 38 as you would be at 90! And the cessation of breathing in your life is but the belated announcement of an earlier death of the spirit.[32]

Quit living as if the purpose of life is to arrive safely at death. Live your life in a way that is worth telling stories about. Go after a dream that is destined to fail without divine intervention.

If not you, who?

If not now, when?

As we near the end of this book, can I speak prophetically over your life? I don't know what setbacks or heartbreaks you've experienced. But I've learned to stand on God's principles and promises. You cannot break the law of sowing and reaping—it will make or break you. If you keep doing the right things day after day, God is going to show up and show off. That doesn't mean you won't get knocked down a time or two or ten. Such is life! But you have to believe that God is planning His work and working His plan. You have to believe, as the psalmist said, "Those who sow in tears shall reap with shouts of joy!"[33]

I've experienced my fair share of failure. I recently found the incorporation papers for a business that went belly-up. It was painful at the time, but I can laugh about it now. Just because it rhymes—Godipod—doesn't mean it will work!

I've weathered disappointment and discouragement. I've got emotional and spiritual scars, as well as physical ones. I've endured plenty of setbacks, but I've also experienced seasons of blessings where you buckle up and keep your hands inside the ride at all times.

"In that day I will restore
  the fallen tent of David.
I will repair its gaps, restore its ruins,
  and rebuild it as in the days of old. . . ."

"Behold, the days are coming,"
  declares the LORD,
"when the plowman will overtake the reaper."[34]

God is promising productivity that is nothing short of supernatural—a sovereign acceleration. You could even call it a multiplication anointing that reaps thirty, sixty, hundredfold. The NLT says, "The grain and grapes will grow faster than they can be harvested."

This past year, the Capital Turnaround was rented out more than 150 times by a wide variety of groups and produced $2 million in revenue. That's more than our first five years of income as a church combined. Maybe twice as much! That's nothing short of sovereign acceleration.

Remember the Culturehouse? We didn't pursue it, it pursued us. We never even thought we'd own property, much less seven properties worth more than $100 million debt-free. A few weeks after purchasing the Culturehouse, we assumed ownership of another historic church in our city by eliminating their debt. We have no intention of using that church building for our purposes. We simply wanted to secure it for the five ministries that currently use it.

That last paragraph makes my head swim, and that's precisely what God promises in Amos 9:13. There are seasons of pruning, no doubt. Of course, pruning is a form of growth too! When I step back and look at what the Lord has done, I can't help but ask *how*. I sure hope you know the answer by now. Blessings and breakthroughs happen two ways—gradually then suddenly!

Regardless of what season you find yourself in, the challenge is this: Enjoy the journey—every age, every stage, every page. If you focus on gradually, God will take care of suddenly! Sooner or later, sovereign acceleration will take you by storm. Like the perfect storm that hit the Sea of Galilee, you can rise above the wind and the waves. You can make the same pronouncement: "Peace! Be still!"

SIDEWALK THROUGH THE SEA

On October 5, 2009, Lora and I were on a coffee date when I made the mistake of answering my phone. The call was from the manager of the movie theaters at Union Station where National Community had met for thirteen years. When the manager informed me that the movie theaters were shutting down, it felt like a sucker punch. She said it was happening in *one week,* and I almost had a panic attack.

How do you move a congregation—more than a thousand people at that point—in one week? The future flashed before my eyes—we had no clue where to go or what to do. I honestly wondered if our best days were behind us. But open doors are often preceded by closed doors! Sometimes sovereign accelerations begin with subtraction.

Remember when the Israelites were trapped between the Red Sea and the Egyptian army? That's what it felt like. And that's the text I preached from on our last Sunday at Union Station. "Do not be afraid," Moses said to the people. "Stand firm and you will see the deliverance the LORD will bring you today."[35]

"I don't know what we're going to do," I said on that last day. "But I know what we're *not* going to do. We're not going to panic. We're going to stand still and see the deliverance of the Lord."

Did I have moments of doubt? No doubt. For many months, we wandered in the wilderness. But God was writing a bigger story. God was making a sidewalk through the sea. It didn't happen overnight, but God did for us what He did for the Israelites.

We would have been content meeting at Union Station forever, but God had some pieces of promise land we knew nothing about. Remember the seven properties worth $100 million? All of them were acquired, except for Ebenezers, after God closed the door at Union Station. Praise God for closed doors!

"When a train goes through a tunnel and it gets dark," said Corrie ten Boom, "you don't throw away the ticket and jump off." What do you do? You do what the woman who survived a Nazi concentration camp did: "You sit still and trust the engineer."[36]

I don't know what challenges you face—physical, emotional, spiritual, or relational. Maybe it's a closed door that got slammed in your face unceremoniously. Maybe the storm clouds are hovering overhead right now. Maybe it's time to do what Jesus did. At some point, you have to stop talking to God about the storm. You have to start talking to the storm about your God. You have to pitch your tent in the land of hope. You have to declare the goodness and greatness of God. If God is for us, who can be against us?[37] He who began a good work will carry it to completion.[38] We can do all things through Christ who strengthens us.[39]

Keep calm and carry on!

FAN INTO FLAME

n 2012, a fourteen-year-old girl named Lola Anderson was watching the Olympic Games in London. When two rowers from the UK won a gold medal, a dream was conceived in her heart. Lola pulled out her diary and wrote these words with a pink highlighter:

> My name is Lola Anderson and I think it would be my biggest dream in life to go to the Olympics in rowing and if possible win a gold for GB.[1]

After writing those words in her diary, Lola felt so self-conscious, so embarrassed, so unsure about what she had written that she tore that page out of her diary and threw it in the garbage. Many of us have done the same thing. Self-doubt causes us to second-guess the dream God has given us. We give up on the dream before we even give it a go! That's when we need someone who believes in us more than we believe in ourselves! Enter Lola's dad, Don Anderson.

The day after Lola discarded that page of her diary, her dad retrieved it from the trash. He didn't tell Lola, but he kept that note in a safety deposit box. Seven years later, two months before dying from terminal cancer, Don Anderson gave that note to his daughter and challenged her to go after her dream. Fast-forward to the Paris Olympics in 2024.

Lola Anderson made the UK Olympic team in rowing. In the finals of the quadruple scull, her team trailed the entire race by a sizable margin. It seemed insurmountable, but in the last few meters of the race, they pulled even for a photo finish. Somehow, someway, Lola and her team pulled out a win, by fifteen hundredths of a second. Lola won the gold medal she had dreamed of since she was fourteen years old.

Lola's dad wasn't there to witness it, but he was there in spirit. It was Lola's father who fanned into flame the gift of God in his daughter. Honestly, I don't think they won that race without him. You can be a skeptic and call me a romantic, but I think the page he saved from Lola's diary shaved fifteen hundredths of a second off their winning time!

WHATEVER THE WEATHER

After winning that gold medal, Lola Anderson reflected on the twelve years of sacrifice that made it possible. As you might imagine, Lola lived a very regimented life as an Olympic athlete. But if you want to live a life that is anything but routine, it starts with routine! Part of that routine was a daily touchstone—the diary page her dad retrieved from the trash.

That precious piece of paper is in a tin box in my bedroom, along with a couple of Dad's rowing medals from his days at university in Durban, South Africa. The tin is one of the first things I see when I wake up at 6am. Then I make coffee and peanut butter on toast, drive to the Redgrave Pinsent Rowing Lake at Caversham, South Oxfordshire, and meet with the rest of the crew.[2]

After that daily dose of inspiration, it's time for perspiration. Lola and her crew would start the day with a two-and-a-half-hour, high-intensity row. "We row 18 miles a day, six days a week," said Lola. And she added, "Whatever the weather."[3] It was rise and shine, rain or shine!

Want to venture a guess as to how many miles Lola rowed over twelve years? I did the math, and it's more than a Magellan! Eighteen miles a day, six days a week, for twelve years adds up to 67,392 miles! That's twice the circumference of the earth. Remember the gold medalist Rowdy Gaines? Lola lapped him. Of course, she did have a boat.

"People say rowing is boring," said Lola's teammate Hannah Scott. "Rowing is not boring."[4] Especially if you win a gold medal, right? No one understands GTS—gradually then suddenly—better than world-class athletes. There is no other way to become the best of the best. You have to pay the price day in and day out, for years on end. And that kind of drive is born of intrinsic motivation—doing what you love and loving what you do.

That gold medal race lasted less than seven minutes, but I think Lola and her teammates would trade twelve years for seven minutes all over again. That's a trade all of us make, one way or the other. We can choose the path of least resistance or we can trade pain for gain. The choice is yours.

IT'S TIME TO DREAM AGAIN

When Lola penned the words in her diary—"It would be my biggest dream in life to go to the Olympics in rowing and if possible win a gold medal"—it became a self-fulfilling prophecy. Words create worlds! That certainly includes dreams written in diaries by fourteen-year-old girls, but nothing inspires like the inspired Word of God. His Word does not return void.[5] Why? God is watching over His Word to perform it.[6]

"Fan into flame the gift of God, which is in you," said the apostle Paul to his protégé, Timothy.[7] Then Paul added this exhortation: "God has not given us a spirit of fear and timidity, but of power, love, and self-discipline."[8] Paul was exhorting Timothy to tap his God-given potential and run his God-ordained race.

Who fanned into flame the gift of God in you?

And whose gift are you fanning into flame?

Most stories in Scripture end with an ellipsis. The unsung heroes of Scripture—people like Rufus, Barzillai, Shiphrah, and Puah—walk off the pages of Scripture and we're left wondering what happened. But there are rare occasions where history fills in the blanks, and such is the case with Timothy.

When Paul wrote this letter, Timothy was a timid twenty-something.[9] And that's what makes the last chapter of his life so amazing. According to church tradition, Timothy became the bishop of Ephesus and served in that capacity until the age of eighty. That's long obedience in the same direction, but his legacy was cemented by twenty seconds of insane courage that resulted in his martyrdom.

Ephesus was a city filled with idols, but their hometown hero was Artemis—the goddess of fertility. Once a year, the Ephesians would parade those idols with great pride. They would carry the statue of Artemis down to the harbor where they would ritually restore her virginity by baptizing her in the Aegean Sea. By the time they got back to the temple of Artemis, which doubled as a brothel, many of them had lost their virginity all over again.

According to Eusebius, Timothy was killed trying to stop one of those pagan parades. That doesn't sound timid, does it? That sounds awfully courageous, and that's where I want to connect the dots. Timothy embodied long vision, long obedience, and long legacy.

We read the Bible in the third person, but Timothy heard those words in the first person. Why? He had been discipled by the man who spoke them, the apostle Paul. Just as Lola Anderson kept the diary entry her dad saved, these prophetic words—"Fan into flame"—echoed in Timothy's ears forever. They inspired Timothy to fight the good fight, to finish the race. Just as a diary entry shaved off fifteen hundredths of a second, that verse of Scripture gave Timothy the courage to do what he did.

I have no idea what page or paragraph of this book pricked your conscience, intensified your convictions, or stretched your faith. But it's time. Time for what? It's time to dream again! You know how dreams become reality—gradually then suddenly! Don't worry about suddenly; that's the lag measure. If you get to work on gradually, God will take care of suddenly.

Go, set, ready!

ACKNOWLEDGMENTS

I t takes teamwork to make the dream work. I'm grateful for the all-star team at WaterBrook & Multnomah and the way you've rallied around each and every book we've published together. Thanks to Tina Constable, Campbell Wharton, and Laura Barker for their constant encouragement. The way you champion books is a gift to authors and readers alike.

Thanks to Drew Dixon for your editing eye. And your patience in the process! Thanks to the bookmaking team—Jessica Choi, Julia Wallace, Richard Elman, Kevin Garcia, Madison Trammel, Simon Sullivan, Tracey Moore, Bailey Utecht, Carrie Krause, and Ruth Chung. You all have an eye for excellence! Thanks to Liz Shapiro for her work on the cover and Jeff Miller for the jacket design.

If a tree falls and no one hears it, did it make a sound? That old axiom is certainly true of dead trees called books. Thanks to Ginia Croker and Johanna Inwood for your marketing genius. Thanks to Brett Benson for opening doors of opportunity to get this message out. And thanks to Lori Addicott for selling with a smile!

A special thanks to my agent, Esther Fedorkevich, and the entire dream team at The FEDD agency. Grateful for the tag team on more than twenty books!

I'm eternally grateful for my favorite people on the planet—my wife and kids and grandkids. To me, books are time capsules I write for future generations. I hope this book blesses you the way you have blessed me! Being a husband and father and grandfather is the greatest joy and privilege of my life.

Finally, thanks to the church I've had the privilege of leading for nearly three decades! This book is dedicated to National Community Church. I'm grateful for each and every person who has called NCC their church home. Everything I write comes out of that crucible! It's been an absolute joy ride, and I believe the best is yet to come!

NOTES

PROLOGUE: PLAYING THE LONG GAME

1. Ernest Hemingway, *The Sun Also Rises* (Simon & Schuster, 2006), 141.
2. Crawford Loritts, "Wind in My Sails—Dr. Crawford Loritts," Passion City Church, March 2, 2021, YouTube, 32:47, www.youtube .com/watch?v=itAmjm2HuzU&t=8s.
3. Rowdy Gaines, quoted in Angela Duckworth, *Grit: The Power of Passion and Perseverance* (Scribner, 2016), 132.
4. Friedrich Nietzsche, *Beyond Good and Evil*, trans. Helen Zimmern (Macmillan, 1907), 107–8.
5. Those three phrases are said to have been found inscribed in the Bible of William Borden, a missionary who died at the age of twenty-five from spinal meningitis.
6. This saying is attributed to theologian Lynn H. Hough.
7. Mike Miller, email message to author, May 11, 2025.
8. Lewis Carroll, *Through the Looking-Glass: And What Alice Found There* (Macmillan, 1882), 100.
9. J. Hudson Taylor, quoted in Tim Keesee, "Beginning with Impossible," *Tabletalk*, November 2021, https://tabletalkmagazine.com/article/2021/11/beginning-with-impossible.
10. Wikipedia, "Muggsy Bogues," last modified June 9, 2025, https://en .wikipedia.org/wiki/Muggsy_Bogues.

11. Wikipedia, "Brachistochrone curve," last modified June 21, 2025, https://en.wikipedia.org/wiki/Brachistochrone_curve.

12. Seth Godin, *The Dip: A Little Book That Teaches You When to Quit (and When to Stick)* (Portfolio, 2007), 23.

13. Eugene Peterson, August 31, 2016, at Glen Eyrie Castle, Colorado Springs, Colorado.

14. Eugene Peterson, *A Long Obedience in the Same Direction*, 20th anniversary ed. (InterVarsity, 2000), 202.

15. Wikipedia, "Pablo Picasso," last modified June 23, 2025, https://en.wikipedia.org/wiki/Pablo_Picasso.

16. Note: This story may be apocryphal. While the story cannot be confirmed, that doesn't make the principle untrue.

17. Wikipedia, "*Guernica* (Picasso)," last modified June 11, 2025, https://en.wikipedia.org/wiki/Guernica_(Picasso).

18. Carl Jung, quoted in Thomas Oppong, "Carl Jung: Life Really Does Begin at 40," Medium, November 11, 2024, https://medium.com/personal-growth/carl-jung-life-really-does-begin-at-40-424dc4fe3cae.

PART I: LONG VISION

1. Wikipedia, "L'Enfant Plan," last modified June 16, 2025, https://en.wikipedia.org/wiki/L%27Enfant_Plan. Argon gas is used in museums to create an inert, oxygen-free environment for preserving delicate artifacts, documents, and artworks.

2. Pierre Charles L'Enfant, letter to George Washington, June 22, 1791, in *Records of the Columbia Historical Society*, vol. 2 (1899), 35, Bartleby, www.bartleby.com/lit-hub/respectfully-quoted/pierre-charles-lenfant-17541825.

3. William Tindall, *Standard History of the City of Washington* (Wentworth, 2019), 18.

4. Tindall, *Standard History of the City of Washington*, 9.

5. Henrik Johansson, "Visingsö Oak Forest," Atlas Obscura, June 14, 2017, www.atlasobscura.com/places/visingso-oak-forest.

6. Stewart Brand, *The Clock of the Long Now* (Basic Books, 1999), 162.

7. Psalm 2:8.

8. Jeremiah 29:11.

9. Jeremiah 29:7.

10. "Longevity in the Ancient World," Early Church History, accessed June 30, 2025, https://earlychurchhistory.org/daily-life/longevity-in -the-ancient-world.

11. Thanks to David Grizzle for this insight. David is a friend, longtime member of National Community Church, and former COO of the FAA.

12. Wikipedia, "Whakapapa," last modified May 30, 2025, https://en .wikipedia.org/wiki/Whakapapa.

13. James Kerr, *Legacy: What the All Blacks Can Teach Us About the Business of Life* (Constable & Robinson, 2013), 169.

14. Kerr, *Legacy,* 171.

15. Kerr, *Legacy,* 171.

16. See Revelation 11:15.

CHAPTER 1: SIXTEEN MILES UPSTREAM

1. Wikipedia, "Norman Borlaug," last modified May 23, 2025, https:// en.wikipedia.org/wiki/Norman_Borlaug.

2. Charles C. Mann, *The Wizard and the Prophet: Two Remarkable Scientists and Their Dueling Visions to Shape Tomorrow's World* (Vintage Books, 2019), 105.

3. Congressional Tribute to Dr. Norman E. Borlaug Act of 2006, Pub. L. No. 109-395, 120 Stat. 2708, www.congress.gov/bill/109th -congress/senate-bill/2250/text.

4. Edgar Allan Poe, "A Dream Within a Dream," Poetry Foundation, accessed June 30, 2025, www.poetryfoundation.org/poems/52829/a -dream-within-a-dream.

5. Andy Andrews, *The Butterfly Effect: How Your Life Matters* (Thomas Nelson, 2010), 77.

6. Wikipedia, "George Washington Carver," last modified June 1, 2025, https://en.wikipedia.org/wiki/George_Washington_Carver.

7. Andy Andrews, "The Butterfly Effect," Life Today, October 31, 2010, https://lifetoday.org/words-of-life/the-butterfly-effect/.

8. "George Washington Carver—The Artist: Yucca and Cactus," National Park Service, last updated December 17, 2021, www.nps.gov/teachers/classrooms/george-washington-carver-the-artist-yucca-and-cactus.htm.

9. "Etta Budd," Grade 4, Lesson 1—Biography Cards, George Washington Carver National Monument, accessed June 30, 2025, www.nps.gov/gwca/learn/education/upload/Grade-4-Bio-Cards_Etta-Budd.pdf.

10. "Etta Budd."

11. Dan Heath, *Upstream: The Quest to Solve Problems Before They Happen* (Avid Reader Press, 2020), 175.

12. Matthew 7:12.

13. Jack Canfield and Mark Victor Hansen, "Love and the Cabbie," in *Chicken Soup for the Soul: Stories to Open the Heart and Rekindle the Spirit* (Backlist, 2012), 31.

14. Canfield and Hansen, "Love and the Cabbie," 31–32.

15. Isaiah 58:12.

16. William Shakespeare, *Othello*, act 3, scene 4, accessed June 30, 2025, https://shakespeare.mit.edu/othello/full.html.

17. *Merriam-Webster Dictionary*, "futurity," accessed June 30, 2025, www.merriam-webster.com/dictionary/futurity.

18. Joshua 3:15–16.

19. George "Æ" Russell, "Germinal," quoted in Graham Greene, *The Power and the Glory* (Penguin Books, 1977).

20. Mann, *Wizard and the Prophet*, 450.

21. Mann, *Wizard and the Prophet*, 451.

22. Mann, *Wizard and the Prophet*, 451.

23. "Module 412: William Wilberforce," Christian History Institute, accessed July 1, 2025, https://christianhistoryinstitute.org/uploaded/50b649ccc5e960.06979983.pdf.

24. Romans 16:13, NLT.

25. Mark 15:21.

26. Wikipedia, "Rufus of Thebes," last modified May 15, 2025, https://en
.wikipedia.org/wiki/Rufus_of_Thebes.

27. Elizabeth O'Gorek, "National Community Church to Lead 2023
Easter Sunrise Service," HillRag, March 31, 2023, www.hillrag.com/
2023/03/31/national-community-church-to-lead-2023-easter-sunrise
-service/.

28. Matthew 25:21.

CHAPTER 2: THE LOST WEEKEND

1. Neal Gabler, *Walt Disney: The Triumph of the American Imagination*
(Vintage Books, 2006), 506.

2. Werner Weiss, "The 'Lost Weekend,'" Yesterland, April 29, 2020,
www.yesterland.com/ryman.html.

3. Weiss, "'Lost Weekend.'"

4. 2 Corinthians 10:5.

5. Wikipedia, "Disneyland," last modified June 24, 2025, https://en
.wikipedia.org/wiki/Disneyland.

6. Joshua Meyer, "The Unexpected Reason Disney World's Iconic Jungle Cruise Ride Uses Dyed Water," Explore, November 14, 2024,
www.explore.com/1714152/unexpected-reason-disney-world-iconic
-jungle-cruise-magic-kingdom-dye-water/.

7. Jody Jean Dreyer, *Beyond the Castle: A Guide to Discovering Your
Happily Ever After*, with Stacy Windahl (Zondervan, 2017), 31.

8. Miguel Ortiz, "This Army General Helped Walt Disney Build His
Magic Kingdom in a Swamp," We Are the Mighty, October 14,
2022, www.wearethemighty.com/mighty-history/walt-disney-magic
-kingdom.

9. Sunny Fitzgerald, "This Is Why You Rarely See Mosquitoes at Disney World," *Reader's Digest*, February 18, 2025, www.rd.com/article/
no-mosquitoes-at-disney-world.

10. Fitzgerald, "Why You Rarely See Mosquitoes."

11. Andrew Krosofsky, "Why Disney World Doesn't Have Mosquitoes," Green Matters, May 12, 2021, www.greenmatters.com/p/why-no -mosquitoes-disney-world.

12. Ed Catmull, *Creativity, Inc.: Overcoming the Unseen Forces That Stand in the Way of True Inspiration* (Random House, 2014), 196–97.

13. Catmull, *Creativity, Inc.*, 198.

14. Dorothy Sayers, "Why Work?" in *Letters to a Diminished Church: Passionate Arguments for the Relevance of Christian Doctrine* (W Publishing Group, 2004), 132.

15. Catmull, *Creativity, Inc.*, 197–98.

16. Exodus 26:14, ISV.

17. "Red Sea Dolphins Project," Red Sea Project, accessed July 2, 2025, www.redsea-project.com/Education/red-sea-dolphins-project.

18. Marc Gellman, "Dolphin Skins?," Reform Judaism, January 1997, https://reformjudaism.org/learning/torah-study/torah-commentary/ dolphin-skins.

19. Gellman, "Dolphin Skins?"

20. Henry James Jr., "The Madonna of the Future," *The Atlantic*, March 1873, www.theatlantic.com/magazine/archive/1873/03/the-madonna -of-the-future/630318.

21. Andy Stanley, *Next Generation Leader: Five Essentials for Those Who Will Shape the Future* (Multnomah, 2003), 93.

22. Jim Carrey, quote from an interview in *Movieline*, July 1994, Heroic, www.heroic.us/quotes/jim-carrey/ive-always-believed-in-magic -when-i-wa.

23. Josh Hoffman, "Why Jim Carrey Wrote Himself a $10-Million Check Before He Had $10 Million," Medium, January 7, 2019, https://socialmediajosh.medium.com/why-jim-carrey-wrote-himself -a-10-million-check-before-he-had-10-million-361809oc9e.

24. John Hargrave, *Mind Hacking: How to Change Your Mind for Good in 21 Days* (Gallery Books, 2016), 134.

25. Habakkuk 2:2, NASB.

26. Emina Dedic—Hack College, "Why You Should: Write Down Your Goals," *Badger Nation Blog*, Snow College, accessed July 2,

2025, www.snow.edu/blog/Why_you_should_write_down_your _goals.html.

27. Brent Lang, "'The Cable Guy' Turns 25: How Jim Carrey's $20 Million Salary Shook Up Hollywood," *Variety*, June 14, 2021, https:// variety.com/2021/film/news/cable-guy-jim-carrey-salary-1234995346/.

28. *Field of Dreams*, directed by Phil Alden Robinson (1989; Universal Home Video, 1998), DVD; "Field of Dreams: Quotes," IMDb, accessed July 2, 2025, www.imdb.com/title/tt0097351/quotes/?ref_=tt _dyk_qu.

29. 2 Samuel 23:11-12.

30. A drachma was worth a day's wage, and the average day's wage in America is $252; 50,000 x $252 = $12,600,000.

31. Luke 6:38.

32. Mark McCormack, *What They Don't Teach You at Harvard Business School: Notes from a Street-Smart Executive* (Bantam Books, 1984).

33. Tim Walker, "The Big Ideas That Started on a Napkin—From Reaganomics to Shark Week," *The Guardian*, April 10, 2017, www .theguardian.com/us-news/shortcuts/2017/apr/10/napkin-ideas-mri -reaganomics-shark-week; Nick Hines, "5 Genius Ideas That Were Born on a Cocktail Napkin," VinePair, January 12, 2017, https:// vinepair.com/articles/cocktail-napkin-ideas/.

34. "Albert Einstein Quotes," BrainyQuote, accessed July 2, 2025, www .brainyquote.com/quotes/albert_einstein_384440.

CHAPTER 3: OPPORTUNITY COST

1. Adam Grant, *Originals: How Non-Conformists Move the World* (Viking, 2016), 1.

2. Grant, *Originals*, 2.

3. Luke 14:28, NLT.

4. Ephesians 5:16, NLT.

5. Thanks to Andy Stanley for this idea.

6. Matthew 7:7.

7. Thomas Gilovich and Victoria Husted Medvec, "The Temporal Pat-

tern to the Experience of Regret," *Journal of Personality and Social Psychology* 67, no. 3 (1994): 357–65, https://doi.org/10.1037/0022-3514 .67.3.357.

8. Etymonline, "decide," accessed July 2, 2025,www.etymonline.com/ word/decide.

9. Tip of the cap to Marshall Bruce Mathers III. Eminem, "Lose Yourself," on *8 Mile,* Shady Records/Interscope Records, 2002.

10. Tony Campolo, *Who Switched the Price Tags?* (Thomas Nelson, 1987), 28–29.

11. Daniel H. Pink, *The Power of Regret: How Looking Backward Moves Us Forward* (Riverhead Books, 2022), 39.

12. Pink, *Power of Regret.*

13. Howard Schultz and Dori Jones Yang, *Pour Your Heart Into It: How Starbucks Built a Company One Cup at a Time* (Hachette Books, 1999), 63.

14. Dan Pilat and Sekoul Krastev, "Why Do We Buy Insurance?," The Decision Lab, accessed July 3, 2025, https://thedecisionlab.com/ biases/loss-aversion.

15. Hebrews 10:39, ESV.

16. Isaiah 58:12.

17. Richard Snow, *Disney's Land: Walt Disney and the Invention of the Amusement Park That Changed the World* (Scribner, 2019), 81.

18. Snow, *Disney's Land,* 81–82.

19. Snow, *Disney's Land,* 82.

20. Snow, *Disney's Land,* 82.

CHAPTER 4: CATHEDRAL THINKING

1. *Britannica,* "Cologne Cathedral," last updated February 7, 2025, www .britannica.com/topic/Cologne-Cathedral.

2. Dictionary.com, "ultracrepidarian," accessed July 3, 2025, www .dictionary.com/browse/ultracrepidarian.

3. Matthew 6:10.

4. Proverbs 29:18, KJV.

5. This idea originates with A. W. Tozer in *The Knowledge of the Holy* (HarperCollins, 1961), vii, 2.

6. Mark 5:9, NASB.

7. "What Does Mark 5:9 Mean?," BibleRef, accessed July 3, 2025, www.bibleref.com/Mark/5/Mark-5-9.html.

8. Thanks to Elizabeth O'Conner for this idea.

9. Mary Catherine Bateson, *Composing a Further Life: The Age of Active Wisdom* (Knopf, 2010), 20.

10. Wikipedia, "Hyperbolic discounting," last modified May 25, 2025, https://en.wikipedia.org/wiki/Hyperbolic_discounting.

11. James L Oschman et al., "The effects of grounding (earthing) on inflammation, the immune response, wound healing, and prevention and treatment of chronic inflammatory and autoimmune diseases," *J Inflamm Res.* 2015:8 (2015): 83–96, https://doi.org/10.2147/JIR.S69656.

12. Kristen Fischer, "Grounding: Techniques and Benefits," WebMD, last reviewed May 3, 2024, www.webmd.com/balance/grounding-benefits.

13. Roman Krznaric, *The Good Ancestor: A Radical Prescription for Long-Term Thinking* (The Experiment, 2020), 23.

14. Krznaric, *Good Ancestor,* 24.

15. David Womack, "Project Platypus: Reinventing Product Development at Mattel, an Interview with Ivy Ross," AIGA, March 6, 2003, https://web.archive.org/web/20150417185707/http://www.aiga.org/project-platypus-reinventing-product-development-at-mattel-an-interview-with-ivy-ross/.

16. Womack, "Project Platypus."

17. Womack, "Project Platypus"; Rimma Boshernitsan, "Ivy Ross: Intuition in Innovation," DIALOGUE, November 2018, https://in-dialogue.co/interviews/ivy-ross.

18. Womack, "Project Platypus"; Boshernitsan, "Ivy Ross."

19. Krznaric, *Good Ancestor,* 21.

20. Krznaric, *Good Ancestor,* 21–22.

21. Genesis 4:21, NLT.

22. See Genesis 4:22.

23. Steven Johnson, *Where Good Ideas Come From: The Natural History of Innovation* (Riverhead Books, 2010), 7–9.

24. Johnson, *Where Good Ideas Come From,* 9–10.

25. Johnson, *Where Good Ideas Come From,* 10.

26. See Genesis 11:6.

27. Cal Newport, *Slow Productivity: The Lost Art of Accomplishment Without Burnout* (Portfolio, 2024), 41.

28. Exodus 23:10–11.

29. John Ortberg once asked Dallas Willard, "What do I need to do to become the me I want to be?" Willard responded by saying, "Hurry is the great enemy of spiritual life in our day. You must ruthlessly eliminate hurry from your life." John Mark Comer, *The Ruthless Elimination of Hurry* (WaterBrook, 2019), 18–19.

30. Newport, *Slow Productivity,* 52.

31. Ronald Rolheiser, "A Crisis Of Imagination," Ron Rolheiser, OMI, December 19, 1997, https://ronrolheiser.com/a-crisis-of-imagination.

32. Ian Bradley, *The Celtic Way* (Darton, Longman, and Todd, 2003), 98.

33. Mark 16:15.

34. Genesis 1:28.

35. "The 15 Most Important Pixar Quotes, According to You," Disney, March 25, 2015, https://news.disney.com/the-15-most-important-pixar-quotes-according-to-you.

36. Wikipedia, "Roman Empire," last updated June 26, 2025, https://en.wikipedia.org/wiki/Roman_Empire.

37. Wikipedia, "Roman Roads," last updated June 30, 2025, https://en.wikipedia.org/wiki/Roman_roads.

38. "Augustus," The Roman Empire in the First Century, PBS, accessed July 4, 2025, www.pbs.org/empires/romans/empire/augustus_religion.html.

39. "What Was Augustus Caesar's Impact on Biblical History?," Got Questions, last updated February 25, 2025, www.gotquestions.org/Augustus-Caesar.html.

40. Rodney Stark, *The Rise of Christianity: A Sociologist Reconsiders History* (Princeton University Press, 1996), 7.

41. Conrad Hackett et al., "How the Global Religious Landscape Changed from 2010 to 2020," Pew Research Center, June 9, 2025, www.pewresearch.org/religion/2025/06/09/how-the-global-religious -landscape-changed-from-2010-to-2020/.

42. "The Arch of Titus—From Jerusalem to Rome, and Back," Center for Jewish History, accessed July 4, 2025, www.cjh.org/visit/exhibit -archive/the-arch-of-titus.

43. 2 Corinthians 2:14.

44. From the preface of Milton Friedman's treatise, *Capitalism and Freedom* (University of Chicago Press, 1982), xiv.

45. Matthew 11:28, MSG.

46. Jim Elliot, quoted in Elisabeth Elliot, *Shadow of the Almighty: The Life and Testament of Jim Elliot* (HarperSanFrancisco, 1989), 108.

PART 2: LONG OBEDIENCE

1. Ashley Westerfield, "Yeast to Wheat: How Boudin Bakery's Yeast Culture Shaped San Francisco's Counterculture," FoundSF, 2019, www.foundsf.org/index.php?title=Yeast_to_Wheat:_How_Boudin _Bakery%E2%80%99s_Yeast_Culture_Shaped_San_Francisco%E2 %80%99s_Counterculture.

2. Stephanie Parker, "Do You Bake Bread? You Just Might Be a Community Scientist," Civil Eats, August 22, 2019, https://civileats.com/ 2019/08/22/do-you-bake-bread-you-just-might-be-a-community -scientist/.

3. Kim Polman and Stephen Vasconcellos-Sharpe, eds., *Imaginal Cells: Visions of Transformation* (Reboot the Future, 2017), 25.

4. Matthew 1:2.

5. Exodus 20:5–6, BSB.

6. Ian C. Hellstrom et al., "Maternal Licking Regulates Hippocampal Glucocorticoid Receptor Transcription Through a Thyroid

Hormone—Serotonin—NGFI-A Signalling Cascade," *Philosophical Transactions of the Royal Society of London. Series B, Biological Sciences* 367, no. 1601 (2012): 2495–510, https://pmc.ncbi.nlm.nih.gov/articles/ PMC3405683/.

7. Hellstrom et al., "Maternal Licking"; Genetic Science Learning Center, "Lick Your Rats," Learn.Genetics, July 15, 2013, https://learn .genetics.utah.edu/content/epigenetics/rats/.

8. Genesis 11:31.

9. "Map of Middle East: Abram/Abraham's journey from Ur to Canaan," Bible Cartoons, https://www.biblecartoons.co.uk/maps/map -of-middle-east-abram-abraham-s-journey-from-ur-to-canaan.

10. Genesis 12:7.

11. Genesis 13:17.

12. Genesis 21:33–34, BSB.

13. Donna Pisani, email message to author, March 19, 2025.

14. Wikipedia, "Robert Laws," last updated June 12, 2025, https://en.wikipedia.org/wiki/Robert_S._Laws.

15. Wikipedia, "Robert Laws." The original name was Virginia Avenue Baptist Church.

16. "District of Culture," Culture House, accessed July 4, 2025, www .culturehousedc.org.

17. "DC's Places of Worship," Sacred Spaces Conservancy, accessed July 4, 2025, https://sacredspacesdc.org/dc-places-of-worship.

18. "George Bernard Shaw > Quotes > Quotable Quote," Goodreads, accessed July 4, 2025, www.goodreads.com/quotes/7047-there-are -those-that-look-at-things-the-way-they. Adapted from George Bernard Shaw, *Back to Methuselah: A Metabiological Pentateuch* (Brentano's, 1921), 6.

CHAPTER 5: THE POWER OF SAME

1. "Casals and the Bach Cello Suites," Vialma Classical, accessed July 4, 2025, www.vialma.com/en/articles/72/Casals-and-the-Bach -Cello-Suites.

2. Eric Siblin, *The Cello Suites: J. S. Bach, Pablo Casals, and the Search for a Baroque Masterpiece* (Atlantic Monthly Press, 2009), 39.

3. Wikipedia, "Pablo Casals," last modified July 4, 2025, https://en.wikipedia.org/wiki/Pablo_Casals.

4. Wikipedia, "Pablo Casals."

5. "Spiritual Quotation: Quotation by Joseph Goldstein," Spirituality and Practice, www.spiritualityandpractice.com/quotes/quotations/view/33825/spiritual-quotation.

6. Rowdy Gaines, quoted in Angela Duckworth, *Grit: The Power of Passion and Perseverance* (Scribner, 2016), 121.

7. N. T. Wright, *Surprised by Hope: Rethinking Heaven, the Resurrection, and the Mission of the Church* (HarperOne, 2008), 193.

8. Jace Frederick, "'That's the Fastest I've Ever Been': Lakeville's Regan Smith Wins Silver with American Record in 200 Butterfly, Advances to 200 Back Final," *Twin Cities Pioneer Press*, August 1, 2024, www.twincities.com/2024/08/01/lakevilles-regan-smith-wins-silver-with-sensational-swim-in-200-butterfly/.

9. Adam Grant, *Hidden Potential: The Science of Achieving Greater Things* (Viking, 2023), 99.

10. Grant, *Hidden Potential*, 99.

11. Grant, *Hidden Potential*, 5.

12. Irving Berlin, "Anything You Can Do (I Can Do Better)," in *Annie Get Your Gun*, Broadway musical, directed by Joshua Logan, 1946.

13. Grant, *Hidden Potential*, 5.

14. Fred Glueckstein, "Churchill as Bricklayer," *Finest Hour* 157 (Winter 2012–2013): 34, https://winstonchurchill.org/publications/finest-hour/finest-hour-157/churchill-as-bricklayer/.

15. Glueckstein, "Churchill as Bricklayer."

16. Duckworth, *Grit*, 39.

17. Duckworth, *Grit*, 39.

18. Ingmar Bergman, quoted in Mason Currey, *Daily Rituals: How Artists Work* (Alfred A. Knopf, 2013), 13.

19. David Blaine, "How I Held My Breath for 17 Minutes," TEDMED,

San Diego, California, October 2009, 19:27, www.ted.com/talks/
david_blaine_how_i_held_my_breath_for_17_minutes.

20. Exodus 23:30.

21. Exodus 23:29.

22. Exodus 23:30.

23. Exodus 23:29.

24. Grant, *Hidden Potential*, 11.

25. James K. A. Smith, "Redeeming Ritual," *Banner*, January 6, 2012,
www.thebanner.org/features/2012/01/redeeming-ritual.

26. Robert Madu, "Hurts So Good," sermon, Social Dallas, April 28,
2024, video, 10:27–11:20, www.youtube.com/watch?v=pz7KHrey6aM.

27. Brian Manning, "Refusing to Fail," *Brian Manning* (blog), November 3, 2022, www.briancmanning.com/blog/2020/8/14/refusing-to
-fail.

28. Smith, "Redeeming Ritual."

29. See Proverbs 17:22.

30. Jacqueline Tempéra and Charlotte Walsh, "How Katie Ledecky
Switched Up Her Training to Make Olympic History in Paris,"
Yahoo Sports, August 2, 2024, https://sports.yahoo.com/heres-exactly
-katie-ledecky-training-154400317.html.

31. Matthew 7:2.

32. Maggie More, "Katie Ledecky Is the GOAT; Here Are the Superlatives She's Earned That Prove It," updated August 1, 2024, www
.nbcwashington.com/paris-2024-summer-olympics/katie-ledecky-is
-the-goat-here-are-the-superlatives-shes-earned-that-prove-it/
3680592.

33. Tempera and Walsh, "Katie Ledecky."

34. Priscilla Blinco, "Task Persistence in Japanese Elementary Schools,"
in *Windows on Japanese Education*, ed. Edward Beauchamp (Greenwood Press, 1991).

35. Blinco, "Task Persistence."

36. Duckworth, *Grit*, 228.

37. Duckworth, *Grit*, 230.

38. "Winston Churchill > Quotes > Quotable Quote," Goodreads, ac-

cessed July 5, 2025, www.goodreads.com/quotes/19742-success-is
-stumbling-from-failure-to-failure-with-no-loss.

39. Scott S. Smith, "Winston Churchill Harnessed His Many Mistakes
    into Victory," *Investor's Business Daily*, February 4, 2021, www
    .investors.com/news/management/leaders-and-success/winston
    -churchill-harness-mistakes-into-victory.

40. Winston Churchill, "Never Give In," speech, October 29, 1941, Har-
    row School, London, https://winstonchurchill.org/resources/
    speeches/1941-1945-war-leader/never-give-in/.

41. Psalm 6:3, BSB.

42. Thanks to Shelly Yost for this prophetic word.

43. Acts 1:7.

44. Acts 1:4.

45. Acts 2:2.

46. Lottie Watters, "Applying to Jobs at the World Bank: An Insider's
    Guide," Devex, updated April 11, 2023, www.devex.com/news/
    applying-to-jobs-at-the-world-bank-an-insider-s-guide-92557.

47. Max Calzada, email message to author, March 18, 2025.

CHAPTER 6: DARE TO BE DIFFERENT

1. Ben Johnson, "The Great Horse Manure Crisis of 1894," Historic
   UK, www.historic-uk.com/HistoryUK/HistoryofBritain/Great
   -Horse-Manure-Crisis-of-1894.

2. Eric Morris, "From Horse Power to Horsepower," *Access* 30 (Spring
   2007): 2–9, www.accessmagazine.org/wp-content/uploads/sites/7/
   2016/07/Access-30-02-Horse-Power.pdf.

3. Morris, "From Horse Power to Horsepower."

4. Peter Drucker, quoted in "Leadership Everywhere Means Reversed
   Leadership by Jane McConnell," 12th Global Peter Drucker Forum,
   September 30, 2020, www.druckerforum.org/blog/leadership
   -everywhere-means-reversed-leadership-by-jane-mcconnell/.

5. Stewart Brand, *The Clock of the Long Now: Time and Responsibility*
   (Basic Books, 1999), 162.

6. A. W. Tozer, *Rut, Rot, or Revival: The Problem of Change and Breaking Out of the Status Quo*, comp. James Snyder (Moody, 2006), 3.

7. Luke 5:38, BSB.

8. Eric S. Hintz, "The Fosbury Flop—A Game-Changing Technique," Smithsonian National Museum of American History, April 8, 2021, https://invention.si.edu/invention-stories/fosbury-flop-game -changing-technique.

9. Ralph Waldo Emerson, *The Essay on Self-Reliance* (Elbert Hubbard, 1908), 10.

10. James P. Carse, *Finite and Infinite Games* (Free Press, 1986).

11. Tip of the cap to John Ortberg who wrote a book with the title *When the Game Is Over, It All Goes Back in the Box.*

12. Hugh Robert Orr, "They Softly Walk," in *Harp of My Heart and Other Poems* (The College Press Publishers, 1922), 18.

13. Simon Sinek, *The Infinite Game* (Portfolio, 2019), 187.

14. Sinek, *Infinite Game,* 185–86.

15. Isaiah 43:18–19.

16. R. T. Kendall, *The Anointing: Yesterday, Today, Tomorrow* (Charisma House, 2003), 133.

17. Kendall, *Anointing,* 44.

18. Exodus 33:15.

19. 1 John 2:27, BSB.

20. Kendall, *Anointing,* 35.

21. In road biking, a century refers to a 100-mile (or 160-kilometer) bike ride completed in a single day.

22. Joshua 14:7.

23. Simon Sinek, *Start with Why: How Great Leaders Inspire Everyone to Take Action* (Portfolio, 2009), 116.

24. Commentary on Numbers 13:22, Hebrew Bible Study, accessed July 5, 2025, https://vi.hebrew-bible.com/en/commentary/Numbers.13.22.

25. Sotah 34b, Babylonian Talmud: Tractate Sotah, accessed July 5, 2025, https://halakhah.com/sotah/sotah_34.html.

26. Numbers 14:24, BSB.

27. See Romans 8:11.
28. Joshua 14:10–11.
29. Proverbs 29:18, KJV.
30. Joshua 14:12.
31. Tip of the cap to the 1981 Journey classic, "Don't Stop Believin'."
    Journey, "Don't Stop Believin'," by Steve Perry, Neal Schon, and Jonathan Cain, *Escape*, Columbia Records, 1981.

CHAPTER 7: THE CREATIVE MINORITY

1. "About: History," Order of the Mustard Seed, accessed July 5, 2025, www.orderofthemustardseed.com/about/history.
2. Traci Watson, "Birds are flap artists, syncing wing beats," *Daily Advertiser*, January 15, 2014, www.theadvertiser.com/story/news/2014/01/16/birds-are-flap-artists-syncing-wing-beats/4498951.
3. Wikipedia, "Moravian slaves," last modified July 3, 2024, https://en.wikipedia.org/wiki/Moravian_slaves.
4. Joshua 3:5.
5. Wikipedia, "List of most populous cities in the United States by decade," last modified May 11, 2025, https://en.wikipedia.org/wiki/List_of_most_populous_cities_in_the_United_States_by_decade.
6. D. L. Moody, quoted in "Our History," The Moody Church, accessed July 5, 2025, www.moodychurch.org/history/.
7. Henry Varley, quoted in Paul Gericke, *Crucial Experiences in the Life of D. L. Moody*, cited in "The World Has Yet to See . . . ," *Christian History* 25 (1990), www.christianitytoday.com/history/issues/issue-25/world-has-yet-to-see.html.
8. D. L. Moody, paraphrased response to Henry Varley, quoted in "The World Has Yet to See . . . ," *Christian History* 25 (1990), www.christianitytoday.com/history/issues/issue-25/world-has-yet-to-see.html.
9. Isaiah 6:8.
10. "Road to Revolution: George Robert Twelves Hewes," Common-

wealth Museum, accessed July 6, 2025, www.sec.state.ma.us/
divisions/commonwealth-museum/exhibits/online/the_boston_tea
_party/the_boston_tea_party_13.htm.

11. "Lydia Barrington Darragh," American Battlefield Trust, accessed
July 6, 2025, www.battlefields.org/learn/biographies/lydia-barrington
-darragh.

12. *Britannica*, "William Crawford Gorgas," last updated June 29, 2025,
www.britannica.com/biography/William-Crawford-Gorgas.

13. William Shakespeare, *The Tempest*, act 2, scene 1, accessed July 6,
2025, https://shakespeare.mit.edu/tempest/tempest.2.1.html.

14. Wikipedia, "Anna Williams (enslaved person)," last modified May
27, 2025, https://en.wikipedia.org/wiki/Anna_Williams_(enslaved
_person); Jesse Torrey, *A Portraiture of Domestic Slavery in the United
States* (Philadelphia, 1817), 43.

15. Torrey, *Portraiture of Domestic Slavery*, 40.

16. Arnold J. Toynbee, *A Study of History*, 12 vols. (Oxford University
Press, 1934–1961).

17. Loren Cunningham with Janice Rogers, *The Book That Transforms
Nations: The Power of the Bible to Change Any Country* (YWAM Publishing, 2007), 62.

18. Bob Briner, *Roaring Lambs: A Gentle Plan to Radically Change Your
World* (Zondervan, 1993), 175, 177.

19. Briner, *Roaring Lambs*, 31.

20. Timothy Gombis, *The Drama of Ephesians: Participating in the Triumph of God* (IVP Academic, 2010), 163.

21. Stanley Hauerwas and William H. Willimon, *Resident Aliens: Life
in the Christian Colony*, expanded 25th anniversary ed. (Abingdon,
2014), 94.

22. Wikipedia, "*Sex and Culture*," last modified July 2, 2025, https://en
.wikipedia.org/wiki/Sex_and_Culture.

23. Brett Waite, "Our Constitution Was Made Only for a Moral and
Religious People," Hillsdale College, December 7, 2023, https://on-
linecoursesblog.hillsdale.edu/our-constitution-was-made-only-for-a
-moral-and-religious-people.

24. R. T. Kendall, *The Anointing: Yesterday, Today, Tomorrow* (Charisma House, 2003), 133.

25. "Hermann Hesse > Quotes > Quotable Quote," Goodreads, accessed July 6, 2025, www.goodreads.com/quotes/8219556-every-age-every-culture-every-ethos-and-tradition-has-a.

26. Hebrews 12:27, NLT.

27. Hebrews 12:27.

28. Phyllis Tickle, *The Great Emergence: How Christianity Is Changing and Why* (Baker, 2008), 16.

29. Exodus 1:15–17, BSB.

30. Exodus 1:20, BSB.

31. Exodus 1:21.

32. Philippians 2:29, BSB.

33. Philippians 2:30, BSB.

34. Bible Hub, "3851. παραβουλεύομαι (*parabouleuomai*)," accessed July 6, 2025, https://biblehub.com/greek/3851.htm.

35. *Barclay's Daily Study Bible*, "Philippians 2," StudyLight.org, accessed July 6, 2025, www.studylight.org/commentaries/eng/dsb/philippians-2.html.

36. *I Can Only Imagine* and *Mom's Night Out* are two of many films he's written, directed, and produced.

37. Elbert Hubbard, "A Message to Garcia," U.S. Army Fort Benning, 1899, www.benning.army.mil/infantry/199th/OCS/content/pdf/Message%20to%20Garcia.pdf.

38. Wikipedia, "Andrew Summers Rowan," last modified May 19, 2025, https://en.wikipedia.org/wiki/Andrew_Summers_Rowan.

39. Hubbard, "Message to Garcia."

40. William Barclay, *The Letters to the Philippians, Colossians, and Thessalonians*, rev. ed. (Westminster Press, 1975), 50.

CHAPTER 8: THE BUTTERFLY EFFECT

1. Wikipedia, "Butterfly effect," last accessed July 3, 2025, https://en.wikipedia.org/wiki/Butterfly_effect.

2. Zechariah 4:10, NLT.

3. Chase Cottle, "2 Crappy Pages Per Day," Medium, November 25, 2017, https://medium.com/@chasecottle/2-crappy-pages-per-day-4a5904b09949.

4. Morgan Housel, *Same as Ever: A Guide to What Never Changes* (Portfolio, 2023), 12.

5. John 3:8, BSB.

6. Acts 27:13, BSB.

7. John Boyd, quoted in Housel, *Same as Ever*, 43.

8. Steven Johnson, *How We Got to Now: Six Innovations That Made the Modern World* (Riverhead Books, 2014), 4.

9. Johnson, *How We Got to Now*, 4–5.

10. Steve Johnson, *Where Good Ideas Come From: The Natural History of Innovation* (Riverhead Books, 2010), 33.

11. *Back to the Future*, directed by Robert Zemeckis (Universal Pictures, 1985).

12. Tim Urban, quoted in Housel, *Same as Ever*, 5.

13. Daniel Kahneman, interview with Tim Adams, "This Much I Know: Daniel Kahneman," *The Guardian*, July 7, 2012, www.theguardian .com/science/2012/jul/08/this-much-i-know-daniel-kahneman.

14. Freeman Dyson, *The Scientist as Rebel* (New York Review Books, 2006), 327.

15. Housel, *Same as Ever*, 51.

16. Housel, *Same as Ever*, 52.

17. Dan Evon, "Is This Cellphone Prediction from 1953 Real?," Snopes, updated April 13, 2023, www.snopes.com/fact-check/cellphone -prediction-from-1953.

18. Michael Crichton, *Timeline* (Century, 199), 10–11.

19. Joe McKinley, "13 Predictions About the Future That Were Dead Wrong," *Reader's Digest*, June 2, 2025, www.rd.com/list/predictions -that-were-wrong.

20. McKinley, "13 Predictions."

21. "H. M. Warner | Warner Brothers, 1927," Industry Central, www .industrycentral.net/node/95.

22. Eli Amdur, "Why the Wright Brothers Flew," *Forbes,* December 16, 2020, www.forbes.com/sites/eliamdur/2020/12/16/why-the-wright -brothers-flew/.

23. Josephine Franks, "10 Predictions About the Future That Turned Out to Be Very Wrong," Sky News, January 2, 2023, https://news.sky .com/story/10-predictions-about-the-future-that-turned-out-to-be -very-wrong-12763530.

24. George Friedman, *The Next 100 Years: A Forecast for the 21st Century* (Anchor, 2010), 10.

25. A. W. Tozer, *Culture: Living as Citizens of Heaven on Earth— Collected Insights from A. W. Tozer* (Moody, 2016), 23, italics mine.

26. Hebrews 11:38.

27. Hebrews 10:39.

28. Carl Sagan, *Cosmos* (Random House, 1980), 282.

29. Adam Hayes, "Recency (Availability) Bias: What It Is, How It Works," Investopedia, August 15, 2024, www.investopedia.com/ recency-availability-bias-5206686.

30. Arthur Lindsley, "C. S. Lewis on Chronological Snobbery," *Knowing and Doing* (Spring 2003), C. S. Lewis Institute, March 5, 2003, www.cslewisinstitute.org/resources/c-s-lewis-on-chronological -snobbery.

31. John Piper, *Don't Waste Your Life* (Crossway, 2003), 19.

32. Lindsley, "Chronological Snobbery."

33. "Ivan Pavlov > Quotes > Quotable Quote," Goodreads, accessed July 6, 2025, www.goodreads.com/quotes/12544536-if-you-want-a -new-idea-read-an-old-book.

34. George Harrison, vocalist, "Got My Mind Set on You," by Rudy Clark, *Cloud Nine,* Dark Horse Records, 1987.

35. Dorie Clark, *The Long Game: How to Be a Long-Term Thinker in a Short-Term World* (Harvard Business Review Press, 2021).

36. Marco Suma, "Have Strategic Patience and 'Be Right a Lot,'" Medium, July 31, 2022, https://marcsuma.medium.com/have-strategic -patience-and-be-right-a-lot-afa24d20c967.

37. Luke 2:37.

38. Housel, *Same as Ever*, 98.

39. Graham Greene, *The Power and the Glory* (Penguin, 2015), 13–14.

40. From an email dated July 10, 2025.

41. Psalm 126:5.

PART 3: LONG LEGACY

1. Anna Kurian, "Oldest Monastery in the West Was Built on the Spot of St. Maurice's Martyrdom," Catholic News Agency, September 22, 2023, www.catholicnewsagency.com/news/255438/oldest-monastery-in-the-west-was-built-on-the-spot-of-st-maurice-s-martyrdom.

2. Kurian, "Oldest Monastery."

3. Wikipedia, "Saint Maurice," last modified June 27, 2025, https://en.wikipedia.org/wiki/Saint_Maurice.

4. Wikipedia, "Saint Maurice."

5. From the film *Gladiator*, directed by Ridley Scott (DreamWorks Home Entertainment, 2000), DVD.

6. Robert Fulghum, *From Beginning to End: The Rituals of Our Lives* (Villard Books, 1995), 29, 33, 38.

7. Fulghum, *From Beginning to End*, 38.

8. Matthew Henry, *Directions for Daily Communion with God: Showing How to Begin, How to Spend, and How to Close Every Day with God* (London, 1830), 121.

9. Derek Coburn with Sara Stibitz, *Let's Retire Retirement: How to Enjoy Life to the Fullest—Now and Later* (Page Two, 2025).

10. Derek Coburn (@cadredc), "Many people take magical moments in their lives for granted every single day," X, March 20, 2025, 1:00 p.m., https://x.com/cadredc/status/1902812443828687268.

11. Coburn, "Many people take magical moments."

12. Coburn, "Many people take magical moments."

13. *The Secret Life of Walter Mitty*, directed by Ben Stiller (20th Century Fox, 2013).

14. Neil Postman, *Amusing Ourselves to Death: Public Discourse in the Age*

of Show Business (Penguin, 1985), 92–93.

15. Richard Halveston, quoted in "There's a Person Down the Road—It's You," *Preaching Today*, accessed July 7, 2025, www.preachingtoday .com/illustrations/2014/august/6081814.html.

16. Crawford Loritts, "Wind in My Sails—Dr. Crawford Loritts," Passion City Church, March 2, 2021, YouTube, 32:47, www.youtube .com/watch?v=itAmjm2HuzU&t=8s.

17. Halveston, quoted in "There's a Person Down the Road."

CHAPTER 9: GOOD ANCESTORS

1. "Harriet Beecher Stowe: Family," Harriet Beecher Stowe Center, accessed July 7, 2025, www.harrietbeecherstowecenter.org/family/.

2. David S. Reynolds, *Mightier Than the Sword: Uncle Tom's Cabin and the Battle for America* (W. W. Norton, 2011), 33.

3. Philip McFarland, *Loves of Harriet Beecher Stowe* (Grove Press, 2007), 81, 83.

4. Wikipedia, "Harriet Beecher Stowe," last updated June 26, 2025, https://en.wikipedia.org/wiki/Harriet_Beecher_Stowe.

5. Galatians 6:9.

6. Roman Krznaric, *The Good Ancestor: A Radical Prescription for Long-Term Thinking* (The Experiment, 2020), 3.

7. Jonas Salk, quoted in Krznaric, *Good Ancestor*, 57.

8. Evelyn Underhill, *Practical Mysticism: A Little Book for Normal People* (E. P. Dutton, 1915), x–xi.

9. Gerard Manley Hopkins, "God's Grandeur," Poetry Foundation, accessed July 7, 2025, www.poetryfoundation.org/poems/44395/gods -grandeur.

10. Nikolai Vavilov, quoted in Peter Pringle, *The Murder of Nikolai Vavilov: The Story of Stalin's Persecution of One of the Great Scientists of the Twentieth Century*, (Simon & Schuster, 2008), 5.

11. Joshua 14:7.

12. Krznaric, *Good Ancestor*, 4.

13. Hayim Nahman Bialik and Yehoshua Hana Ravnitzky, eds., *The*

Book of Legends Sefer Ha-Aggadah: *Legends from the Talmud and Midrash,* trans. William G. Braude (Schocken Books, 1992), 203.

14. Psalm 126:1, ESV.

15. Zechariah 9:12.

16. Pinchas Shir, "Methuselah Date Palm from the Days of Jesus," PSHIR.com, June 5, 2024, www.pshir.com/methuselah-date -palm/.

17. Laura Clark, "Tree Grown from 2,000-Year-Old Seed Has Repro-duced," *Smithsonian,* March 26, 2015, www.smithsonianmag.com/ smart-news/tree-grown-2000-year-old-seed-has-reproduced -180954746/.

18. Mark 4:30–32.

19. Venkat S. R., "What Are the Health Benefits of Mustard Seed?," WebMD, June 2, 2024, www.webmd.com/diet/what-are-the-health -benefits-of-mustard-seed; "Mustard Seeds Nutrition Facts," Nutri-tion and You, accessed July 7, 2025, www.nutrition-and-you.com/ mustard-seeds.html.

20. Mark 4:32, BSB.

21. Psalm 2:8, ISV.

22. "100 Greatest Songwriters of All Time," *Rolling Stone,* accessed July 7, 2025, www.rollingstone.com/interactive/lists-100-greatest -songwriters/#paul-mccartney; "Paul McCartney," Official Charts, accessed July 28, 2025, www.officialcharts.com/artist/18538/paul -mccartney.

23. John 1:45–46, BSB.

24. C. S. Lewis, *The Weight of Glory: And Other Addresses* (Macmillan, 1980), 19.

25. John 1:47–49, BSB.

26. Earl Roe, *Dream Big: The Henrietta Mears Story* (Regal Books, 1994), 252–53.

27. Roe, *Dream Big,* 243.

28. Roe, *Dream Big,* 244–46.

29. Will Graham, "The Tree Stump Prayer: When Billy Graham Over-came Doubt," Billy Graham Evangelistic Association of Canada,

July 9, 2014, www.billygraham.ca/stories/the-tree-stump-prayer
-when-billy-graham-overcame-doubt.

30. Billy Graham, *Just As I Am: The Autobiography of Billy Graham*
(HarperSanFrancisco, 1997), 139.

31. Wendy Murray Zoba, "The Grandmother of Us All," *Christianity
Today* 40, no. 10 (September 16, 1996): 44–46.

32. Ephesians 3:20.

CHAPTER 10: THE DAY WHEN DECADES HAPPEN

1. "CP-1 Goes Critical," The Manhattan Project: An Interactive History, U.S. Department of Energy, accessed July 7, 2025, www.osti
.gov/opennet/manhattan-project-history/Events/1942-1944_pu/cp-1
_critical.htm.

2. "Nobel Laureates," The University of Chicago, accessed July 7, 2025,
www.uchicago.edu/who-we-are/global-impact/accolades/nobel
-laureates.

3. Wikipedia, "Amos Alonzo Stagg," July 3, 2025, https://en.wikipedia
.org/wiki/Amos_Alonzo_Stagg.

4. Amos Alonzo Stagg, quoted in John Wooden and Steve Jamison,
The Wisdom of Wooden: My Century On and Off the Court (McGraw
Hill, 2010), 19.

5. Andy Serwer, "The Legend of Robin Hood," *Fortune,* September 8,
2006, https://web.archive.org/web/20130727104619/https://money
.cnn.com/magazines/fortune/fortune_archive/2006/09/18/8386204/.

6. Paul Tudor Jones, interview by Tony Robbins, in Robbins, *Money:
Master the Game* (Simon & Schuster, 2014), 494.

7. Jones, in Robbins, *Money,* 494.

8. 2 Samuel 15:30.

9. 2 Samuel 17:27–29, my paraphrase.

10. KJV.

11. 1 Kings 2:7.

12. Peggy Campolo, quoted in Matt Garvin, "You Are Called to
Change the World Where You Are . . . You Don't Have to Go to

Africa," *Faith Reflections* (blog), accessed July 8, 2025, https://sermons.logos.com/sermons/15884-the-importance-of-motherhood.

13. The Barkley Marathons is a one-hundred-mile ultramarathon through off-trail terrain.

14. 1 Kings 19:4.

15. 1 Kings 19:15–16.

16. Michael Sprague, "Do It Again Lord," *Christian Grandfather Magazine*, June 2, 2022, www.christiangrandfather.org/2022/06/02/do-it-again-lord/.

17. A. W. Tozer, *Fiery Faith: Ignite Your Passion for God*, comp. W. L. Seaver (Wingspread, 2012), 112.

18. Jon Tyson at National Community Church, January 2022.

19. 1 Kings 19:19.

20. 2 Kings 2:9.

21. 2 Kings 2:9.

22. A. W. Tozer, *The Pursuit of God* (Moody, 2015), 107, 109.

23. Laurie Beth Jones, *The Power of Positive Prophecy: Finding the Hidden Potential in Everyday Life* (Hyperion, 1999), ix.

24. Jones, *Power of Positive Prophecy*, xii.

25. Numbers 11:29.

26. 2 Kings 8:19, BSB.

CHAPTER 11: DREAM FACTORY

1. Steven Johnson, *Where Good Ideas Come From: The Nature History of Innovation* (Riverhead Books, 2011), 25–27.

2. *We Bought a Zoo*, directed by Cameron Crowe (20th Century Fox, 2011).

3. C. S. Lewis, *The Screwtape Letters* (Macmillan, 1942), 148–49.

4. 1 Samuel 14:6.

5. Proverbs 31:28.

6. Edgar Allan Poe, "A Dream Within a Dream," Poetry Foundation, accessed July 8, 2025, www.poetryfoundation.org/poems/52829/a-dream-within-a-dream.

7. Genesis 37:19.
8. Gordon W. Allport, preface to *Man's Search for Meaning*, by Viktor E. Frankl (Beacon Press, 1962), xi.
9. Luke 21:13, NASB.
10. Genesis 50:20.
11. "Fusiform face area," Wikipedia, accessed July 28, 2025, https://en .wikipedia.org/wiki/Fusiform_face_area.
12. Genesis 40:6, NLT.
13. Genesis 50:25.
14. Joshua 24:32.
15. Brandon Lake, "Hard Fought Hallelujah," by Brandon Lake, Steven Furtick, Benjamin Hastings, Rodrick Simmons, Jelly Roll, and Chris Brown, Provident, November 8, 2024.
16. Isaiah 6:1.
17. Abraham Lincoln, "Letter to John Stuart (January 23, 1841)," Lincoln's Writings, June 29, 2013, https://housedivided.dickinson.edu/ sites/lincoln/letter-to-john-stuart-january-23-1841/.
18. "Lincoln's 'Failures'?," Abraham Lincoln Online, accessed July 8, 2025, www.abrahamlincolnonline.org/lincoln/education/failures .htm.
19. 1 Peter 5:10, BSB.
20. Carl Jung, quoted in Andy Murphy, "The Difference Between a Good Life and a Bad Life (According to Carl Jung)," Medium, May 19, 2024, https://medium.com/illumination/the-difference-between -a-good-life-and-a-bad-life-according-to-carl-jung-e9874dda1535.
21. Wikipedia, "Shizo Kanakuri," last modified November 11, 2024, https://en.wikipedia.org/wiki/Shizo_Kanakuri.
22. See 2 Timothy 4:7.

CHAPTER 12: KEEP CALM AND CARRY ON

1. "Bell X-1," Smithsonian, accessed July 8, 2025, www.si.edu/object/bell-x-1%3Anasm_A19510007000.
2. "Henry Ford > Quotes > Quotable Quote," Goodreads, accessed

July 8, 2025, www.goodreads.com/quotes/978-whether-you-think
-you-can-or-you-think-you-can-t—you-re.

3. Phillip B. Childs, "The 'I Can't' Funeral," ed. Gary Amirault, Tent-
maker, accessed July 8, 2025, www.tentmaker.org/newinspiration/
Icant.html.

4. Sarah Williams, "Earning a Good Salary? Thank Your Fourth-
Grade Teacher," *Science*, October 7, 2013, www.science.org/content/
article/earning-good-salary-thank-your-fourth-grade-teacher.

5. Exodus 4:10.

6. Jeremiah 1:6.

7. Genesis 18:13.

8. 1 Kings 19:4.

9. Judges 6:15.

10. Jeremiah 1:7

11. Isaiah 6:8.

12. 2 Corinthians 4:13.

13. Wikipedia, "Ken Jennings," last modified July 6, 2025,
https://en.wikipedia.org/wiki/Ken_Jennings.

14. John 5:4.

15. 2 Kings 5:11.

16. Alexander Solzhenitzyn, "Live Not by Lies," Toward an Honesty
Culture, 1974, https://honestyculture.com/alexander-solzhenitsyn
-live-not-by-lies/.

17. Lewis Carroll, *The Hunting of the Snark: An Agony in Eight Fits*
(Macmillan, 1876).

18. John 8:32.

19. Mark 4:37–38, BSB.

20. Genesis 3:12.

21. Mark 4:39, ESV.

22. Edwin Friedman, *A Failure of Nerve: Leadership in the Age of the
Quick Fix* (Seabury Books, 2007).

23. Edwin Friedman, "*A Failure of Nerve* Quotes," Goodreads, accessed
July 8, 2025, www.goodreads.com/work/quotes/146596-a-failure-of
-nerve-leadership-in-the-age-of-the-quick-fix.

24. Martin Luther King, Jr., "Letter from Birmingham City Jail (1963)," in *A Testament of Hope: The Essential Writings of Martin Luther King, Jr.*, ed. James Melvin Washington (Harper and Row, 1986), 300.

25. See Romans 8:28.

26. 2 Timothy 4:6–7.

27. G. K. Chesterton, *Orthodoxy* (Kassock, 2012), 96.

28. Romans 5:4.

29. "Smith Wigglesworth > Quotes > Quotable Quote," Goodreads, accessed July 8, 2025, www.goodreads.com/quotes/621574-great-faith-is -the-product-of-great-fights-great-testimonies.

30. "James Corbett > Quotes > Quotable Quote," Goodreads, accessed July 8, 2025, www.goodreads.com/quotes/540142-fight-one-more -round-when-your-feet-are-so-tired.

31. Farrell Evans, "How MLK Responded When Segregationists Bombed His Home," History, last updated May 27, 2025, www .history.com/news/martin-luther-king-jr-home-bombing -nonviolence.

32. Martin Luther King, Jr., "But If Not," sermon, Ebenezer Baptist Church, Atlanta, GA, November 5, 1967.

33. Psalm 126:5, ESV.

34. Amos 9:11, 13, BSB.

35. Exodus 14:13.

36. Corrie ten Boom et al., *The Hiding Place* (Bantam, 1971).

37. Romans 8:31.

38. Philippians 1:6.

39. Philippians 4:13.

EPILOGUE: FAN INTO FLAME

1. Jacqueline Howard, "Lola Anderson's Dad Kept Her Diary Dream Alive," BBC, August 1, 2024, www.bbc.com/news/articles/ cndo6pgokowo.

2. Lola Anderson, interview by Jeremy Taylor, "Rower Lola Anderson on the Note Her Dad Gave Her Before He Died," *The Sunday*

Times, September 8, 2024, www.thetimes.com/sport/rowing/article/
rower-lola-anderson-on-the-note-her-dad-gave-her-before-he-died
-times-swoty-mkrcwb25z.

3. Anderson, in Taylor, "Rower Lola Anderson."

4. "Team GB Win Historic Gold Medal in Women's Quadruple
Sculls," British Rowing, www.britishrowing.org/2024/07/team-gb
-win-historic-gold-medal-in-womens-quadruple-sculls.

5. Isaiah 55:10–11.

6. Jeremiah 1:12.

7. 2 Timothy 1:6.

8. 2 Timothy 1:7, NLT.

9. We don't know his exact age, but twenties is a good guess based on
scholarly consensus.

ABOUT THE AUTHOR

MARK BATTERSON is the lead visionary of National Community Church in Washington, DC. One church with a network of churches, National owns and operates Ebenezers Coffeehouse, the DC Dream Center, the Culturehouse, and the Capital Turnaround. Mark holds a doctor of ministry degree from Regent University and is the *New York Times* bestselling author of twenty-five books, including *A Million Little Miracles, Win the Day, The Circle Maker,* and *Chase the Lion.* He also authored the children's books *The Best Worst Day Ever* and *God Speaks in Whispers* with his daughter, Summer Batterson Dailey. Mark and his wife, Lora, live on Capitol Hill in Washington, DC.

ABOUT THE TYPE

This book was set in Caslon, a typeface first designed in 1722 by William Caslon (1692–1766). Its widespread use by most English printers in the early eighteenth century soon supplanted the Dutch typefaces that had formerly prevailed. The roman is considered a "workhorse" typeface due to its pleasant, open appearance, while the italic is exceedingly decorative.

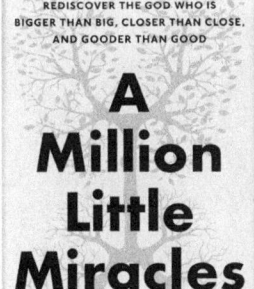